DO YOU MAKE THESE FINANCIAL RETIREMENT MISTAKES?

Low return on your investments?

Running out of money in retirement?

Taking too much risk in the stock market?

Paying too much in taxes?

Not having affordable healthcare when you need it?

Paying excessive fees and hidden costs?

Tsunami Proof Your Retirement

The Top 9 Financial Storms Retirees Will Face in the Next 10 Years

That Their Current Planner Doesn't Know or Won't Tell

John (Jay) E. Tyner Jr.

RFC®

First Edition 2012
Second Edition 2013
Third Edition 2013

Fourth Edition 2015

Tsunami Proof Your Retirement
The Top 9 Financial Storms Retirees Will Face in the
Next 10 Years
by John (Jay) E. Tyner Jr.
Printed in the United States of America

ISBN-10 151775450X
ISBN-13 9781517754501

Unless otherwise indicated, Bible quotations are taken from the New
International Version. Copyright © 1973 by Biblica.

www.xulonpress.com

NOTICE TO READER

In loving memory of:
Jenna Prusia

March 14, 1996
December 28, 2012

www.jennafoundation.com "Heaven"

I want to run in greener pastures.

I want to dance on higher hills.

I want to drink from sweeter waters,

In the misty morning chills.

And my soul is getting restless

For the place that I belong.

I can't wait to join the angels

And sing my heaven song.

-Phil Whickam

Dr. Wallace B. Honeycutt

**A great dentist and client of our firm,
who passed away in 2011**

Jay and Robin Tyner with President George W. Bush in Washington D.C. on January 24, 2014.

Table of Contents

Bonus Chapters

Introduction

As I write this book, my father turns 80 years old and 67% of seniors recently surveyed say they are concerned with taxes. My father's concern becomes my concern, from both a personal and professional stance. It is my desire that this book will give assurance and direction to anyone concerned about their financial future, their child(ren)'s or their parents'.

It takes time and no disturbances to write a book, so I headed to our RV at Holden Beach to write with some seclusion. Early one morning, as I was walking out to get a cup of coffee and passed another camper parked near the shore.

Mrs. Peggy P. Sink from Thomasville, North Carolina, who turned 88 years of age on December 22, 2012, was standing with her two retired daughters. As I passed by, she looked at me and said, "You want to do the twist?" and shook her hips like a 25-year-old! We all started laughing and talking and discovered that after a 4-hour drive from home, we were pretty close neighbors from Davidson County, North Carolina. Later, I asked this new friend of mine, who I'll call a "Senior Senior" (anyone over the age of 75), what advice she would give to me as I wrote this book for pre-retirees and retirees. "Attitude", she said. "Show love and friendship, smile, keep busy, move your body and don't be so serious." I could tell that she enjoyed life and found out later as we talked that she had 11 great grandkids, is widowed, lost a son early, and still attends Zion United Church of Christ.

Some of the content in this book will be downright serious and depressing. So take 88 years of advice from Mrs. Peggy P. Sink and keep a good attitude. To help in this area, I've reprinted some of Derek Johnson's short historical stories he published in his book "Wonder of America." I trust that they will help keep your outlook positive as you continue reading.

To help you better understand the contents of this book, I was once interviewed by a major news promotional agency and have included a copy of the resulting article:

Turning Retirement Savings into Retirement Income:
Transitioning from the
"Working Phase" to the "Retired Phase"

When aspiring retirees reach retirement, they are relieved and excited to have finally achieved the goal they set out for decades prior. However, as newly minted retirees begin to tap their nest eggs, they also need to shift their mindsets from the working phase to the retired phase.

Turning nest egg savings into income is a challenging task that, if not handled properly, can negatively impact a retiree's lifestyle.

"If you make a mistake in early retirement, your portfolio doesn't have adequate time to recover," explains Jay Tyner, president and founder of Semmax Financial Group in Greensboro, NC.

*According to Tyner, it is vital that retirees change from a current advisor who specializes in getting a client **TO** retirement to an advisor who specializes in getting a retiree **THROUGH** retirement with active planning of their investments and nest egg savings to avoid making costly mistakes.*

Retirees can successfully do so by appropriately weighing current and future income needs, long-term care concerns, and the desire to leave a legacy with their savings account balances and plan accordingly.

Most importantly, retirees are highly encouraged to utilize a Registered Financial Consultant who concentrates in income and tax planning — by creating tax-favored "paychecks" from savings accounts to afford and maintain their targeted retirement lifestyle for several decades.

"In order to ensure a successful retirement, a retiree must know how much money they need to live on, but also incorporate strategies to make sure that the income lasts for 25-30 years," says Tyner.

I'm reminded of a recently retired couple, Bill and Anna, who made their annual trip to the county fair. This particular year for the first time, they saw a new attraction: a sign that read "Airplane Rides." Bill and Anna asked the pilot, "How much does the airplane ride cost?" "Ten dollars," replied the pilot. Bill looked at Anna and said very excitedly, "Anna, we've never been on an airplane ride. Let's try it out." Anna looked at him and quickly replied, "Bill, ten dollars is ten dollars. That's a lot of money!" Needless to say, they didn't take the plane ride. Well this went on and on for several years. Each time, Bill would suggest they take a plane ride and Anna would look at him and say the same thing, "Ten dollars is ten dollars."

One year they returned and, as always, the same thing happened. The pilot stood near his sign that read "Airplane Rides." The pilot greeted Bill and Anna with, "Well, it's still ten dollars!" Bill looked at Anna and before he could say anything Anna recited her customary response, "Ten dollars is ten dollars." However, this time the pilot didn't let them walk away. He said, "Wait a minute, folks. I remember you, and I have a deal for you. I am going to let you take a plane ride for free on one condition… that you don't say anything." Bill looked at Anna and Anna looked at bill. A free plane ride! Who could refuse? So off they went! No sooner had they taken off than suddenly the pilot started doing loops and barrel rolls. He was cutting up and down and dancing that plane all over the sky, and he never heard a word. As he started to land the plane, he shouted to his silent passengers, "Bill, why didn't you say anything?" Bill shouted back to the pilot, "It was real hard a few minutes ago when Anna fell out of the plane, but ten dollars is ten dollars!"

Now, the topic that I'm covering in this book is called Retirement Planning. Retirement Planning has changed in the last thirty years. In fact, we have now categorized seniors into three groups. We have the **baby** seniors who are age 55 to 65. Then we have the **middle-aged** seniors; they're 66 to 75. And our **senior** seniors are anyone over age 75. These three different, unique groups of seniors all have different, unique financial needs and concerns. A 62-year-old has different financial planning needs than an 82-year-old. A 60-year-old doesn't have Social Security. An 82-year-old is receiving Social Security benefits; however, she may have lost a spouse's pension, be paying taxes on a forced distribution from an IRA, and now filing a single tax return instead of a joint return, thus putting her into a higher tax bracket.

Have you heard of the "Granny Goes to Jail" law? (See Appendix.) In the 1990s, this law created fear in cities across the U.S. Many people today don't realize that it came into existence. With this law, if you, as a senior, decided to transfer your assets to your children to protect your money from being swallowed up by a nursing home, it would be against the law. Not only was it against the law, but if you did protect your money, you were subject to a fine of up to a $25,000 and up to five years in prison. Basically, if you gave some of your assets to your children, you could go to jail because you were trying to get out of the nursing home spend down.

The good news is that law was repealed under Attorney General Janet Reno, who said there was no way we could keep that law in effect. There was no way we could send an 85-year-old grandma to jail. However, there still is a form of this law on the books as part of the nursing home spend-down transmittal. I'll explain it to you later.

This book title comes from the realization that many seniors and their families will face financial problems as illustrated by a tsunami. In 2011, the tsunami that Japan faced left damaging personal consequences to those locally where it hit. The 2004 Indian Ocean tsunami could rank as the most devastating on record. More than 200,000 people lost their lives — many of them washed out to sea.

A tsunami may be less than a foot in height on the open ocean surface, which is why they are usually not noticed by sailors. But the powerful shock wave of energy travels rapidly through the ocean as fast as a commercial jet. Once a tsunami reaches shallow water near the coast, it slows. The top of the wave moves faster than the bottom, causing the sea to rise dramatically.

You're probably thinking, what in the world does that have to do with *Tsunami Proof Your Retirement*? When you think of a tsunami, you usually don't have pleasant thoughts. Retirees and pre-retirees are often like the sailors who don't notice the tsunami because, in their eyes, it's just a little one-foot wave. Yet underneath, it is moving at more than 500 miles per hour and developing into a 30- to 100-foot mass of powerful destruction. These tsunamis can sink your retirement plans and wash away your peace of mind – your financial peace of mind. Don't be fooled into thinking only someone else will be hit or that you're already protected.

June 01, 2011/by the CNN Wire Staff
IAEA report: Japan Nuclear Plant was not ready for Huge Tsunami Waves

*The United Nations nuclear watchdog agency said Wednesday that Japan **underestimated the hazard posed by tsunamis to nuclear plants** but praised the country's response to the Fukushima Daiichi crisis as "exemplary."*

The International Atomic Energy Agency announced a preliminary summary of safety issues related to the crippled power plant. The plant was damaged after the March 11, 2011 earthquake and tsunami that devastated northern Japan and killed more than 14,000 people and left another 10,000 people missing.

Don't underestimate the hazard posed by financial tsunamis during the next ten years!

Can you guess which financial tsunami was ranked the highest in the April 2011 LIMRA study? If you guessed taxes, you're right. According to a survey of consumers done by eNation, a national online research service, LIMRA extrapolated the results from a large polling of retirees. When asked the question, "Do I worry that my taxes will increase?" nearly 67% agreed. That's up from 62% in a previous study by the same group when more than 400 retirees with at least $100,000 in investable assets were surveyed.

In the 2011 compiled data report, these are the 10 financial concerns that surface to the top on retiree's and pre-retiree's minds as "major concerns" they will face in the next 10 years. We'll explore these top 10 financial concerns in detail in the pages that follow.

> 67% - Tax Hikes

> 58% - Reduction in Medicare Benefits

> 55% - Social Security Cuts

50% - Inflation

44% - Prolonged Stock Market Downturn

43% - Health Care Costs

37% - Declining Interest Rates

35% - Prescription Drug Costs

35% - Long-term Care Costs

21% - Possibility of Outliving Assets

Associate Managing Director of Retirement Research at LIMRA, Matthew Drinkwater, said he was not surprised by these results. Drinkwater commented, "*For one thing, we know that retirees don't want to hear about cuts to Medicare or Social Security or tax increases as a budget balancing option.*" And as I scan the digital morning news, the following article pops up.

July 7, 2011 7:32 AM
Obama proposes cuts to Social Security
By Corbett B. Daly
President Obama answers questions during a "Twitter town hall" on July 6, 2011.
(Credit: CBS)

*President Obama has said he wants to use a looming deadline over raising the amount Congress is allowed to borrow to work a deal with Republicans on something "big." And now he **plans to propose major changes to Social Security as part of that "grand bargain**," which he hopes will reduce the deficit by as much as $4 trillion over the next decade, administration sources tell CBS News.*

President Obama is scheduled to meet at the White House Thursday morning with congressional leaders from both parties, including House Speaker John Boehner, to negotiate a deficit reduction deal.

It appears that one-foot tsunami waves are everywhere. According to a Bloomberg report by Sangim Han from May 8, 2011, South Korea says it will double the height of sea walls protecting its oldest nuclear reactor to quell unease about the risks of atomic power, and drawing on the lessons of the Fukushima disaster in Japan. I suggest you use this book to detect your own one-foot tsunami waves and, with the help of a professional financial guide and coach, quickly start "doubling the height of your sea walls" to protect your retirement from irrevocable damage.

Sincerely,

Jay Tyner, RFC®

Pepper by Sea

It was 1453 when the Turks conquered Constantinople and cut off the commerce between the East and West. In so doing, they deprived Europe of silks, jewels, and one other vital item – the spices of Asia Thus, modern history, says Alistair Cooke, began with the problem of how to bypass Turkey and get to the Spice Island of Indonesia by sea. One man believed it could be done, and that he was providentially chosen to do it. He was a six-foot, redheaded, fast-talking dreamer, filled with great quantities of curiosity, stubbornness, and a sense of mission. A Christian of almost maniacal devoutness, he also longed for the secular trappings of pomp and power He was determined to convert every prince and pauper in the Indies and have himself proclaimed governor of every land he discovered. Finally, after more than twenty years of searching for a royal sponsor, he set sail under the flag of Spain in three tiny ships with forty men. On October 11, 1492, he sighted what he believed to be the mainland of Asia. In reality, it was San Salvador in the Bahamas. To his dying day, he never knew that he had not touched the Orient, or that he, Christopher Columbus, on a voyage to discover pepper by sea, had stumbled on the New World. Yet, he possessed an unsinkable spirit that exemplified the wonder of America!

Chapter I: Inflation Tsunami

"The budget is like a mythical beanbag. Congress votes mythical beans into it, then reaches in and tries to pull real ones out."
--Will Rogers

"If you would like to know the value of money, go and try to borrow some."
--Benjamin Franklin

"Whoever said money can't buy happiness simply didn't know where to go shopping."
--Bo Derek

"When a man retires, his wife gets twice the husband but only half the income."
--Chi Chi Rodriguez

"The question isn't at what age I want to retire, it's at what income."
--George Foreman

2006 - Ibbotson Study
Source: retirementthink.com

Found that systematic withdrawals from retirement savings can be problematic if individuals withdraw more than 3% - 4% annually.

- 5% withdrawal rate can be expected to last 22 years
- 7% can only be expected to last 9 years

Alternate Inflation Charts

John Williams makes it clear that inflation for pre-retirees and retirees is not only out of control but is also being reported by the government differently than it used to be. The lower line on the following chart represents the inaccurate government reporting of inflation to be around 3.5%. If this were the 1980s, the government would be using the same input but reporting accurate inflation to be currently at over 10%. This means that today, you as a retiree will need double the income you now rely on to maintain the same standard of living only 7.2 years from NOW.

The CPI chart on the home page of shadowstats.com reflects their estimate of inflation for today as if it were calculated the same way it was in 1990. The CPI on the Alternate Data Series tab reflects the CPI as if it were calculated using the methodologies in place in 1980. In general terms, methodological shifts in government reporting have depressed reported inflation, moving the concept of the CPI away from being a measure of the cost of living needed to maintain a constant standard of living.

I have included part of John Williams' report substantiating his reasoning. I suggest you visit his website, www.shadowstats.com, for a complete and thorough read.

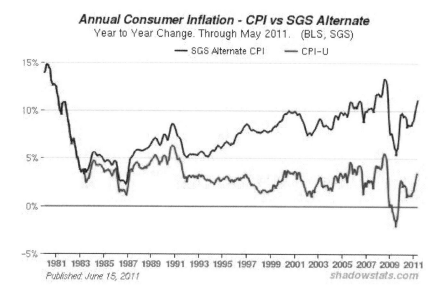

Annual Consumer Inflation - CPI vs SGS Alternate
Year to Year Change. Through May 2011. (BLS, SGS)
— SGS Alternate CPI   — CPI-U

Published June 15, 2011   *shadowstats.com*

Hyperinflationary Great Depression

Even with the government's spending, debt, and obligations running far beyond its ability to cover with taxes or its political willingness to cut entitlement spending, the inevitable inflationary collapse, based solely on these funding needs, could have been pushed well toward the end of the current decade. Yet, the effects of extraordinary economic downturn and the government's response to the same have advanced the timing of Social Security funding from being in net surplus to net deficit by several years, to the present day.

The printing presses are already running and the Fed is working actively to debase the U.S. dollar, effectively funding fully net U.S. Treasury debt issuance to the public. Global rejection of the U.S. dollar and criticism of U.S. government fiscal actions and Federal Reserve monetary policy are accelerating, along with calls for a new world reserve currency.

Actions already taken to contain the systemic solvency crisis and to stimulate the economy (which have not worked), plus what should be a renewed devastating impact of unexpected ongoing economic contraction on tax revenues, have set the stage for a much earlier crisis. Risks are high for the hyperinflation beginning to break in the months ahead, and it likely cannot be avoided be-yond 2014; it already may be beginning to unfold.

It is in this environment of rapid fiscal deterioration and related massive funding needs that the U.S. dollar remains open to a rapid and massive decline, along with a dumping of domestic- and foreign-held U.S. Treasuries. The Federal Reserve would be forced to monetize further significant sums of Treasury debt, triggering the early phases of a monetary inflation. Under such circumstances, current multi-trillion dollar deficits would feed rapidly into a vicious, self-feeding cycle of currency debasement and hyperinflation.

With the economy already in depression, hyperinflation kicking in quickly would push the economy into a great depression, since disruptions from uncontained inflation are likely to bring normal commercial activity to a halt.

What happens next is anyone's speculation. How long would a hyperinflation last before the government brought its fiscal house into order and established a sound currency? I would be surprised if the hyperinflation crisis lasted beyond a year or two, since the system is not positioned to handle the crisis well and pressures for rapid resolution would be extremely strong. All that depends, however, on what evolves out of highly unstable political, economic, financial, and social environments. Accordingly, the best individuals can do is to take actions to protect themselves and their families through the worst of foreseeable circumstances – both in terms of personal safety and in terms of the purchasing power of pre-crisis assets. The following is an exploration of certain problems that likely would have to be handled in a hyperinflation.

Lack of Physical Cash

The United States in a hyperinflation likely would experience the quick disappearance of cash as we know it. In Zimbabwe, there was the back-up of a well-functioning black market in U.S. dollars, but no such back-up exists in the United States. Shy of the rapid introduction of a new currency and/or the highly problematic adaptation of the current electronic commerce system to new pricing realities, a barter system is the most likely circumstance to evolve for regular commerce. Such would make much of the current electronic commerce system useless and add to what would become an ongoing economic implosion. It also could take a number of months to become reasonably functional.

Some years back, I was in San Francisco, having dinner with a former regional Federal Reserve Bank president and the chief economist for a large Midwest bank. Market had rumored that day that there was a run on a major bank in the City by the Bay. So I queried the regional Fed president about what would be happening if the rumors were true.

He had had some personal experience with a run on banks in his region and explained that the Fed had a special team designed to handle such a crisis. The biggest problem he had had was getting adequate cash to the troubled banks to cover depositors, and having to fly cash in by helicopters to meet the local cash-flow needs.

The troubled bank in San Francisco, however, was much larger than the example cited, and the former Fed bank president speculated that there was not enough cash in the vaults of the regional Federal Reserve Bank, let alone the entire Federal Reserve System, to cover a true run on deposits at the major bank.

Therein lies an early problem for a system headed into hyperinflation — adequate currency. Where the Fed may hold roughly $150 billion in currency outside of roughly $50 billion in commercial bank vault cash, the bulk of roughly $930 billion in currency outside of the Banks is not in the United States. Back in 2000, the Fed estimated that 50%–70% of U.S. dollar cash was outside of the system. That number probably is higher today, with perhaps as little as $300 billion in physical cash in circulation in the United States, or roughly 1.7% of M3. The rest of the dollars are used elsewhere in the world as a store of wealth, or as an alternate currency — free of the woes of unstable domestic financial conditions. Those conditions would change severely in the event of a U.S. hyperinflation.

Given the extremely rapid debasement of the larger denomination notes with limited physical cash in the system, existing currency would become worth more as kindling for a fire than as currency, and would disappear quickly as a hyperinflation broke.

For the system to continue functioning in anything close to a normal manner, the government would have to produce quickly an extraordinary amount of new cash, and electronic commerce would have to adjust to rapidly changing prices.

In terms of cash, new bills of much higher denominations would be needed, but production lead time is a problem. Conspiracy theories of recent years have suggested the U.S. Government already has printed a new currency of red-colored bills, intended for some dual internal and external U.S. dollar system. If such indeed were the case, then there might be a store of "new dollars" that could be released at a 1-to-1,000,000 ratio, or whatever ratio was needed to make the new currency meaningful. But such a solution would not resolve any long-term problems — as seen in the multiple Zimbabwe devaluations — unless it was part of an overall restructuring of the global currency system, and unless the U.S. government first put its fiscal house in order.

From a practical standpoint, however, currency would disappear, at least for a period of time, in the early period of a hyperinflation.

Possible Short-Term Electronic Relief for Individuals

For those who have foreign-currency denominated bank accounts outside of the United States, something along the lines of a debit card against that account — let's say a Swiss franc account could help, in theory. In the U.S., one could buy $100,000 worth of groceries with the debit card and 50 Swiss francs would be deducted overnight from the account in Zurich, based on the then-current exchange rate. Such presumes, though, the ongoing functioning of a system in the U.S. that could handle the transaction.

Where the vast bulk of today's money is not physical, but electronic, however, chances of the system adapting there are virtually nil. Think of the time, work, and effort that went into preparing computer systems for Y2K, or even problems with the recent early shift to daylight savings time. Systems would have to be adjusted for variable, rather than fixed pricing; credit card lines would need to be expanded daily; and the number of digits used in tallying dollar-denominated transactions would need to be expanded sharply. I've received assurances from some in the computer field that a number of businesses have accounting software that can handle any number of digits.

From a practical standpoint, however, the electronic quasi-cashless society of today would likely shut down early in a hyperinflation. Unfortunately, this circumstance would also rapidly exacerbate an ongoing economic collapse.

Barter System

With standard currency and electronic payment systems non-functional, commerce would quickly devolve into black markets for goods and services and a barter system. Gold and silver both are likely to retain real value and would be exchangeable for goods and services. Silver would help provide smaller change for less costly transactions. One individual indicated to me that he had found airline bottles of high-quality scotch to be ideal small change in a hyperinflationary environment.

Other items that would be highly barterable include full bottles of liquor or wine, or canned goods. Similar items that have a long shelf life can be stocked in advance, and would otherwise be consumable if the terrible inflation never came. Separately, individuals, such as doctors and carpenters, who provide broadly useable services, could barter with their already valuable services.

A note of caution was raised once by an old economics professor who had spent part of his childhood living in a barter economy. He told a story of how his father had traded a shirt for a can of sardines. The father decided to open the can and eat the sardines, but found the sardines had gone bad. Nonetheless, the canned sardines had taken on a monetary value.

Howard J. Ruff, who has been writing about these problems and issues since Richard M. Nixon closed the gold window, rightly argues that it would take some time for a barter system to be established, and suggests that individuals should build up a six-month store of goods to cover themselves and their families during the difficult times. Such an option is within the scope of normal disaster planning in some areas of the country. Stories from the great Japanese earthquake reinforce those common-sense principles.

It's hard not to discuss any financial topic without taking note of the debt that has taken over the globe. Most people think that the U.S. Government debt is high. Incredibly, the debt picture is much more than that. Just take a look at the following screen shot from the U.S. Debt Clock.

In the Old Testament, one of the judgments for doing wrong was that a nation would be strapped with debt. HMMM!! Another whole book could be written on the FIAT money system we use globally that is completely based on debt. For a good read on how this came into being check out *THE CREATURE FROM JEKYLL ISLAND - A Second Look at the Federal Reserve* by G. Edward Griffin - American Media, 2003.

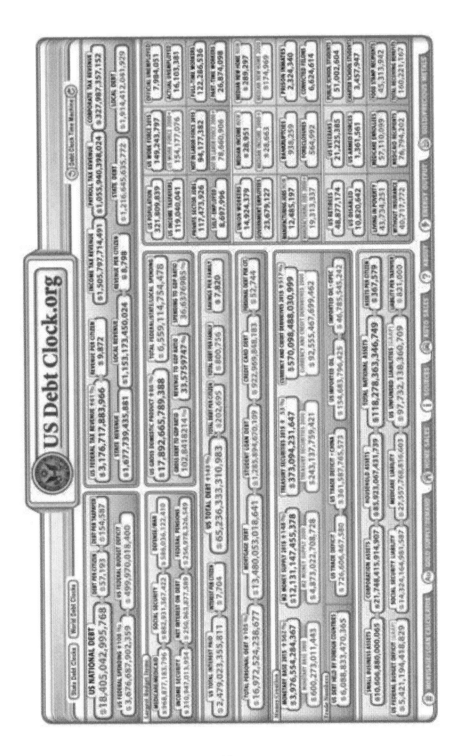

Strawberry Lemonade

During the summer of 1857, the Mabie Circus was touring through the South. One of the clowns suddenly decided to leave the troupe. The manager called on Pete Conklin, one of the sideshow barkers, to fill in. Pete did well, so well that he asked for a raise. The manager said he hadn't done that well. Pete was mad, and quit. But he was broke, so he tagged along with the circus as a lemonade-seller. Lemons were scarce and expensive in 1857, so Pete made his lemonade with tartaric acid and sugar. One hot day, he did such a brisk business that he ran out of his thirst quencher. Rushing to a nearby tent, he picked up the first bucket of water he could find, stirred in some tartaric acid, and was back in business again. It wasn't until he poured the first glass that he noticed his new lemonade was pink. He couldn't imagine how the color had changed, but with good old-fashioned American ingenuity, he made the most of it. "Strawberry lemonade," he shouted. "Try my new strawberry lemonade." People did, and they loved it. Today there's not a circus anywhere without pink lemonade. And how did Pete Conklin's lemonade get that color? Well, after 119 years I guess it's safe to tell his secret — a performer's red tights had just been soaking in that bucket of water and turned the lemonade pink.

Chapter II: Financial Advisor Tsunami

During the 2007–2008 crash, researchers surveyed retirement account owners who used professional financial advisors. At that time, more than 80% said they were unhappy and were looking for another financial advisor. When the market goes up, most retirees don't give much thought to their retirement accounts. However, when the tide changes and the tsunami hits, the accounts start going down and they start looking. May I suggest you start looking now? After you realize your income is not enough, your taxes are too high, you're spending down your retirement accounts for a nursing home, your spouse has passed, and you don't have that extra social security or pension check coming in, it may be too late to undo the damage done by an unknowledgeable or uncaring advisor who is more concerned about his/her pocketbook than yours.

Six Sure-Fire Steps to Hiring the Best Advisor

Step 1: Don't go it alone!

The rules of the retirement planning game are changing rapidly today. You need trusted professionals who focus on solving these types of financial and legal problems. These trusted professionals won't be found in the form of your favorite bank teller, nor at the local coffee shop, beauty salon or golf course. The most complete review available will be with specialized teams of professionals who have a qualified elder law attorney, a registered investment advisor, and a licensed insurance architect who all specialize in asset protection.

Step 2: If it sounds too good to be true, it probably is.

It's a common and scary trend today to hear retirees who have made poor decisions based on "buying into great opportunities." For instance, if a financial salesperson tells you about a 9% CD when you know darn well the bank down the road is paying 1.25% on CDs, guess what — that's a giant, waving red flag. When you hear something that sounds good and you want to believe it, ask more questions, such as, "What strings are attached?" If they say "no strings," then most likely, you need to turn and run. There are many great financial products with attractive features. But even the greatest opportunities come with "rules" (a.k.a. "strings" attached). You need to know what those strings are, if they are acceptable to you, and in line with your planning goals. Always use and trust your own good judgment and common sense.

Step 3: Watch out for legal advice from non-lawyers.

I know the value of integrating trust documentation and specific financial products. However, be very cautious when the purchase of a financial product also entitles you to free legal documents to support the plan. This is where you can be penny-wise and fortune-foolish. The business model of the firm should be de-signed for collaboration among like-minded professionals focused on meeting the goals and objectives of the client. No one professional can wear all of these hats and be good at all of these jobs. A key is to realize legal documents cost money, and a packaged offer with legal documentation included (based on the purchase of a product) should be a giant red flag.

Step 4: Beware of online "resources."

Information online should be viewed with a very skeptical eye. Today, it is not uncommon for retirees to jump online to do "research."

The critical question is, are you getting information from a credible source? The credibility of a source can be very difficult to decipher online.

Information overload is another problem. If you enter the keyword "revocable trust" on Google, you'll find about 962,000 articles, websites, and "resources." Yes, you need to do research, but on the right thing – finding the right help. Focus your due diligence on finding the right planning team to assist you (as discussed in Step One).

Step 5: Demand proof!

There's nothing worse than getting sold a bad idea. Slick talk can be very persuasive, but it may prove financially disastrous. When seeking professional advice, we recommend that you assess just how accomplished your potential advice-giver really is. How that person answers the following questions should give you a good idea of their qualifications and passion for their work.

Have you ever been published in an industry periodical?

Industry magazines look for real experts because they want their readers to receive credible and accurate information. Both you and the publication need someone who doesn't just talk a good game, but someone who really knows his or her stuff.

Are you an author on this subject?

Though many trustworthy financial professionals are not published authors, professionals who take the time to write clearly have a passion for what they do. They've taken time to spell out their planning methods and beliefs. It's not easy to write a book, and doing so demonstrates that they are dedicated and serious about their profession and proud of what they do. Plus, you'll be able to obtain their book, read it, and then check that the advice that they are giving you is in line with the message they published in their book.

Do you invest in your professional knowledge?

This question is a great way to gauge the prospective advisor's commitment to staying current on new laws, tax code changes, and cutting-edge ideas to help preserve and grow your wealth. The same logic goes for lawyers. If you have a large IRA, you might be swayed knowing an advisor has trained with Ed Slott, a recognized expert CPA in the area of IRA planning. Likewise, a multi-disciplinary advisor who invests nearly $24,000 a year to belong to an elite advisor coaching group is certainly educated on the latest and most effective long-term care planning strategies available to preserve and protect their clients' life savings.

Which professionals refer business to you?

It's common to ask for references, but I believe this is a loaded proposition. It wouldn't be too hard to find three or four people who like an advisor or lawyer and would give them a good reference.

Step 6: Be smart and trust your feelings.

Much is revealed when you meet face to face. See how you feel. Every person who walks through the doors of a financial consultation needs to be treated as if they are a member of the firms' own family. There should be no cost or obligation for a client to have a Complete Planning Review (CPR).

Maps from Memory

Benjamin was born in 1731 near Baltimore, Maryland. Early in his life, he showed great mechanical ability by taking his father's farm tools apart then reassembling them so they would work better. His grandmother taught him to read. His Quaker schoolmaster said he was an exceptionally bright pupil. He was a wizard in mathematics, and he was a naturalist with great understanding about crops and weather. He even conducted one of the first studies of bees, and he completed mathematical research on the seventeen-year locusts. Benjamin made the first clock in America, even though he'd never seen one. Borrowing his mother's watch and working with only a small knife as a tool, he took it apart, spread out the tiny wheels, and then reassembled it time and again. From this experience, he gained the idea for a chiming clock for which he carved all of the parts from wood. A neighbor taught Benjamin about surveying, and in 1790, the United States government hired him for one of the most important jobs ever. President George Washington had appointed Major Pierre Charles L'Enfant to draw plans for a brand new city, but Major L'Enfant, in a fit of anger, packed up all of the maps and plans and returned home to France. We would have lost that city forever except for the memory of that brilliant black surveyor, Benjamin Banneker, who redrew all of the maps from memory and gave us our Capitol, Washington, D.C.

Chapter III: Tax Tsunami

In his book *Comeback America*, David M. Walker, seventh Comptroller General of the United States, discusses the federal deficit. Below is an excerpt from his book:

Let's take the example of kids born in early 2000, when our national budget was in balance and the technology-powered future seemed bright. During the first eight years of their lives, we have learned, the nation's financial hole grew by 176% to $56.4 trillion. And the number is not standing still. That was its size as of September 30, 2008—before the official declaration of a recession, before the significant market declines of October 2008, and before the big stimulus and bailout bills designed to jump-start the economy and address our immediate financial crisis. In fiscal 2007, recall, our budget deficit was $161 billion, or 1.2% of the economy. By 2009, the deficit soared to $1.42 trillion, which is about 9.9% of the economy. Just think about that for a second. Our federal deficit grew by almost nine times in the past two fiscal years! Given our scenario—no benefit cuts, no tax hikes—the government would have to finance this gaping hole mainly by borrowing money from domestic and foreign investors, with interest. Don't forget, according to the GAO's latest long- range budget simulation, even without an increase in overall interest rates, our interest payments would become the largest single expenditure in the federal budget in about twelve years. And what do we get for that interest? Nothing! Of course, something will have to give before we get to that point. However, the govern-

*ment has over-promised and under-delivered for far too long. **How can we fix things? Will we cut benefits, those mandatory payments that are chiseled into law? Or will we raise taxes to onerous levels? We will probably have to do some combination of both. That is, we will have to renegotiate the social contract with our fellow citizens and raise taxes.***

DAVID M. WALKER has more than thirty-six years of experience in the public, private, and not-for-profit sectors, and is currently President and CEO of the Peter G. Peterson Foundation. He has received three presidential appointments, one each from Ronald Reagan, George H. W. Bush, and Bill Clinton, including as the seventh Comptroller General of the United States and CEO of the U.S. Government Accountability Office from 1998–2008. Walker is a frequent speaker, writer, commentator, and congressional witness, and has appeared in many major publications and on a significant number of television networks, cable channels, and radio programs. He is chairman of the United Nations Independent Audit Advisory Committee, serves on several boards and advisory committees, and is a member of the Sons of the American Revolution and the Trilateral Commission.

The tax tsunami could be the worst tsunami for many people. Often, we fail to see the fatal tax wave coming until it's too late. Sometimes the tax tsunami comes by surprise. It sneaks up on you and all of a sudden, you've just lost a big part of your estate. Taxes indeed nibble away at our assets a little at a time for many years. Then comes the last big bite when, upon your death or the death of a spouse, for example, your heirs are hit with the federal estate tax.

Before we go on, ask yourself if you are up to date on changes in tax laws. More importantly, are your advisors following the changes? Are they informing you about the changes, and do they help you truly understand what those changes mean to you? In other words, do your advisors help you stay abreast of tax changes?

We all know that taxation is one big financial tsunami, but here's the bottom line: **How do we reduce taxes, or eliminate them altogether?**

There are many types of taxes, but we'll concentrate on the major interpretation of taxation that affects senior citizens.

In all, there are four major types of taxes you want to watch for. Later, you'll learn the four major ways the Internal Revenue Service crashes down on your hard-earned savings. First, let's try to understand the basics of taxes. Here's how it works: taxation is based on politics, government, basic societal needs, "pork barrel" issues often defending the needless, and more.

Unfortunately, our tax system has turned into a tool allowing the government to take from anyone and spend stupidly. Equally unfortunate is the lack of a watchdog that could protect us from our government taking too much (especially when you consider federal taxes, state taxes, county taxes, city taxes, and district taxes).

Sure, we're all patriotic citizens. We know taxes must be paid to maintain the many wonderful benefits of living in America. However, when we watch the various ways our government uses our hard-earned tax dollars, it can be appalling.

If you paid taxes in 2008, part of your money went to the fund these federal programs:

- $150,000 to improve ways of killing rats on an island in Alaska
- $460,752 to improve the ingredients in beer
- $583,000 to the Montana World Trade Center in Missoula, Montana
- $50,000 to establish a museum honoring pack mules in California
- $98,000 to develop a walking tour of the tiny southern Virginia town of Boydton

- $188,000 to help keep lobsters from getting sick at the University of Maine's Lobster Institute
- $1.92 million of tax breaks for rum imported from Puerto Rico and the U.S. Virgin Islands
- $1 million for a museum commemorating the 1969 Woodstock music festival
- $1.9 million for the Charles B. Rangel Center for Public Service dubbed the "Monument to Me"
- $2 million for companies that make children's wooden bows and arrows

(Source: www.time.com Top 10 Outrageous Earmarks by Katie Rooney)

Therefore, we want to utilize every exception, exclusion, deduction or credit available — legally available — of course, and that's the nuts of it.

While government spending often seems out of line, that very same government has given us a wide range of methods to reduce and eliminate taxes. Unfortunately, many of us never bother to learn about these methods. Too many of us are afraid to take a peek at tax advantages built into the tax code on our behalf.

Many seniors would agree on this point: the last places they want to give their money to would be the government and nursing homes. Most say they would rather give all of their assets away than make Uncle Sam the ultimate inheritor. But at the bottom line, Uncle Sam only wants part of our assets. To ease the storm, he grants us numerous tax breaks in the federal tax code and, again, they are documented as "exemptions, exclusions, deductions, and credits." Yet, it's up to us to find them in the IRS code book and use them.

Many of us rely on our tax preparers to do this, but they often do not help to *reduce* taxes — they just add up taxes and tell us how much we owe.

Allow me to condense this entire tax subject to one simple word. In the margin, write this one word: **GAIN**. I know you're probably thinking, why the word *gain*? Years ago before they retired, many seniors thought that when that wonderful retirement day came, they wouldn't be working any longer. So taxes wouldn't have to be paid, right? The reality, as many seniors have learned, is that it doesn't work that way. There's a high probability that you have additional taxes now in retirement that you didn't have before.

Let me see if I can illustrate this for you. Uncle Sam has grown bigger and bigger over the years. Everyone knows Uncle Sam. But what about all of his brothers? We've got the Federal Uncle Sam, the State Uncle Sam, and the County Uncle Sam – and they all got together years ago and created a best seller. Do you know the name of it? It's a very big book called the Internal Revenue Code Book. The reason they call it a Tax Code Book is because you've got to know the code to get the tax breaks. You have to break the code to take advantage of this book.

In fact, if you went to the back of the code book and looked up tax breaks what will you find? Nothing. You'll find a footnote. Do you know what that footnote says? Actually, if you looked up "exclusions, credits, deductions or exemptions" in the index, guess what you'd find. You would find a plethora of tax breaks; however, it's not that easy. Simply because there is a potential tax break, you may not be eligible to use it.

You might need to combine certain rules with others to maximize your deductions. You may need to rebalance, reposition or restructure your current retirement plans to exercise your right to pay fewer taxes. We call this using TAX STRATEGIES. Just because you make one move in a chess game doesn't mean that you win. And making many moves in a chess game doesn't mean you win either. Most seniors make minimal moves in the tax chess game by going to a tax preparer or CPA. In order to win the chess game, you need to make multiple moves with a planned strategy. It's similar in the financial tax game. You need to utilize tax strategies and, hopefully, do that with a coach known as a Registered Financial Consultant. You may need a group of professionals – usually tax, financial, insurance, and legal specialists that take a focused, coordinated business effort to navigate you through these storms.

You've got to "know the code" or employ someone who does. I learned Morse code back in the 1980s to take my advanced class for an amateur radio license. Although I don't use it regularly now, I occasionally tap out letters and numbers in "dits" and "dahs" just so I don't forget. Let's try to break the code a little for you by exploring some simple tax strategies that may help retirees and pre-retirees. I'm not concerned with the insignificant taxes we pay each and every day. I stayed in a hotel the other night and paid an occupancy tax. You run to Wal-Mart and pay a sales tax. Put tags on your car, truck or RV, and you pay a tax. Simply drive on some roads and you pay a toll road tax. The taxes can go on and on and on.

Let's look at some of the big taxes that can completely re-shape a senior's retirement plans. There are five major taxes that we all face... one of them is a tax just for seniors. This one's specific to middle-aged and senior seniors. What comes to your mind as a Senior-only tax? What tax only affects seniors? If you said Social Security tax, you got it. Moreover, there are five major triggers that cause seniors to pay taxes.

The **first** tax of course is the tax triggered by receiving Social Security benefits. **Second** is the capital gains tax. If you sell something that you've held for a long time and make a profit you incur what is known as a capital gains tax. The **third** tax trigger that we all deal with is what I call interest income tax. That's the tax on your money when your money made money (ref: IRS form1099). Your bank sends you a 1099 on your CD earnings annually. Of course **fourth**, federal tax, and then the **fifth** one that I'd like to talk about is the tax on your 401(k)/ IRAs. Put it all together and it starts to sound like TAXFLATION! This last one's a time bomb, ladies and gentlemen. And when this tsunami hits, it is going to be severely detrimental to your IRA. We'll talk about that later.

These are the big storms coming for most retirees and pre-retirees. Many of us spent all of our lives working in our profession, and we became quite proficient at what we did. However, we all knew that some of the responsibilities in our work environment needed to be supervised by other specialists who spent their time studying, consulting, and expanding their knowledge base and experience in their associated related fields.

Most of us left our financial nest eggs in the hands of other specialists, while some did very little to plan for retirement. My concern is that most of what you have, whether left or moved to the hands of specialists, is currently being managed by those who knew how to get you **TO** retirement, but are not specialists in how to get you **THROUGH** retirement.

If you are retired, do you realize you are now facing up to 30 years of "unemployment?" You need to be working with an Advisory Group that specializes in how to secure you THROUGH retirement. Many of you have an IRA, 401(k), 403(b), 457 deferred compensation, KEOGH, and/or a ROTH. You may have heard of some of these retirement savings plans. These are all accounts that are normally used in individual retirement savings plans that have special tax treatment until the 30-foot tsunami smashes into your account. Then you're in survival mode. We'll talk more about that in just a moment. (Yes, even ROTHs have strings attached... little storms.)

Let's take a look at the social security tax.

In 1983, Congress started taxing Social Security benefits. Many of us protested, but Congress didn't seem to hear. When the dust settled, Uncle Sam increased the Social Security tax through the 1993 Omnibus Reconciliation Act, otherwise known as "OBRA." The last increase was supposed to affect wealthier Americans. Instead, the tsunami turned once more toward middle-class seniors and increased their taxes — business as usual. (Ref: http://en.wikipedia.org/wiki/Omnibus_Bud get_Reconciliation_Act_of_1993)

Here's the good news: You may be able to reduce or eliminate much of the government's Social Security tax rather easily. But first, let's find out if your benefits are being taxed. In the Income Section on the front page of your tax return, you will find a line that says "Social Security Benefits." That line shows how much you get from Social Security every year.

Let's say you get $10,000 a year from Social Security. Beside the Social Security benefits line, another line says, "Taxable Amount." Does that ring a bell? It should because if a dollar figure sits in the "Taxable Amount" column (under "Social Security Benefits") you are being taxed on your Social Security benefits.

In 1935, when Social Security was enacted, the government went to the social security and life expectancy tables created by actuarial scientists to see how long one should live by assessing the life expectancy tables. When they looked in these tables, guess how long an individual was supposed to live?

Before I answer that question, let me ask another...At what age were they going to start paying Social Security? Back then, it was to start at age 65. Now, the answer to the first question... life expectancy tables back then stated you were supposed to die at age 59.7 – five years before you were to receive those Social Security benefits! It seems to me, that the government never intended to have to pay much Social Security benefits in the first place. According to the life expectancy tables, most people would be dead 5 years before the government had to pay them their money back. Now what's the case nearly 80 years later?

According to a study done by Allianz (Ref: White Paper ENT-1132), the average woman's life expectancy is 80 years, and men's life expectancy has increased to 75.4 years. Today people are living longer, they're healthier, they have better medical facilities, and they're eating a little better. This is very important. In fact, when my dad drives down his driveway and he sees me or I see him, he says, "Wait a minute, Jay. You keep going to work. You keep paying in to social security so I can get my check!"

What triggers tax on a senior's social security income? The answer is income – plain and simple. If you make or create a gain, you have income. Now, many seniors think that when they retire taxes decrease, and they don't have to worry about it because they don't have any more money coming in. Well, you do have income according to the tax man. Let's look at that.

First of all, are you currently receiving social security benefits? Many of my clients have started receiving social security since they have been with our firm. Did you know that your social security income goes into the formula to tax your social security? Let's repeat that: *Your social security income goes into the formula to tax your social security.*

Number two, if you're receiving a pension, that's income. Third, if you're taking out IRA distributions, that's income. So what can you do to reduce your income? Send your social security back? Send your pension back so you won't have to pay the tax? Not take your IRA distribution? If you don't take the distribution and are over 70½, the IRS will hit you with a 10% penalty on the amount you should have taken and will still make you take it as income.

If you are still working and receiving a paycheck or a 1099 miscellaneous income — even though you might be retired — this also goes into the formula to calculate the tax percentage on your social security income. So we've covered one, two, three, four, five ways that money is coming in, and it all adds up. If your earnings hit the first hurdle of income, which is quite low, a senior must pay tax on his or her social security check.

If you're single and earning $25,000, or if you're married earning $32,000, do you know what percentage of your social security gets taxed? Fifty percent! Half of your social security gets moved into the taxable column and gets taxed. You don't lose that social security; half of it rolls over to the taxable column and then gets taxed at whatever marginal tax rate you fall in. The rate is higher if you file a single return and lower if you file a joint return.

If you're married, you and your spouse's income all add up. If you hit $32,001 of total income, then your social security income is taxed at the applicable rate. For example, maybe you have $12,000 in total social security income and you hit the 50% level, thereby resulting in $6,000 of your Social Security moving into the taxable column.

Paying income tax on Social Security benefits
www.socialsecurity.com

Do I have to pay income taxes on the benefits I receive?

You will have to pay federal taxes on your Social Security benefits if you file a federal tax return as an individual and your total income is more than $25,000. If you file a joint return, you will have to pay taxes if you and your spouse have a total income of more than $32,000.

Use the Internal Revenue Service (IRS) Notice 703 shown on the back of the Social Security Benefit Statement, Form 1099, to determine if any of your benefits may be taxable.

Social Security has no authority to withhold state or local taxes from your benefit. Many states and local authorities do not tax Social Security benefits. Contact your state or local taxing authority for more information.

I just gave you the formula on the law passed in 1983. Here's the law as it was passed in 1993. If you are single and earning $34,000, or married earning $44,000 or more, how much of your social security rolls over and gets taxed? What percentage? 85%! If you've triggered this level and you have $10,000 in social security benefits, $8,500 is taxable. That's how it works.

Taxes and Your Social Security Benefits

Some people have to pay federal income taxes on their Social Security benefits. This usually happens only if you have other substantial income (i.e., wages, self-employment, interest, dividends, and other taxable income that must be reported on your tax return) in addition to your benefits.

No one pays federal income tax on more than 85% of his or her Social Security benefits based on Internal Revenue Service (IRS) rules.

If you file a federal tax return as an individual and your combined income is…

- between $25,000 and $34,000, you may have to pay income tax on up to 50% of your benefits.
- more than $34,000, up to 85% of your benefits may be taxable.

If you file a joint return, and you and your spouse have a combined income that is…

- between $32,000 and $44,000, you may have to pay income tax on up to 50% of your benefits
- more than $44,000, up to 85% of your benefits may be taxable.

If you are married and file a separate tax return, you probably will pay taxes on your benefits
(Ref: www.socialsecurity.com)

Now, what can you do to keep your social security from being taxed? You can reduce your income. We've already covered all of your income, and there's a **preferable** way that we can reduce the big taxation. If you have money growing in a tax-deferred annuity or other tax advantaged asset, like oil and gas, none of those gains show up on a tax return; therefore, it reduces your overall income. With these options, you may be able to lower yourself under one of these levels and not have to pay a tax. We recently met with a lady who was just $400 away from not being taxed. We showed her how to remove the $400 the next year from her tax return by using one of the tax exclusions that I mentioned earlier. Now she's not paying any taxes on her social security this tax year. This is not tax evasion; this is tax deferral. This strategy prevents you from paying tax on your Social Security each and every year you use it.

Did you know that even tax-exempt interest income reported on line 8b can trigger a tax on your social security income? Now, you might be thinking, wait a minute, why would you have to report your tax-exempt interest if it's tax-exempt? Good question. It goes into the formula that calculates taxing social security; that's why they call it "sneaky tax." Of course, you could rebalance your income from taxable accounts to tax-free or tax-favored accounts and avoid most or all of this tax tsunami that 67% of seniors say is their biggest concern. You put into action this thought: why don't you take some of this money that's being taxed, take those CDs and move them from pocket A to pocket B. See, pocket A has a tax hole — a big tax hole. Pocket B doesn't. That's why you put those CDs and tax-exempt accounts into a tax-preferred account. You can still have safety, continue to get the return, and still have your hands on it, but not have it show up on next year's tax return because the government gives you exemptions, deductions, exclusions, and credits. If you use them, you get a tax break; if you don't, you pay the tax.

Let's talk now about capital gains. The old capital gains tax rate was 28%, then dropped to 20% and now, at the time of this book printing, it's 15% for some and approximately 10% for a few depending upon overall income. In my opinion, it's still a hefty tax to pay. Now, the good news is coming. If you sell your primary residence, the home which you live in, you can have a gain and not pay capital gains tax. A lot of seniors are down-sizing lately. If you're single, you can sell your primary house and make $250,000 and have no capital gains tax to pay. If you're married, you can sell your primary home and not pay capital gains tax as long as you don't go over half a million dollars in gains. If you sell that big house you've had for 30-40 years, you're going to have taxes to pay unless you use this tax break, and then you won't have anything to pay. There are some restrictions, so check with a good financial/tax planner for details.

Now, what about other assets: stocks, bonds, lumber, property, collect-ables? I had a lady from Greensboro, NC, who had valuable lumber cut down and taken off her land. She sold the lumber and received $100,000. She then turned right around and wrote a check for $28,000 back to the government because capital gains tax rate was 28%. Was there a way to prevent this situation using tax strategies? Yes!

Why didn't she do it? Her advisor didn't tell her how.

Let me share with you what you can do. If you take items that may have capital gains on them and you place them inside a special tax-favored financial legal account, like stocks, bonds, a beach house, may-be a mountain home, lumber, etc. We put all of this stuff into a special vehicle and you sell it in this special vehicle. You may avoid paying capital gains tax altogether. It's a Charitable Remainder Trust (CRT). Now, the key word here is the word **remainder**. It's what you leave af-ter you die that goes to charity. A lot of people think, "Oh no, I'm go-ing to do a charity thing and I'm going to lose everything I have." No, you won't. You'll get tax benefits and income for life.

Let me explain how it works. We have a couple that came to us and they had a farm that had been in their family for three generations. The local utility company offered them $1,000,000 for their farm. The couple asked us if they would have to pay any taxes. So we took their tax returns and gathered the appropriate financial information to assess the situation. We found out that they owed nothing on the farm and had owned it for many years. It had been in the family for many generations. We determined they were going to have to pay taxes — possibly $100,000 in taxes. Obviously they wanted to know if there was anything they could do. Of course one option is to put it in a Charitable Remainder Trust, then sell it to the utility company and they wouldn't have to pay all that tax.

What else should they do? How about taking advantage of a tax credit on the income tax for the next five years? Here's how that works. Once they take the million dollars and place it inside the Charitable Remainder Trust, the trust then pays them back $75,000 every year. And it pays that on a yearly basis as long as one of them is living. *As long as at least one of them lives, they get the $75,000 each year in income.* So now they have this lifetime of income. They had a million dollars that was leveraged for charity after they died; for this couple, that was their answer. Everything was great. We were getting the papers ready when all of the sudden the phone rang, and it was the kids. The children were panicked saying, "Wait, we hear you're giving away the farm!"

Mom calmly explaining that, indeed, they are because they're trying to take care of their retirement business. All paperwork stopped and the couple called a family meeting with their children and us. We all sat down together and we asked the kids, do you really want the farm? Do you want that cow kicking you upside the head? Do you really want to keep it in the family? Their response, no they didn't want the farm, just the value of the farm! They had no intention of farming the farm because they all had their own educational degrees and careers; everyone was doing something else. They just wanted the money.

After listening to the children and their concerns, we advised the couple to take a little bit of that $75,000 coming in every year and buy a one million second-to-die life insurance policy, place it inside a life insurance trust, and then when they both die, one million dollars goes to the kids, tax free! One million dollars is leveraged for charity. Mom and Dad are getting $75,000 every year. Now everybody was happy.

I'm just giving you examples of ways to take capital gains and do something with it – make it disappear.

I once told this story in a financial seminar, and a gentleman asked, wouldn't you have to pay a lot of taxes on the extra $75,000 in CRT income next year? Wouldn't it cause you to go into a higher tax bracket? Yes, it probably would, but the government sees that you're going to leave money for charity. Uncle Sam will give you a tax break on your income tax for up to five years. With proper planning, one can get a capital gains tax break and an income tax break, and leave money to the kids tax-free. The government will do a whole lot of things for you if you'll do something for charity. It just takes the right advice given to a coachable retiree.

Now what about interest income? Before we jump there let me pause.

Biblical Roots

The Parable of the Talents (a Biblical unit of money where a talent equals approximately $1,150,000 today per Max Lucado) appears in Matthew 25. The boss goes on an extended journey and turns over $5.75 million to one employee, $2.3 million to another employee, and $1.15 million to the third employee. The first two employees double the money entrusted to them and are commended and rewarded. The third man "was afraid" and hid his money.

In those days, an extended journey usually meant five to seven years. Interest rates historically don't change much. Three to five percent a year is probably a good estimation of rates in that time. Therefore, using what you know about money doubling from the rule of 72 (Be Attitude #7*), the first two servants must have found a way to make 10 or 15 percent per year. In other words, if the boss was gone five years, it would take a return of 14.4% to double his money. The worthless, lazy, wicked servant who buried the money was told: that's a terrible way to live! It's criminal to live cautiously like that! If you knew I was after the best, why did you do less than the least? The least you could have done would have been to invest the sum with the bankers, where at least I would have gotten a little interest. (Ref: Matthew 25:26-27)

> * David B. White, JD, CPA, CLU, ChFC is President of David B. White Financial, Inc. As a well-known speaker, David has addressed numerous groups including Fortune 500 corporations, civic groups, senior organizations, churches, and various universities. He has been a repeat speaker on ethics for the accountants and auditors for the State of Michigan. In his book *The 11 Be Attitudes of Prosperity*, he brings to light a story from the Bible. As a good friend of mine and financial colleague, David, has allowed me to quote a portion from his book. I recommend that you get a copy of from his website: www.the11BeAttitudes OfProsperity.com.

Let me tell you about Carl and Marie, who have decided to take a trip to visit friends. Carl and Marie hop in their car and head to Virginia to see some friends from high school many years ago. After driving for several hours, Carl notices that the car is running low on gas. He sees a station ahead and he pulls in. As he's filling the gas tank, he sees a sign: "Virginia Lottery." Carl has never bought a lottery ticket, but decides to buy a one dollar ticket, just in case. He scratches the lottery ticket and, lo and behold, Carl wins $1,000! That's almost enough money to fill a gas tank. Seriously, though, he pays for the gas and puts the winning ticket in his pocket.

When he returns to the car, Marie says, "What are you smiling about?" Carl says, "I just won a thousand dollars!" She replies, "You better put that in a safe place when we get back home." So when they return to North Carolina after visiting friends, Carl drops in to his local, friendly bank. After grabbing a doughnut and coffee in the front lobby, he checks in with the bank teller and tells his story of good fortune. Just as he's wrapping up his story, she says "Carl, I've got the perfect place for that thousand dollars. Let's put it into a one year CD."

Now what is the technical definition of CD? What does that stand for in banking terms? Certificate of Disappointment. Certificate of Depreciation. During the last years of Federal Reserve Chairman Alan Greenspan's term, he lowered rates. And now that Ben Bernanke is in his place, Bernanke has lowered rates to between 0% and .25%. By the way, I met with one lady who showed me her bank statements. When I asked her what she thought she was getting, she said a 2.5% return on her money. The bank had included the percentage sign, so she misread the .25% thinking all along she was getting 2.5%; she was only earning a miserable ¼ of a percent.

Banks can't seem to give a good return — at least not now. Although, if your son needs a business loan, they will loan him your 1% CD money at a rate of 7%. So, let me go ahead and finish my story about Carl. This was during a time when you could get 3% on a CD. Well, a whole year goes by and the banker calls Carl to let him know that his one year CD has matured. Now how much did he make? Thirty dollars. Well, $30 is a lot of money in anybody's mind. So Marie and Carl decide to get dressed up and go to Greensboro to Ruth's Chris Steakhouse, or maybe the Village Tavern in Winston-Salem for a nice place to eat.

As they are getting dressed, he hears a knock at the front door. It's the IRS — the tax man. "Did you make or create a 'gain' today," Mr. IRS man asks. He gets his calculator out and he runs the numbers and finds that they are in the 28% marginal tax bracket. Carl slams the door shut and says, "That's highway robbery. We had gangsters in the old days who didn't charge that much."

Minutes later, there was another knock at the door. Who is it this time? It's the State of North Carolina. Now they want up to 8% of that thirty dollar gain. This time, Marie slams the door and says, "Carl forget the steakhouse. Let's split a cheeseburger." But before she can turn around, she hears another knock at the door. Who is it this time? It's the social security man. On the national average, he gets about 3% of your overall taxed income. When we add all of this up, we are getting close to 40%. I haven't even mentioned inflation, or the other small taxes. We just talked about the three big ones. This time, Carl says, "Hey let's find one of those free lunch seminars." Now for those of you who crunch numbers, you will know this is not exact. However, I'm trying to make a point about the taxes that we pay, so bear with me.

If you take these taxes out of your small interest gains, you'd get what is called your net rate of return, or your real rate of return. And in this case, it's a little over 1%. So if they start at 3% CD interest (which you can't even get today), they'd be a little over 1% in real rate of return by the time they pay all of the taxes and throw in a little inflation, which the government is falsely reporting to be 3.5% when it's incredibly over 10%. (See www.shadowstats.com)

Now remember I'm not figuring to the exact mathematical penny. I'm just trying to point out areas that affect both your income and your gain. Has anybody heard of the Rule of 72? The Rule of 72 says, if you take your net rate of return and divide that number into 72, it tells you how many years it will take for your money to double. So using Carl's example, we take interest rate of 1— remember we started at 3 – after taxes and we got a real rate of return a little over 1. Divide 1 into 72, and it comes up to 72. So Carl's $1,000 CD will take 72 years to turn into $2,000. We've got to get a better rate of return and pay fewer taxes.

Now, if Carl is 60 years old, he'll be 132 years old before his money doubles. What can they possibly do? Well, this time Carl goes to see a local Registered Financial Consultant who considers carefully and reviews his retirement needs, after which he provides Carl with several solutions. I'm going to put four in writing, and this is all public information. You can research this on your own, but I recommend seeking the advice of good financial advisors before you implement any major financial solution. The whole idea is to use tax strategies to reposition your assets from left to right on the following chart. All of your assets end up in one or more of these buckets.

The more you move to the right, the less tax you pay and the more you have to spend, gift, and enjoy.

A BIT OF HUMOR...

"And now, if you can answer the following question, you'll win a million dollars. Question: If you actually won the million bucks, how much would you have left after federal taxes, state taxes, capital gains, county taxes, school taxes, excise taxes, alternative minimum taxes, Social Security taxes, Medicare taxes, FICA taxes, regional taxes, death taxes...?"

Equity index annuities (where you can capture gains of the market without risking your principal), or variable annuities, offer much higher returns. The income earned each year by annuities is not counted; it's subtracted. That's important… really important. In fact, one could earn thousands of dollars of income each year in tax-deferred annuities, and there is no 1099 issued. This has been called preferential treatment, according to the government accounting report.

Another method of lowering your taxable income is to put interest-bearing accounts into Series EE bonds. That's because, like annuities, as your money grows in Series EE bonds, the income is not counted for Social Security Income tax calculations.

For example, let's say your total taxable income comes to $37,000 for a married couple. That's $20,000 from pensions, $10,000 from Social Security, and $7,000 from interest-bearing accounts, such as CDs. If the $7,000 from interest-bearing accounts is put into Series EE bonds or annuities, the $7,000 is not counted. It is subtracted, leaving only $30,000 for taxable Social Security calculation. That's under the $32,000 threshold, thus the Social Security tax is eliminated.

And there are many different annuities available including "fixed" annuities, "variable" annuities, and "equity indexed" annuities. The money you make from these annuities is not counted against you for Social Security tax calculations each year. So, what happens when you take out the earnings from Annuities and Series EE Bonds? You will pay roughly 20% taxes on the gain. So, what good are the annuities/bonds? The positive effect is that your money accumulates faster and in greater amounts because your money is compounding by earning interest on principal, or interest on interest on interest on the money you would otherwise pay in taxes. So, even when you take money out of the annuities/bonds, you will have more money after taxes because it compounded effectively. This is a wise principal of money dynamics. Again, ask a tax professional for guidance on tax issues.

Consult an insurance professional for the array of available annuities. Know that spreading some of your hard-earned investment dollars into an annuity or two could lower that "taxable" income just enough to lower, or even eliminate, your Social Security tax. The savings is substantial.

Chapter IV: Catastrophic Illness Tsunami

Let's talk about catastrophic illness. Do you now have, or have you ever considered a long-term care insurance policy? If you haven't, then you should know that you really do have a long-term care policy; it's called the State of North Carolina, or whatever state you live in. Here's how your plan works. If you go to a nursing home, they're going to ask one major question. Who's paying? And they're going to do a financial asset test. They want to know everything that you have. How much is your house worth, how much is in your IRA, your checking account, your savings account. If you've got more than the limit, you've got to pay your own way, right?

Well, here's a joke. Somebody said, "Hey, I know how to fix that. If I give all of my money away and don't have any left, and then I'll be okay, right?" ***Do you remember the granny goes to jail law?*** To qualify for your nursing home to be paid by the state or federal government, they are going to look back five years. If you've given your house away, if you've given some money away, if you have given assets away, they're still accountable assets. You must spend down your assets or be disqualified for care.

Yes, you can put your money into a trust. This gentleman did just that, and they had a 60-month look back, as well. Anything that's been placed inside the trust is considered accountable assets. Then they divide the assets by placing countable assets on one side and noncountable assets on another side.

Here's how it works in the most simplest of ways. I call it the one-one-one-one rule. Here's what they let you keep. They let you keep one house, one car, one wedding ring, one burial plot, and $1,500 cash value in life insurance policy. If you're the surviving spouse, you fall under the Community Spouse Resource Act (CSRA), which says you keep a little over $90,000. That has to include your house and your car. So, there's not much of a break. The rest of your money must be spent down. In the state of North Carolina, you'll have to spend your assets down to $2,000. That's your own money. And North Carolina can put a lien on your property to recover your home and sell your home after your death to recoup any amount they spent to keep you in a nursing facility.

In March of 2000, I had a client reveal that her mom had been keeping her dad in a home and self-paying for the cost every month. She had had her husband in a nursing home since 1986, and he had died in 1999. I asked her if she would write me a handwritten note of how much it had cost her to keep him there. About two weeks later, I received that handwritten note basically stating that she had spent up to $442,000. She spent down her estate using the spend-down option.

There are ways to prevent or slow down the spending in the event you or your spouse has to stay in a home. Some of you might be thinking, "I don't really like what you're saying. **It sounds like you're cheating the government.**" Here's my response, and I want to get this off my chest so you know where I stand. How many of you have paid a Federal Tax, State Tax, County Tax, Medicaid Tax or Medicare tax in the last forty years? Some of those taxes went to Medicare, and some went to Medicaid to pay for your health care. In 1983, they changed the law and took away much of your Medicaid and Medicare benefits that you paid into the system.

Now, let me show you some ways that you don't have to spend your money. Avoid the Medicaid tsunami without buying long-term care insurance. Before I give you a solution, we had a lady and her husband that were found dead in their home from suicide. He had left a note saying, "I have been taking care of my wife for 44 years. I can't do any more than I have done in all these years." This is not the solution. This is serious and needs to be planned for.

First of all, prior to mentioning a good nursing home insurance policy, find an independent advisor who can help you look at a few options. Being independent, he's not forced to show you just one company, but can shop around and get you the best plan for the best price.

Next is a home health care policy. Have you been turned down because you have poor health? Or did you apply for a policy, but couldn't afford it? With costs topping $1,500 – $3,000 per year, either it's too expensive or it's not enough help. A home health care plan is less expensive, easier to qualify for, and it only covers you in your personal home. So if the kids can look after you, or your spouse can look after you during the evening, this policy will pay to have professional care during the day. It's just an alternative.

Last, let's talk about Medicaid Planning. That's where you sit down with an Elder Law attorney and a financial professional and apply their legal and financial planning to an estate to protect, preserve, and secure as much of your estate as is possible. I've noticed a shift in thinking lately about long-term care insurance. Here is blog from one financial professional who helps seniors in this area:

Real-time commentary and analysis from The Wall Street Journal

Financial Adviser
News and insight for financial advisers, wealth managers, and their clients.

Voices: Matt Zagula, The Trouble with Long-term Care Insurance

Matt Zagula is the president and founder of the Estate & Elder Planning Center in Weirton, WV.

The largest risk faced by the American retiree is the cost of long-term care. We know from the AARP that one in two Americans will face some sort of disability. And the cost of that care can be significant: Home health care costs can reach $14 to $15 per hour, and a nursing home can cost north of $7,000 a month.

A client who's worked hard to accumulate their life savings could be wiped out in a relatively short period of time. For that reason, all of our planning is geared toward preventing that from happening. Because when you're out of money, you're out of options.

Our priority is to devise plans that help clients build on their retirement savings and meet their objectives for lifetime income without the need to purchase long-term care insurance.

In my opinion, long-term care insurance is a bad buy. It is experience rated, just like homeowner's or car insurance, and ultimately the premium is not fixed. That's a big risk when you have a retiree on a fixed income. If they're faced with a premium increase of possibly 20% or more, they won't be able to afford it. Then they either have to reduce their coverage, or they have to let it lapse altogether.

It's challenging for financial advisers because the advice in manuals, and in the literature that's put out into the adviser community, is to sell long-term care insurance. But there aren't many Americans over the age of 60 who haven't been pitched long-term care insurance. And the percentage of buyers is still less than 10%. You have an audience that's saying, "This is not what we want."

So we, as advisers, struggle for answers to the problem of long-term care. And clients suffer as a result of different people in the industry not being consistent in their approach. Some advisers believe in 'magic' trusts developed by estate and elder law attorneys, and some believe in insurance-based products as a stand-alone solution.

Frankly, the sweet spot is a combination of the two. But unfortunately, America's retirees are underserved when it comes to accessing these types of services from teams of professionals knowledgeable in how to create a protected financial environment.

You may or may not agree with his comments, but I've included them here for your review.

Remember Franklin

Alaska is the largest state and Rhode Island the smallest. California has the largest population, and New York is not far behind. All of these we recognize with ease as different states of our Union. Many school children can recite all fifty states with little trouble. But have you ever heard of Franklin? No, I don't mean the man's name. I mean the state. It is unrecognized and unofficial; still, from a practical aspect, it is an important part of the great family of American states. Franklin's original land charter was in western North Carolina. The people there had pushed out into the wilderness to make new homes. In a primitive way, they belonged to each other and they were held together in a bond of defense against the wild land. With a fierce independence, they clamored for a separate identity. They wanted their own state. On August 23, 1784, the men of the west river country met at Jonesboro, North Carolina, and proclaimed the state of Franklin. John Sievers was elected governor. No one contested their try for statehood; many simply ignored it. That wasn't the reason for us not having a state of Franklin. The real problem was that they simply did not have enough money or manpower, and in four short years it was all over. The little brother state was lost. It quietly returned home to North Carolina. Now, it's only a memory. But they tried, and for that we owe them. You see, in large part, America is the chance to try, even at the risk of failure.

Chapter V: Legal Estate Planning Tsunami

Building a Solid Legal Foundation

Although 20 plus years in the financial services industry have given me a great understanding in the world of estate planning and elder planning, I wouldn't want to mislead anyone that I qualify as an attorney. Therefore, I have called on my friends, associates, and mentors — a leading planner/attorney team from West Virginia: Attorney Pam Smoljanovich, a practicing elder law/estate planning attorney and her brother, Matt. They published a book titled *Invasion of the Money Snatchers*, in which Pam has dedicated a chapter to building a solid legal foundation. With their permission, I am reproducing a portion here for your reference. Thank you, Matt and Pam!

One of the most important things you can do to develop a plan that will withstand a future disability is to build a solid legal foundation. While many see the wisdom in getting their legal "ducks in a row," most don't realize that not all legal documents are the same. In fact, common errors in your basic legal documents can actually trap your money and wipe out your life savings if disability strikes.

When conducting estate planning, the most common course of action is to visit the family attorney and obtain a Will. Everyone knows that someday they are going to die, and are generally concerned with who gets their assets when they are gone. Too often, that document sums up most estate plans, because people continue asking the old estate planning question. "What happens to my stuff when I die?" That kind of obsolete planning really misses the mark today. AARP, MetLife, and GE Financial all predict that at least 1-in-2 of us will need some type of long-term care in the future. Now that doesn't mean that 50% of us are headed for the nursing home, but at least half of us will require some kind of long-term health care — so we better have a plan to pay for it without going broke.

Are you prepared for a future of expensive home health, assisted living, or nursing home bills? If not, perhaps you need to start asking the new question in estate planning... "What happens to my stuff if I become disabled before I die and need long-term care?" You may have given some thought to temporary illness or a trip out of the country, and asked your lawyer to draw up a Power of Attorney — maybe you even printed one off of the Internet. If so, are you certain that document is powerful enough to protect your money and your house from being lost to nursing home bills?

You will be shocked to learn how traditional estate planning documents can create insurmountable problems if you or your spouse becomes sick — problems that can never be fixed unless caught in time. Be sure that your legal documents don't destroy your ability to protect your life savings if disability strikes. Read on to learn how to identify the most common errors contained in almost all traditional estate planning documents. We'll tell you how to spot them right away, and help you to avoid being the architect of your own future financial disaster.

What about All of These Bad Documents?

You are probably asking yourself why so many of these "bad" documents exist. Surely there can't be that many lawyers out there who don't know how to draft Wills, Trusts, and other basic estate planning documents. Well the problem isn't that these lawyers are incompetent, but they are practicing traditional estate planning, and that is really death planning. When a client visits an estate planning attorney, their biggest concern is that their money and their home go to whom they want without dispute or delay. You will see in the next few paragraphs how traditional "death planning" can actually have the opposite result.

The "I Love You" Will: Love It or Leave It?

The most basic of all legal estate planning documents is a Last Will and Testament, and many single folks without children don't even bother to get one. As for most married couples, you can bet they have traditional "I love you" or "Sweetheart" Wills. The husband's will states that when he dies all of his just debts and expenses are to be paid, and the remainder of his estate goes to his beloved wife. If his wife dies first, then his estate goes to the children. The wife's Will is a mirror image of her husband's, devising all of her assets first to her husband, and then to the children. Each spouse is named to serve as each other's Executor, and the oldest child is typically named as the alternate. These Wills often comprise a married couple's entire estate plan.

So what is wrong with that? Well, first of all, if your goal is to leave assets to your loved ones without dispute or delay, you will probably not accomplish that with an "I love you" Will — or with any Will, for that matter. A Will forces your estate into probate, which can cause great delays and disputes, and can be very expensive. But there's a bigger concern with the old "I love you" estate plan. Today, we know that one in two Americans face the need for some type of long- term care assistance — and some of those people will end up in a nursing home. The average cost of a nursing home today is about $6,000 per month, and as you have now learned, Medicaid won't help you pay that bill until you have spent virtually all of your assets down to $2,000. That's right — your entire life savings could be wiped out before the government helps you with your biggest health care expenses.

Let's revisit John and Mary. They have been married for 48 years. The family lawyer drafted their "I love you" Wills 30 years ago to ensure that their children (and future grandchildren) were taken care of when they died. Many years later, John suffers a debilitating stroke and is forced to go to the nursing home. Remember what happens to their money?

Mary is overwhelmed with worry about her husband's health care and with how she is going to pay the $6,000 nursing home bill and still maintain her home. She is spending down a large portion of their assets on the nursing home and is trying to live on a reduced income and half of their assets. The stress of her husband's poor health and the financial burden prove to be too much for Mary, the supposed "healthy" community spouse, and guess what happens? She dies first. What happens to John and Mary's money?

Well, Mary's traditional "I love you" Will leaves everything she owns to her beloved husband, who is in the nursing home. It all becomes the sole property of John, who is racking up that $6,000 per month health care expense. He will be forced into a "spend down" that ends in most states when there is only $2,000 left. The question now is this: Have John and Mary's estate planning goals been met? Of course not, because now their children and grandchildren will get nothing.

If only John and Mary had asked the new question in estate planning and obtained an "I love you dearly BUT" estate plan. They could have utilized special Trusts that direct assets away from a disabled spouse if the other passes away first. They could have preserved their money for Mary and passed on assets to their children, instead of losing everything to the nursing home. When doing planning, be sure you are asking the right question. Don't just plan for death, plan for disability, too. Otherwise, the nursing home might end up being your biggest heir.

Is There A Bear Trap In Your Trust?

Maybe you have discovered a viable alternative to those traditional "I love you" Wills - and transferred your home and your bank accounts into a Revocable Living Trust. A Trust is a document containing specific instructions concerning how your money and property should be managed when you are alive and ultimately distributed when you die. Trusts can either be revocable (you can change, amend or eliminate it at any time) or irrevocable (more permanent and unable to be changed) or sometimes a unique hybrid of the two.

Conceptually, a Revocable Living Trust (RLT) makes perfect sense. Traditional estate planning attorneys will explain that this Trust helps you to avoid probate — and that is true. The cost and delay associated with probate make an RLT a very attractive tool. Even if a married couple owns their accounts jointly (which avoids probate between the spouses) this trust avoids probate for their children, too. A Revocable Living Trust is typically structured so the Grantor (who created the trust), the trustee (who manages the trust), and the beneficiary (who benefits from the trust through income or access to principal) are all the same person or persons.

So, consider another couple — Fred & Wilma — who have transferred their bank accounts and home into a Revocable Living Trust so that when they die, their daughter, Pebbles, will inherit everything without the delay and expense of probate. Before their deaths, Fred and Wilma have full access to the money in the Trust. They can modify the terms of the Trust, spend all the money in the Trust, change the beneficiaries or even get rid of the Trust altogether (revoke it). They have complete control. It's truly a Revocable Trust.

Because Fred and Wilma were such good savers and Fred had a strong pension from the rock quarry, they have accumulated $300,000 in their Flintstone Family Revocable Trust when Fred passes away. After Fred's death, Wilma continues to have complete control over everything in the Trust. Like before, the problem comes when disability strikes. Years later, Wilma is diagnosed with Alzheimer's disease. She is no longer able to manage her own affairs, and despite her daughter's best efforts to keep her at home, Wilma now requires 24-hour skilled nursing home care for her own safety. Pebbles takes charge of the assets in the Trust because her parents had designated her as the successor Trustee.

What else has changed about the Trust? Although the Trust was revocable by Fred and Wilma, the original trustees, it is NOT revocable by the successor trustee. Pebbles is required to follow the terms set forth in the Trust, and will breach her fiduciary duty if she doesn't. So, is there a problem? If the Flintstone Family Trust looks like most Revocable Living Trusts out there, you can bet your bottom dollar there is. Traditional estate planning attorneys almost always include health, education, maintenance, and support language (often referred to as HEMS provisions) in the successor trustee section of the Trust.

The Trust actually dictates that the Successor Trustee (Pebbles) must use the Trust assets for the health, maintenance, and support of the Grantor (Wilma). What is the true impact of this language? Well let's consider Wilma, who is mentally incapacitated but physically in good health. She may spend years in a nursing home at a monthly cost of more than $6,000. Her daughter will be forced to spend almost ALL of the $300,000 to pay everything in the Trust. Like be- fore, the problem comes when disability strikes.

HEMS provisions appear in almost every RLT ever drafted; we see them all of the time. If they are in your Trust, it may be impossible for your family to protect any of your assets if you end up in a nursing home. Just a few sentences in a document that you PAID FOR can literally trap your life savings and force your children to give all of your hard-earned money to the nursing home. Without them, Pebbles could have preserved a significant amount of that $300,000 — which her parents worked a lifetime to save — and kept it in the family where it belongs.

Here is a cautionary word about Revocable Living Trusts; they are NOT asset protection Trusts and do NOT protect your "stuff" from the nursing home. How can you tell if your Trust is protected from long-term care costs? If you have direct access to the Trust assets, can reach into the accounts and withdraw money or sell your real estate and keep the sales proceeds without any assistance from anyone else, then those assets are NOT protected. If you can get to the money, you will be required to get to the money and spend it on your care before getting any help from the government.

Do You Have A Powerless Power of Attorney?

A power of attorney may be the single most important document in your estate planning toolbox — yet, most people don't ever obtain them. If you get sick and can't communicate or make decisions for yourself, the agent you appoint in your health care power of attorney will have the right to talk to your doctors, authorize medical treatment, and have full access to your medical records. A financial or general durable power of attorney gives your agent the right to access your bank accounts and sell real estate. This appointment is especially important if you become disabled because without it, it will be very difficult for anyone to protect your assets from being wiped out by long-term care costs.

If you have a financial power of attorney, how can you be sure that it is really powerful? We've all heard that the road to ruin is paved with the best intentions. Many well-meaning estate planning attorneys add gift-giving limitations to the document, such as: "My agent is hereby prohibited from making gifts to himself or herself." So if you become incapacitated and your wife is your agent, she will not be allowed to use any of that money for herself. Many powers of attorney will only permit your agent to make gifts "up to the annual exclusion." That refers to an IRS rule that allows you to gift $13,000 per year per person without it counting toward your lifetime gift tax exclusion. Most people know they can give away $13,000 a year (it used to be $10,000) without a penalty — what they don't know is that referencing that rule in their power of attorney can trap all of their money to pay for their future long-term care.

Let's think about John and Mary again. Suppose John has a $275,000 IRA (individual retirement account). Because IRAs cannot be jointly owned, the IRA is in John's name only. John has designated Mary as his primary beneficiary so when he dies, Mary gets the money. But that kind of planning doesn't address the new question in estate planning, does it? Because what happens to John's IRA now that he is disabled and entering the nursing home? As a beneficiary, Mary has no right to John's IRA until he dies.

If prior to becoming mentally incapacitated John did not sign a power of attorney appointing Mary as his agent, she cannot access that IRA and try to protect it. She will be forced to seek guardianship and con-servatorship rights over her disabled husband. She has to hire a lawyer, go to court, and ask that John be declared incompetent, which can be a horrible and expensive process. Then, a judge gets to decide what Mary can do with John's IRA (that she was supposed to inherit) and could order her to use the money to pay for John's health care instead of pre-serving it for her and her husband.

Good thing John had the foresight to get that Power of Attorney and appointed Mary to handle his finances. But is it truly powerful? Well, if John's lawyer included those gift-giving limitations in his document, Mary may be able to protect only $13,000 of his IRA — and the rest could be lost to the nursing home! This is an example where language designed to protect you (from a tax standpoint) can create much more harm than good... and by the time you realize this costly mistake is in your documents, it will be too late to fix it.

So look carefully at your legal documents. Look for limitations on gift-ing in your Powers of Attorney and look for Bear Trap language in your Revocable Trust. Seek advice from an experienced elder law at-torney who can help you fix these problems before it's too late, and build a solid legal foundation that you can truly count on if disability strikes.

It's not all bad news! There are things you can do to protect yourself. Here are some powerful solutions that you can put into action.

Get Out Your Tools and Build a Fortress around Your Money

Your first line of defense from all of the money snatchers we've discussed is to build a solid legal foundation. The sooner you start laying the groundwork, the better. You accomplish this by having a powerful power of attorney and carefully designed Trusts that specify how your money and property should be handled in the face of disability and the crushing financial burden of long-term care costs. If you have large IRAs or other qualified accounts, be sure your Power of Attorney doesn't contain gift-giving limitations that prevent your spouse from accessing and protecting your assets. If you have a Revocable Living Trust, look carefully for those HEMS provisions and get them removed! And remember, be aware — or BEWARE — that not all legal documents are constructed the same. Finding the right legal assistance from an experienced elder law attorney is the key to avoiding legal mistakes in your documents that could trap your money and make the nursing home your biggest heir.

Your Last Will and Testament and wealth transfer documents should be constructed to "disinherit" a disabled loved one who may be receiving public benefits. If receiving an inheritance will ultimately cost your loved one valuable assistance in the form of government benefits, then it is better to direct your assets to a protected account that can be used for your loved one's needs without disqualifying them from benefits.

Otherwise, your money will be used in place of those benefits until it runs out, which is probably not what you intended when you had your Will drafted. If your goal is to preserve assets for you and your spouse, and to transfer wealth to your children when you die, this is best accomplished through the use of special Trusts that will safeguard your money if disability strikes. Because when dealing with long-term health care, when you're out of money, you're out of options. And being broke and at the mercy of the government is a place you never want to be.

The right Trust planning can pave the way to a solid estate plan that truly protects your wealth and your health! Your own set of instructions, chosen in advance, can direct your money to your family and away from creditors, nursing homes, your son's unpaid credit card companies, your daughter's bankruptcy predators, divorce and your bad daughter-in-law, high-priced probate lawyers, and a government gone wild (taxes, estate recovery, etc.).

Planning From Both Sides of the Coin

After constructing a solid legal foundation, it is important to target the financial outcome you desire. This is best accomplished by integrating carefully drafted trusts with very specific financial and insurance products. This is not commonplace in the retirement planning community for two very silly reasons. First, most lawyers think they know everything and don't need any help. Second, most financial advisors think they know everything and resent the lawyers who often oppose what they perceive to be risky financial strategies (and counsel their clients to reject them).

The Financial Advisor is portrayed as a product pusher with no real value to add to the estate planning equation. In reality, the proper coordination and cooperation between these two specialties can greatly contribute to a sound estate planning process. But this big personality clash and a continued lack of understanding of how each can benefit the other, perpetuates this outdated, one-sided planning that leaves your assets at risk and the door open for the invasion of the money snatchers to barge in and swipe precious dollars right out of your bank accounts. (See, we told you it was silly, but that is the truth!) When conducting your estate planning, be sure you have a multidisciplinary team of professionals working for you. That way, you'll have all the bases covered (financial and legal) to help make your plan a home run.

If Gift You Must... Gift to a Trust

Transferring money within the family, especially to family members you trust, is a great strategy to protect assets from long-term care risk. But the money-snatching risks associated with gifting are so high that we need to summarize them again... and then craft a better plan.

BIG Gifting Risk Number One: Your children's problems can bump into your money. One in two marriages ends in divorce; drivers have auto accidents; your children or their spouses may have huge professional liabilities; the younger generation has much more debt than you do, and they love to use those credit cards. Your children may strap themselves with high mortgage payments, open-ended lines of credit and car loans, leaving them overextended and ripe for lawsuits from money-snatching bill collectors. Don't forget: If you put your children's names on your bank accounts and real estate deeds, you are paving the way for their creditors to get reimbursed — with your money and property!

BIG Gifting Risk Number Two: Thinking that Big Risk Number One isn't a concern for you because your children and their spouses are perfect?! If that is true, you are very fortunate. But no matter how wonderful your children may be, they still drive, work, and get married, all of which can expose your assets to money snatchers beyond their control. And remember, outright gifts to your perfect children may cause them to pay large capital gains taxes, receiving a less than perfect inheritance.

Making gifts to revocable Trusts with your children as named beneficiaries is a smarter way to keep wealth in the family by avoiding probate and preventing a disabled spouse from inheriting assets that will be lost to the nursing home. Using irrevocable and "hybrid" Trusts can protect your assets from future long-term care costs. We utilize a proprietary technique we call the Protected Gift Account. This strategy permits you to make completed gifts to family members without exposing your money to their creditors or creating large capital gains. Gifted funds are held in a "safe harbor" account designed to work with a specially drafted protective Trust. Taxes are deferred, probate is avoided, and assets are protected...a smart way to make gifts that keep on giving!

If Your Home Is Your Castle, You Better Build A Moat!

For many folks, the family home is often their largest asset. When you consider the added sentimental value, it's easy to see why this is one of the largest areas of do-it-yourself planning. Unfortunately, it is also the area where the some of the biggest mistakes are made. While it makes good sense to protect your home from all of those money snatchers, we hope that Chapter Four has opened your eyes to the dangers of deeding your home directly to your kids. If you want to avoid probate, transferring your home to a properly drafted Revocable Living Trust is a smarter way to accomplish that goal. Likewise, the proper asset protection Trust can protect your home from nursing home bills and estate recovery.

But remember, not all Trusts are the same. The wrong language in your Trust can turn into a powerful Bear Trap; if disability strikes, that trap will clamp down so hard you will never get your money out, and the nursing home will become your biggest heir.

Life estate deeds, once a very popular estate planning tool for probate avoidance and asset protection, should be used with caution. A life estate interest is the right to occupy, possess and use property during your lifetime. This right exists as long as the owner of the life estate interest is alive; when they die, the life estate interest dies with them. If you deed your home to your children and reserve a life estate interest for yourself, you will retain the right to live in the home. That right cannot be compromised by your children's debts, divorce, or lawsuits. As the owner of a life estate, you will have a present right of ownership (life estate interest) and your children will have a future right of ownership (remainder interest).

Unfortunately, life estate deeds are overused and misunderstood, and the protections they afford are often exaggerated. Big problems can arise if your house is sold while you are still alive. If you are a healthy senior who intends to use your sales proceeds to purchase new property, travel the world, or make investments, you may not realize that your children are entitled to a portion of the proceeds (which increases as you age). They are entitled to keep part of the money, leaving you with less money than you may have been expecting. The older you get, the less your life estate interest is worth, and the less you will be entitled to keep if the house is sold. In order to transfer ownership to the new buyer, your children (and in many states, their spouses) must sign the Deed. If they refuse to sign, they can interfere with your ability to sell your own home!

If you are a disabled senior now living in a nursing home, and your children sell your house, they may not realize that you are entitled to a portion of the sales proceeds. The percentage of your ownership interest is legally set by state statute (but if you're on Medicaid, federal life estate valuations may be used). When the house is sold, your portion of the proceeds will be at risk of being lost to the nursing home (and can cause you to lose your Medicaid benefits until the money is spent down). And if you have a lengthy nursing home stay and your home isn't sold until after you die, the new estate recovery rules will require the state to come and snatch your life estate proceeds... even though you are no longer alive! It's crazy, but it's true. The states are permitted to value your life estate right before you die and file a lien against your home for that amount.

In order to fully protect your home, don't rely on outdated planning methods. Properly drafted asset protection trusts can avoid probate and protect your home from future long-term costs while still keeping a roof over your head.

Bringing Dead Equity Back To Life

Millions of seniors are struggling to make ends meet without realizing they are surrounded by available money. It's all around them: in the walls, floors, and ceilings of their home. They just need to pull it out. Unfortunately, less than 20% of retirees ever use their homes to help fund their retirement and, of those, only 5% ever do so with a reverse mortgage. This is a severely underutilized and totally misunderstood financial tool that, if used properly, can be a real powerhouse estate planning strategy.

Contrary to popular belief, a reverse mortgage does not require you to sell your home to the government. Instead, you are loaned money based on the value of your home, and you are never required to make a monthly payment. The accrued interest on the loan is rolled into your total mortgage balance. The house remains in your name until it is sold. When you pass away, your heirs can choose to pay back the loan and keep the house, or walk away and let the bank sell it. Either way, your family will never be personally responsible for that debt. When your home is ultimately sold (by you while you are living or by your heirs after you die), none of you will ever be required to pay back more than the market value of the home at the time of the sale, regardless of the loan balance.

Pulling the equity out of your home to pay off all of your debt or go on a mad spending spree are probably not the most advisable uses of a reverse mortgage. And most retirees, who take pride in the fact that their home is paid off, would never even consider using their home as collateral. But the fact is, if you are pinching pennies and still drowning in bills, this strategy could be the proverbial life raft that gets you safely to shore.

For those who are living comfortably, reverse mortgages present unique planning opportunities to protect your future health care (and keep you out of the nursing home) and guarantee a tax-free inheritance for your family. This is the essence of the "Spend It Twice" strategies proposed by Matt Zagula in his book of the same name. A reverse mortgage is utilized and funds are paid out in one lump sum payment (an allowable distribution option). A portion of the mortgage proceeds are then used to purchase a life insurance policy with a special long-term care rider. Enough life insurance will be purchased to replace the value of your home that would have been inherited by your children mortgage-free. If you become disabled, and begin failing routine activities of daily living, you can turn on the switch and the rider starts paying out a set monthly amount for home health care, assisted living or even skilled nursing care. Unlike long-term care insurance, however, if you never need the long-term care money, the policy remains intact until your death, at which time it is distributed to your heirs — tax-free and without probate.

A Word about Long-Term Care Insurance

Another gigantic warning! Long-term care insurance doesn't usually cut it. It is experience rated, like your auto and homeowners insurance. If the experience of the insurer is unfavorable and they are losing money, they can increase your premiums. This is typically done when you are older, on a fixed income, and approaching the age where long-term care is a real risk factor. Suddenly, you may be faced with the decision to either increase your premium (which swallows up more of your income) or reduce your coverage, at a time when the costs of long-term care are going to be much higher than when you originally bought the policy. Coverage is generally inadequate, and if you never use it, you lose it.

In theory, long-term care insurance sounds great. In reality, it may wind up snatching more money than it protects. It may become too expensive to maintain, may provide inadequate coverage, and may give you a false sense of security that prevents you from planning appropriately. The smarter solution is to avoid the marketing hype. Steer clear of long-term care insurance and opt for life insurance with fixed premiums and long-term care riders. That way, you'll know just what to expect in terms of costs and benefits.

Income and Inheritance Trust Planning

You've read about the dreaded spend down and how skilled nursing home costs can be financially devastating to a surviving spouse. It is very sad to see the aftermath of financial ruin that long-term care costs can unleash on a family: hundreds of thousands of dollars spent. Then pensions and Social Security checks die right along with our loved one, leaving the surviving spouse in a financial crisis. Add in the final blow, courtesy of your State and Federal Government, when those hidden medical taxes (estate recovery liens) come and snatch your home from your children. It's easy to understand why retirees and seniors today just want to stick their heads in the sand and do nothing. Confusion and fear often lead to inaction. That, unfortunately, is the path to certain failure, with so many snatchers lurking in the wings ....that's why it's an invasion. Not one snatcher, but many snatchers, all coming from a different perspective or from a different governmental agency, can wreak havoc on a surviving spouse.

What can we do to protect a spouse's income and then ultimately pass wealth on to their family? We utilize a strategy we call Income and In-heritance Trust Planning. Just like the Protected Gift Account, success comes from a carefully crafted trust document paired with a specific insurance-based product. (Again, legal and financial concepts com-bined to produce the best results.) Here, the solution is reverse engi-neered. Consider a husband who is age 70, and his wife of 48 years is a healthy vigorous 68-year-old woman. Statistically we know that from birth, she has a seven year life expectancy advantage and can reasonably live nine years longer than her husband. The good news is, if he is alive and in fairly good health right now, we have the benefit of time and the power of compounding interest in our favor. Planning opportunities exist — even at age 70 — to protect a surviving spouse from the inevitable income loss created by her husband's passing.

Step one is doing some simple math. We discount back to present value dollars how much income we need to replace when the husband dies. Let's say his wife's income will drop $1,500 after his death. He is currently 70 years old, so his life expectancy is about 15 years. The question is: "How much do we have to put aside today so that in 15 years his wife is guaranteed from a highly rated insurance company to get $1,500 a month for her life?" In essence, the planning replaces her income she is sure to lose when her husband dies. Then, because we don't want that "pension value" to die with her, the unused value remaining is transferred without probate to their children. The solution is actually income THEN inheritance planning.

Financial advisors love to "round up." We totally disagree with that practice. If it takes exactly $82,437 to fix the income problem in the future, then that is the amount to fund into the strategy. You should never position more money than you need to use to solve your financial planning problems. Before you embark on any estate planning financial strategies, you should develop the attitude going in that you are going to solve your retirement planning problems with the least amount of money possible — whatever that number is... and not a penny more!

At first glance, this appears to be a purely financial solution. But remember, money snatchers come from all angles. Although the right insurance product can solve the problem of future income loss for your spouse when you die, you still must address what happens to your money if you become disabled before you die. Again, this is rarely analyzed because of the ongoing friction between legal and financial professionals (Remember, lawyers vs. financial advisors). By working with qualified attorneys, specific points of the insurance product are matched to specially designed Trusts, allowing for future income, as defined by the insurance product, to be available to your spouse after your death. BUT don't allow them to use all of your money in this planning strategy! Because if all of the money is available to your spouse when you die, and your spouse ends up in the nursing home, then your plan is seriously flawed! Unless the plan properly defines that income and NOT principal as available, your planning may lead you straight into the "spend down," and your children can kiss that inheritance goodbye!

Be sure you are working with a qualified lawyer who knows how to tailor your beneficiary designations to fit your overall financial plan. With a customized asset protection trust, your beneficiaries can be divided as income beneficiary, principal beneficiary, and final beneficiary (at death). This way, your money can be legally directed and protected. REMEMBER: Don't be a victim of the word processor. Not every Trust is the same. Income & Inheritance Trust planning creates a targeted solution specifically designed to replace lost income for your spouse and protect wealth transfer to your kids. Done correctly, this is a powerful strategy.

Heck, It Ain't Even Easy To Die These Days!

If a pre-paid funeral is not already in place when an ailing senior applies for Medicaid, the emotional impact of later trying to take advantage of this exemption cannot be ignored. When a loved one enters a nursing home, it is an extremely difficult time for the entire family. Family members are usually fraught with guilt over placing their loved one in a nursing home. They are often afraid that their spouse or parent may be ignored or unnecessarily medicated in a strange environment out of their control. But some families may hold onto another emotion — hope. Hope that their husband will get better and come home, or hope that their mother will progress enough to move to a less restrictive, assisted living facility. Nothing will destroy your hope of recovery faster than heading to the funeral home to plan your loved one's funeral. And for those who have accepted that their loved one will never come home, meeting with the undertaker and picking out a casket may be too overwhelming during what is already an unbearable emotional time.

Again, the importance of early planning cannot be emphasized enough. Making your funeral arrangements in advance, when you are 81, healthy, and able to participate can spare your family a great deal of unnecessary grief in the future. Pre-need planning can also save you money, not only because earlier purchased funeral contracts are sold at a discounted price, but because it helps prevent unnecessary up-sales by overzealous funeral directors looking to cash in on your family's emotions.

Be warned: pre-need funeral contracts don't come without their share of risks. Because despite the best intentions of most funeral home directors, each year we hear of unscrupulous funeral home operators and outrageous actions connected to the funeral home industry. In 2008, for example, Robert Helms, the owner and president of a company that owns and operates funeral homes and cemetery property, was discovered to be conducting a trust fund scheme that defrauded residents in Osceola, Indiana, of $27 million — money that was ultimately transferred to Mr. Helms and his wife. In the same year, the Ziomek Funeral Home in Livonia, Michigan, closed without warning, leaving an estimated 20-100 people with no funeral contracts and no refund of their money. The funeral home had been in business in the community for 16 years. While some have recovered their money, many others lost thousands of dollars and have no funeral plan in place. Seriously, how could someone do this?

Even in the absence of fraud or intentional wrongdoing by the funeral home, your pre-paid funeral contract could be in jeopardy, particularly if it was purchased before 2002. In Bessemer, Alabama, for example, pre-planners lost thousands of dollars when Bessemer Brown Service

Funeral Home filed for Chapter 11 bankruptcy. The bankrupt funeral home found a buyer who refused to honor the pre-paid funeral contracts already in place. Since 2002, the law has required funeral operators to place pre-paid funeral payments into individual trust funds which cannot be touched. This should help protect later purchased pre-need contracts from the devastating effects of a bankrupt funeral home. Again, this is a perfect example of why you need knowledgeable legal counsel, because these pre-need arrangements are contracts and are legally binding.

An alternative to pre-paid funerals is the purchase of a Final Expense Trust. This is essentially a fully pre-paid single premium life insurance contract that is specifically designated for your final (funeral and burial) expenses. There is no requirement that you choose a particular funeral home, and your family is spared the unsettling task of selecting your casket and planning your funeral while you are still living. Medicaid treats Final Expense Trusts as non-countable resources as soon as they are purchased and, in most states, these Trusts are considered exempt assets up to $12,500 (you must confirm this with a qualified specialist in your state). Final Expense Trusts are backed by highly rated insurance companies and ensure payment of your funeral expenses when you need them.

The attraction is that you are in control of your money. The scandals discussed above were created by the relinquishing of control of the funds. The Final Expense Trust is an account established by you, which is much more advantageous than an arrangement where an account is established by a third party vendor (funeral home) ultimately for your benefit, in the future, when you die. Not only do Final Expense Trusts protect you from the difficult task of planning a loved one's funeral, they alleviate the potential risk of funeral home fraud or collapse in connection with your pre-need funeral contract.

So while pre-planning for funerals is an advisable asset protection strategy, proceed with caution. Investigate the funeral home thoroughly before writing them a check, and consider the use of a Final Expense Trust to insulate your money from the future financial instability of the funeral home and the unethical practices of the greedy money snatchers who could be in charge of them.

Named for a Horse

It was a long time ago in England when a sportsman went to the race-track to win just one big one. He'd had a poor day and was down to the last race. He couldn't make up his mind on which horse to bet. So, his beautiful lady companion made up his mind for him. As a whim, she placed a few pounds on a particularly handsome animal that struck her fancy. Of course, it didn't matter to the lady that this beautiful horse had never won a race in its life. To her, he just looked good. In the language of the turf world however, he was just a plug. In any case, guided by her hunch, the English sportsman wagered all of his money on that horse to win. Well, as you can probably guess, the horse did win, and paid a great deal of money. With this newly won fortune, the man journeyed to America, settled in California, and invested his entire riches in real estate. He prospered and reinvested. His holdings mushroomed and became extensive. He kept buying and holding, then buying some more. Finally as a mark of honor, he named his immense real estate holdings after the English racehorse that made it all possible. For you see, from those holdings were born a community and a town that have become known and glamorized all over the world. You'd never remember the name of the bettor, but I'll bet you'll never forget the name of his winning horse: HOLLYWOOD.

Chapter VI: Wall Street Tsunami

A Message about Risk and Reward

If you're 55 to 85 years of age, here is a message for you about risk and reward.

Why am I writing about this now and asking you to pay close attention? Because today, people over the age of 55 face economic conditions much different than previous American retirees. The media attempts to make parallels to past decades, but this situation is different — much different.

I want to make sure that I explain to retirees (and those soon to be retired) important facts like the true impact of investment risk. I want to be sure that people over the age of 55 understand the return needed after a loss just to get back to even. This math is simple and important to understand.

As we age, the amount of time required to recapture our losses and the large gains needed become very difficult. It may take years of gains just to get back to where we started. (See the exercise and chart on the following pages.)

There are retirees who fear being embarrassed by their lack of investment knowledge, and thus, blindly trust an advisor. The question is, do you truly have an advisor to guide you through the turbulent times, or do you fear you are in the hands of a financial salesperson with motives tied to his or her own best interests, rather than yours?

Tom Brokaw called your age group "the Greatest Generation" for a reason. You worked, you saved, you raised your family, you sacrificed, and went without to accumulate the money you now have for your retirement and eventually for your family. Please have the courage to do something positive about it.

By the way, I don't mean to sound like an alarmist; nor do I want to profess that I possess all of the answers. (No one does.) However, I've been convinced that encouraging you and others in a way that no other broker, banker, advisor, lawyer or accountant could ever do is a worthy cause.

Frankly, I was a little reluctant to mention that many advisors are, in fact, financial salespeople and not advisors at all. But again, my colleagues persuaded me to explain the truth about how the money system in our country really works, so that you can lend the courage to take action.

Anyway, this really shouldn't be about me at all. It's all about you, your life with your family and sense of security. And it's about a terrific team of people eager to assist you — eager to serve you and provide plans which are simple, straightforward, and easy to understand.

SOUND FAMILIAR?

If you invested $100,000 into a mutual fund that experienced a 20% loss, you would lose $20,000. The account value on your next statement would be $80,000.

Question:
For you to get your statement balance back to $100,000, will a 20% gain recoup your loss?

Let's crunch the numbers:

$80,000 x 20% = $16,000
$80,000 (beginning balance) + 16,000 = $96,000

Answer:
No. A 20% loss followed by a 20% gain does not get you your principal back. In fact, to regain your original principal balance you will need to get a 25% return.

Required Return to Regain Your Principal

% Lost	% Gain Needed
20%	25%
30%	42.85%
40%	66.7%
50%	100%

Our process starts with a proven set of diagnostic reviews — a process we call the Complete Planning Review (CPR), to identify potential financial and family planning problems. We identify problems that may stop you from meeting your goals. Depending on the issues we identify, we have solutions available to help. The reassurance my team and I offer you is that our experience has allowed us to help others in these situations with ease.

You will never receive a high-pressure sale pitch. Our success is based on one simple key element: ***goodwill***. We want people in our community to know that we are here for them. After they meet with us, we want them to tell their family, friends, and neighbors how well they were treated and how thorough our review process and planning truly is.

Way back when, most of us thought getting a better value for our money meant buying the CD at the bank with the highest rate. Estate planning meant having a will. Things have come a long way since then. Although the economy is turbulent and some believe the government has gone wild with our money, opportunity still exists.

It takes courage to face things like volatile markets, fast-talking financial salespeople, long-term care concerns and Wall Street "money traps." It might seem easier to ignore it or deny it or to just hold on, tough it out, and see where it all goes. But I honestly believe that you and your family deserve better. If you're worried, unsure, unhappy, or losing sleep about what your money, your retirement and your financial future will be, then do something about it.

Wall Street

Who is always smiling when it comes to your portfolio? Who? Your broker. He's always smiling because you're always paying him — no matter if you're losing money or gaining money. You mean to tell me if my broker, what's his name, loses my money he still gets paid? Yes! When the stock market's going up he's buying positions and making a commission. If the market is dropping, he's put in stop loss orders which trigger the sale of my stock positions and he makes a commission. He makes money either way. If you think the big guys don't get caught in the psychology of the market, think again. They also get caught "buying" the top and selling the "lows" as revealed in the chart that follows. Here is a reprint from Elliot Wave International:

The process is being driven by an emotional, unconscious response by investors who look at the market subjectively and impulsively and who must make decisions under conditions of ignorance and uncertainty. Most people tend to engage in what we call herding. They follow the actions of others, whether those others are on the right side of the market or not.

The result is that prices move up and down according to investors' optimism and pessimism. Investors use the news to rationalize their emotional decisions, and most people lose money.

Even the big boys do it. Stock mutual funds tout their investing know-how, yet this chart shows that they also succumb to buying at tops when prices are high and selling at lows. It compares 40 years of the S&P 500's price moves with the changes in stock mutual funds' cash vs. assets ratio. When the percentage of cash is low, it means that the funds are buying stocks and keeping less cash (marked as "Bought" on the chart). When the percentage of cash is high, they are selling stocks and converting to cash (marked as "Sold" on the chart).

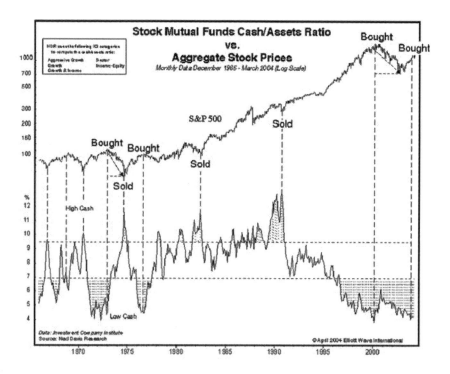

Mutual Funds

Planning for our financial future — whether for retirement, our children's college education, leaving behind an inheritance for our loved ones or simply building financial peace of mind — is something millions of Americans do. We invest our hard-earned dollars with the intention of making money. No one goes into an investment with the intent of losing money or even breaking even – what's the point in that? The goal is to invest wisely and make as much profit as possible in a vehicle that's as secure as possible.

Consider this. You hire a professional in the field of finance —whether a broker, adviser or fund manager — whom you trust and have faith in the fact that he will represent your best interests in the investments he makes on your behalf. He introduces you to an investment which is supposed to be a safe haven for your money, and with full faith and blind trust (because he's the educated professional) you pull the trigger and invest, expecting, of course, wonderful results.

Beneath the surface, however, the investment is not what it appears to be. It is built on a group of industry professionals who buy based on past history of a company's performance; thus paying a premium price based on perceived value from past performance. They sell when the once-high value comes to true-reality value, and drops. The for-profit companies involved in your invested industry face conflict of moral consciousness between producing profits for their owners and generating profitable results for their investors. They can't do both and have historically delivered inferior results to their investors while creating market-beating results to their owners. Profits for their owners and extravagant salaries for themselves were chosen over their duty to serve their client, their investor…you!

All the while, this industry continues to get away with such despicable and self-serving tactics because it promotes itself widely, pouring lavish amounts of money into marketing campaigns for themselves, as well as making campaign contributions to influence politicians and lobbying to avoid regulation. There's no regulating authority to hold them to a "fiduciary standard" — one that puts the client's interests first.

You'll be surprised to know that you probably have a portion of your financial investment tied up in this industry at this very moment. What is it, you ask? Mutual funds. As defined by Webster's Dictionary, a mutual fund is *an open-end investment company that invests money of its shareholders in a usually diversified group of securities of other corporations.* Part of the problem is the selection of the "diversified group of securities of other corporations."

Morningstar, a Chicago-based arbiter of investment performance, rates corporations on a one- to five-star basis: one being the lowest and five the highest. Brokers, financial advisors, and mutual fund companies aggressively and consistently seek out to invest in corporations with a four- or five-star rating. Sounds practical, the higher the star rating, the higher the past market performance. But read that statement again: *past market performance.* Investments are made by financial *professionals* based on a rating from *past* performance, not current, nor anything taken into account for the future. It only looks at star ratings based on past fund performance.

The rating system, itself, appears to convey such credibility in investors' minds that, even in years of financial crisis, millions of dollars of investments are being made in the upper-star rated funds. In 2010, investors redeemed $252 billion from the lower rated one-, two-, and three-star funds, while during the same time placing $304 billion into four- and five-star funds. In 2008, as the financial situation of the U.S. became crisis-like, investors pulled $174 billion from one-, two-, and three-star rated funds, but ADDED $47 billion to the higher-rated funds. Consistently, investments in the higher rated four- and five-star funds have remained resilient, while consistent investments in the lower-rated funds have not fared as well.

Many people are under the assumption that constant buying and selling is necessary to profit in the market. However, the constant changing of investor mutual fund portfolios mostly hurts, not helps, investor returns. The mutual fund industry uses both this misconception and the skewed view of the star-rating system to its own advantage. First, brokers and sellers use and even encourage what they know to be pointless buying and selling to increase and justify their extravagant compensation. Second, they use the star-rating system by Morningstar to stimulate "performance-chasing." In layman's terms, they encourage selling funds that perform poorly and buying funds that perform well, thus buying high and selling low. Where's the profit for the investor in that formula?

American investors are losing phenomenal sums of money each year due to the industry-encouraged unnecessary buying and selling of funds. In 2005, Morningstar examined and published a study of 17 categories of stock funds over a ten-year period. Not surprisingly, after taking into account the unnecessary, poorly advised buying and selling, the actual returns in each category fell short of the returns that were advertised to the public. As is fact at any time, the funds that were volatile performed poorly, while those which were more stable performed much more successfully.

In 2010, Morningstar reported that if mutual fund investors of 2000 as a whole had bought and held their funds for 10 short years, their investment outcome would have improved by an average of 1.6 percentage points per year. That adds up to tens of billions of dollars per year!

While volatility in the market causes losses to the investing public, the mutual fund industry sees no such suffering. There is always — and always will be — fund companies that have some temporary strong performance that causes it to rise to the cream of the crop and obtain a four- or five-star rating, thus providing the self-serving broker, adviser or fund manager with yet another offering to market to a gullible investment public. Of course, the opposite can happen, and does. However, there is always the "Cinderella" fund in the mix that starts in the basement with a one- or two-star rating until they receive their glass slipper (the four- and five-star ratings), thus ensuring them to skyrocket to the top of the upper echelon and becoming a new favorite to be sold to a blind, gullible, and trusting investor.

Mutual Fund Fees

Another blemish in the mutual funds system is the fees. Upon initiation of any financial transaction with a Registered Investment Advisor, they are required to disclose all fees related to said investment transaction. These fees will typically average 1.5%. Mutual funds salespeople capture their unknowing victims many times with the allure of disclosing that their fees for a mutual fund are on average .25%. Unfortunately, disclosed fees aren't the only fees involved in mutual funds management; there are many undisclosed fees. Some of those fees include a fund's brokerage commissions, tax costs, and market-impact costs.

Here's the basis of how it works: your fund manager/broker sells you a mutual fund investment disclosing his fees are .25%. And those are HIS fees; he's not being dishonest – just not fully disclosing ALL costs involved. Because built into the mutual fund, itself, is a management fee probably around 1%; there are also broker fees around 1%. (But wasn't he paid in that .25% he told you about upfront?) There are fees related to the number of times a fund is traded, additional costs involved if the fund is under traded (causing your fund manager to make several transactions to purchase a large number of stocks on your behalf), then there's also the instances where your manager obtains a less-than-advantageous price for your fund's securities. These all add up and you incur and pay for them all – as undisclosed fees.

So let's go back and tally where we stand. Our Registered Investment Advisor was going to charge 1.5%; our funds manager/broker is charging .25% in disclosed fees, plus undisclosed fees of 1% funds management fee built in, plus 1% broker fees built in, putting us at 2.25%, without yet calculating any market-impact costs. So where's the best arrangement again?

Mutual Funds: The Solution

Part of the problem in this whole scenario is the fact that investors are not involved enough in their own financial portfolios or they aren't educated regarding their investments. When it comes to our finances, most people would rather believe the best even when the worst is happening. It's the visual effect of an ostrich sticking its head in the sand. If I don't see my financial future is in disarray, I won't have to face the fact that it is.

There are several critical things that are going to have to happen to change the dynamics of the mutual fund industry to force them to put the investor's best interest at the forefront of their business. First, you, as an investor, must get educated and involved. Don't blindly trust — get involved. Just as the actual definition of "mutual fund" states, invest in a well-diversified portfolio, preferably low-cost index funds. Even Morningstar, the star ratings company itself, states in a very candid study that low costs do a better job of predicting superior performance than do the firm's own five-star ratings. Investing with this type of strategy, lower cost funds not only put more money in the hands of the investing public, but they take money out of the hands of the mutual funds industry.

A government entity such as the SEC (Securities and Exchange Commission) must get involved with some stringent rules and regulations to encourage such agencies to put the individual investor's money into a low-cost index fund instead of relying on a broker who will only invest in the higher-priced, ratings-related funds and thereafter jump onto the bandwagon of unnecessary buying and selling. There should also be some form of policing agency requiring the mutual fund industry to fully disclose an apples-to-apples comparison of their recommended fund and the alternative index fund; thus allowing the individual investor to make an educated personal choice for his or her own investment.

Most importantly, the mutual fund industry must be held to a higher standard and forced to put their clients' interest before their own, something commonly known as a "fiduciary standard." As new laws have come into effect and will in the future, the SEC must require that brokers act as fiduciaries, not just as an agent offering their clients what they deem to be "suitable" investments.

It's time to put a stop to the parasitic actions of the mutual funds industry. The lax actions and attitude of the general investing public over the past 20 years has allowed an industry we trust to help us and take advantage of our finances that we rely on not only for the current day, but also for our future. We've allowed it to happen. It's time to get educated, get involved, force changes to be made by the governmental agencies, and stop allowing the wealthy and powerful mutual funds industry to continue to take advantage of the less-fortunate — the investor, those whom they are supposed to be serving.

You can completely opt-out of this scenario by using a Registered Investment Advisor. This type of planning consists of a managed portfolio using only stocks and ETFs, not mutual funds. By opting- out you reduce the disclosed and undisclosed fees, and should see better portfolio results.

Red Zone

I had one lady recently tell me during a consultation that her other financial broker seems to have a one-size-fits-all planning attitude to her portfolio. If you're 57 years old and want a distribution out of your IRA or 401(k), you might end up paying a 10% penalty! Of course, a good advisor knows that Section 72 of the IRS code book lets you take it out without the penalty if you follow the rules.

Many early retirees make this costly mistake because their advisor/banker did not know or just did not care. The baby senior is the one that is in the RED ZONE. This area is one of the biggest financial tsunamis that pre-retirees will face. It's the zone that sets the stage for the rest of your 25 to 35 years of retirement. If you make a mistake here in the early years, you're most likely not to ever recover.

Let me give you an example. I met with a couple some years ago in the mountains that came to see me literally with tears in their eyes. They had been working and saving away in their retirement accounts for nearly 38 years. About a year before they were talking to me, their broker called and said, "Congratulations you guys are millionaires! Your portfolio just topped one million dollars!" So they decided to move from up north to the pleasant, southern Bible Belt, as they called it, to retire. The broker set them up for monthly distribution paychecks of a little over $4,166 for an annual retirement income of $50,000. At the time, they said this seemed like a good plan. As it ended up, their broker, who was from a widely respected brokerage firm, never thought to protect any of the account when they transitioned from the working phase to the retirement phase.

You see, many financial planners are specialists in getting you TO retirement but not getting you THROUGH retirement. Within a year, their IRA portfolio crashed downward to just under $357,000 and now they were sitting in front of me in shock, wondering what they were going to do. Listen, what you do in the first few years of retirement is so important; it's what we call the RED ZONE. Of course, each age group must not make the common mistakes typical for their age.

Let me give you some words of advice. The first one is, the Dow is going to go up, and it's going to go down, and I don't know in which order or how much — neither does your broker, neither does the money manager, nor do the gurus of the world. Nobody knows.

Can you afford to risk your life savings — your retirement money that you've worked 40 years saving? Can you afford to risk that in the stock market after you retire? That's the key question.

If you'll notice here, in the last 30 years we've had single year declines of 20% in 1987, 47% in 2002, and 57% in 2009. If you had decided to retire during any one of these years, your portfolio would have lost so much in value that you may have never recovered.

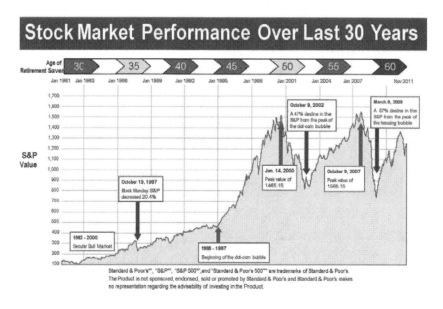

Let me give you the Wall Street Rule of 100s. You've probably never heard of it, but here it is. If you're 68 years old, you should have 68% of your assets out of harm's way and not at risk. When you turn 70, 70% of your assets should be out of harm's way. The older you get, the more you start pulling out of risk.

When I turned 15, I got my first driver's license, got a motorcycle, and drove it as fast as I could, not telling my mother, of course. Then my first car was a yellow Nova with the big V8 engine, tires that were huge on the back, sitting like a plane getting ready to take off down road. Well, again, I went fast. What was I doing? I was taking a lot of risk. But I was young. I had the rest of my life ahead of me. Then I met my wife and we had children and I slowed down. We got a minivan with some car seats to strap in the children.

As a senior, most of us drive slower and more carefully. When you were younger, that was your risk-taking time. That's when you were accumulating the nest egg while at the same time holding a job, acquiring assets like homes, cars, and personal property, and hopefully reaching for retirement in a reasonable time frame.

My dad visited me a few months after the 9/11 market crash and wanted me to read an article in *AARP Magazine*. In it was an article by Colin Powell with his photo on the front cover. My dad is a military man who served in the Korean War 73rd tank division. He said, "You may want to read this article about Colin Powell. He talks about the Seven Laws of Power." I went straight to the "Seven Laws of Power" article and scanned it. I then returned to the front of the magazine and noticed an article with a picture of a boat that looked like the Titanic going over the edge of Niagara Falls. It was a pictorial analogy, like these tsunamis. They were using this picture, and the caption read, *"Back from the brink. Terrorist attack pushed the economy to the edge."*

If your money is in the stock market, you're sitting on the edge of Niagara Falls in your financial portfolio ship that, at any moment, could get wiped out. Some of you served in the Navy. My sister's a nurse in the Navy. My father-in-law of 29 years served in the Navy on the *USS Essex*, which you can still see replicas of at the National Naval Aviation Museum in Pensacola, Florida. If you were the captain, how long could you keep that ship on the edge? Not long, I would guess. You are the captain of your own financial ship. You need to keep your money and your retirement plan from going over the edge.

Chapter VII: Bank Tsunami

B anks like money. They say they offer a kind of "safe harbor" through certificates of deposit. But how safe is a harbor infested with tsunamis? To find out, let's take a casual stroll through the history of banks and their treatment of senior citizens.

First, we'll put the infamous certificate of deposit, or CD, under a microscope.

Frankly speaking, the CD has performed miserably for seniors. Let's imagine a CD kept in the same bank since 1926. When tracking that same CD through years of taxes and inflation, the average return is a whopping minus .1% — the sum total and bottom line of the CD's history! Yet, bankers still hawk CDs like the last word in good financial planning.

Second, the advice you get at the bank may be poor to downright dangerous for your money. Many banks have even been known to tell widows and widowers to place their assets with their children. However, bankers often fail to remind you that your children might get sued in the most litigious era in history, or they may get divorced or file for bankruptcy. If those tragedies occur, you've lost the game. Your money falls prey to creditors, former spouses or plaintiffs in a lawsuit.

Third, lobbyists in Washington are in a desperate struggle to coax Congress to dump the Truth in Savings Act. The Act essentially protects us from interest rate manipulation, specifically the interest income on our bank accounts.

The Savings and Loan disaster in the late 1980s was a close call for many savers. If it happens again, who will pay for bank losses and how? Last time taxpayers paid, and next time taxpayers will, too. Only the next time, because of various pressures that have built up in the banking system, it could be worse.

Here's another one. We all know about the FDIC, the Federal Deposit Insurance Corporation. It insures the money we have in the bank — up to $100,000 — in case the bank fails. But the FDIC is a private corporation. In 1991, the FDIC was in the hole to the tune of $7 billion. Basically, the FDIC was broke.

So, what did the government do to fix the FDIC's leaky bucket? They lowered interest rates so the FDIC could increase their "spread." In business jargon, the "spread" is the difference be-tween two prices, or the difference between what the investment banker sells a security for and the amount of money the issuer of the security receives.

Putting it another way, if a farmer wants to sell a bushel of apples, he probably needs a middleman. So, the middleman takes the apples and sells them to you. The "spread" is the difference between the amount you paid for the apples and the amount the farmer eventually receives.

But what happened in the early 1990s when they lowered interest rates to bail out the FDIC? You would know if you had any CDs at the time. The amount of money you were making from your CDs dropped like an apple into an empty basket. It didn't do much for the weekly grocery budget either. Seniors all over America felt the pinch.

These are only a few reasons to pick on banks. One more example re-volves around the new desks that started appearing in bank lobbies a few years ago. Behind the desks sat insurance or securities salespeople.

If you sit down with one of these people, realize that the salesperson is not a bank employee. He or she works for another company outside of the bank. Just like a bank employee, however, they spin around in their chairs and put your name into a computer. It must be a computer cheer-fully provided by the bank because, lo and behold, they can pull up all of the bank's information about how much money you have in the bank.

In a nutshell, the bank freely gives an outside company — a stranger — all of the information about your private finances. In some instances, banks give your financial records to someone selling stock or insur-ance, although some banks are getting in trouble for the practice. It might even be against the law, depending upon where you live.

A BIT OF HUMOR...

> *"And make sure, no matter what, that you don't let those old folks know what the real returns are once taxes are taken out of their CDs."*

The main problem with banks is not that they are "risky places" in which to place your money; it's that they are places where your money can go to sleep. Banks simply haven't paid very high rates of return on savers' money, and this trend has not changed since the 1970s.

Someday that might change and banks might again become repositories of people's excess capital. But for a variety of reasons, that may not happen soon, if at all, without a full-fledged reshaping of the larger domestic and international financial systems.

Inflation is what really puts banks at a competitive disadvantage, and unless the international banking community makes big changes to the monetary system, inflation is here to stay — and has been ever since President Nixon basically pushed the world into floating currencies in 1972.

Without getting too complicated, when currencies float central banks can print lots of money, which fires up inflation. And savers don't do well in inflation. That's why in the 1980s and 1990s, savers turned to Wall Street and to innovative financial products that offered increased returns over stodgy savings bonds and certificates of deposit.

Over the past 20 years, stocks have outperformed virtually every other kind of investment. While banks have begun to offer securities through outside brokers, by law banks haven't been able to offer people the kinds of equity opportunities that have garnered big returns for investors in the past two decades.

Senior savers, who want to take advantage of strong returns for at least part of their portfolio, should look somewhere other than banks. Some basic instruments hold more promising returns:

- Stocks
- High-yielding bonds
- City and state tax-free bonds
- Zero-coupon bonds
- Variable annuities

Of course, most of the above options may vary considerably when it comes to value throughout the life of the investment because they ultimately offer higher returns. Another way to say this is that high-yielding instruments are considered "riskier." That's why Tsunami-Proof Senior Savers diversify and never put more than a portion of their savings into one kind of instrument or one investment strategy.

Take It or Leaf It

When it first arrived in America, nobody knew what to do with it. Some people buttered and salted the little dried leaves and munched on them as special treats on cold New England nights. Others just boiled it for an hour or more and drank the bitter, black brew without sugar or milk. It was said that this plant could raise spirits, soothe nerves, give comfort, and offer cures. As a drink, it was refreshing, bracing, calming, and cheering. It was touted as an aphrodisiac guaranteed to produce "ferocious love bouts" and "lusty desire." To others, it was a miracle liquid said to aid insomnia, asthma, and fertility. We're not really sure of its origin. It could have come from China or India or Tibet or Burma. But we do know that it spread all over Southwest Asia, Africa, Russia, and even South America. When it finally arrived in Europe, medical men called it "pernicious to health." The clergy denounced it as the "demoralizer of the working man." But the colonists in our New World finally figured out how they liked it, and the brew became our national beverage. It very likely would have remained that way if the English hadn't decided to tax it. We loved those little leaves so much by then that we were prepared to fight over them. "Taxation without representation" was our battle cry, and the Revolutionary War was fought, in part, at least, because of tea.

Chapter VIII: IRA/401(k) Tsunami

$\longrightarrow$

Okay, let's talk about the IRA 401(k).

Most seniors own some form of a retirement account: 401(k), SEP, EOGH, deferred compensation from a past employer, and IRAs. My birthday and your IRA have something in common. On January 11, 2001, the IRS changed the laws of IRAs (Publication 590 from the IRS website: www.IRS.gov). This is the exhaustive manual for qualified money, the bible on your IRA account.

Here we go… Your IRA, now can be taxed easily up to 50%, and in many cases up to 70% upon your death. Say you have $400,000 in IRAs. Upon the death of the last spouse, the kids might trigger what's known as "forced distribution," and they must pay taxes on all of it.

Suppose a husband and wife have a large IRA, and the husband passes away. Under normal situations, if the IRA beneficiary forms for their accounts are set up correctly, the wife will take advantage of a spousal rollover, which allows her to receive the IRA and not pay any tax on it. If the husband was over 70½ and taking distributions, she will still have to take out a distribution for the year he passed away. However, this is where it gets touchy. Many accounts have the proper structure to ensure that the kids get their portion without paying taxes.

But I've often seen another situation happen. When mom dies, she hands it over to her son, in which every dollar of that IRA floods the son's tax return. As it goes into forced distribution, every penny is going to be taxed at the son's marginal tax rate — every penny. It's a new law, so you've got to be careful. I'll give you a solution: it's what we call a "double tax."

I suggest at least an annual review to make sure that you take out the right amount. If stocks go up and you don't take enough out, you get a penalty. If your IRA value goes down, you might take more than you wanted to, which could push you into a higher tax bracket. And make sure you designate your beneficiary. Be careful and remember that your trust, if you have one, does not control or manage your IRA accounts unless you have one specifically drawn up for that purpose.

Let me explain it another way. I have two daughters: one of them lives in Kansas and the other lives in Winston-Salem, NC. I'm going to illustrate a $100,000 IRA account's distribution through the tax code: if I died and passed some of my IRA money to one of my daughters, this is how it would be taxed. Imagine that I'm talking about your daughter or granddaughter.

Let's say she's in college and every college student in America has at least three of "these." Know what *these* are? They're credit cards. And they're all maxed out. If I die, and Candace gets $50,000 from my IRA — or in your case, your daughter or granddaughter gets $50,000 — that floods her tax return as income. She happens to be working a part-time job while going to school, so she has a little of her own income besides the inheritance. Unfortunately, she has to turn around and pay more than $14,000 right away to Uncle Sam. Then, she is going to have to pay more than $3,500 in taxes to the State of North Carolina. And then she's going to do like every good student should do, she pays off one credit card at $7,500 because the car dealership she visited said that would help her qualify for a new car loan.

Now she's got $25,000 left of the $50,000 IRA inheritance and she is going to do what most college students are going to do, buy a new

BMW. There's only one problem. She runs down to the local dealership and she finds out that $25,000 won't buy her a new BMW. So she settles for a used convertible with tax, tags, and title at just $25,000. A year later, her boyfriend borrows the car and wrecks it and she forgot to pay the insurance premium because she was studying really hard for the final exams for nursing school and the state exams. Wow...in short order, $50,000 is GONE with wind.

Alright, let's start over. This time I set my IRA up as a multi-generation IRA. In this case, she gets a $50,000 multi-generation IRA, and now she won't have to pay tax on the whole amount. She can take money out based on a distributional process and not pay taxes, except for what *she will use*. Now this money can grow over half a million dollars during her life — from just $50,000. So it does make a difference.

I had a client that I showed this to and he said, "There's just no way. Why would the government let you not pay taxes?" Let me ask you a question: if you were a tax man, would you like to collect taxes one time on $50,000 or on a half million over many years? Taxes are paid either way; however, with the multi-generational IRA, they are paid based only on what is used annually from the IRA, instead of a lump sum on the $50,000. That's a multi-generational IRA, or MGA. You can stretch the tax distribution over the life expectancy of your children and/or grandchildren, allowing them to have tax-deferred growth and protect any spend-thrifty kids or grandkids you might have.

In a recent show on Rush Radio, I was asked to provide what I saw would be the top ten mistakes one would make with their 401(k) when they retire. I've listed them here:

10 Mistakes to Avoid When Rolling Over Your 401(k)

Planning for and securing the retirement of your dreams requires advanced preparation and knowledge. Overcoming the financial obstacles that could lie ahead is easier if you know what to look for. In order to reach your financial goals, it is important to understand the benefits of a 401(k) when used correctly, when and how to effectively rollover a 401(k) to an IRA, and how to avoid the 10 most common mistakes that could happen in the process. Proper rollovers can help you maximize your retirement assets, avoid unnecessary taxes, reduce expenses, and add ease, simplicity, and security to your retirement years. Avoid the common pitfalls of 401(k) rollovers and turn your nest egg into a golden egg.

1) Allowing the rollover check to be issued in your name

Retirement planning begins at understanding the procedures and options available to you. Don't take the rollover process lying down. How you rollover your 401(k) is just as important as choosing the product to roll into and the custodian, or money manager, of your funds. An improper transition can cost you 20% or more in taxes and penalties. Making certain that your rollover check is directly transferred into the new account is crucial to facilitate a smooth, penalty-free transition. Never allow your rollover check to be issued in your own name. Keep it simple and work with a qualified rollover specialist to help conduct an efficient transfer that can maximize your assets and minimize your tax liability and fees.

2) Neglecting to repay loans to your 401(k) before rolling over your account

Unexpected situations may cause a need to borrow money from your 401(k) plan; however, unless you are ready to lose additional funds, you must settle any outstanding loans before leaving the company. Commonly, when loans are not repaid prior to a rollover, the loan is considered a distribution and is subject to being taxed at the regular income tax rate, as well as a potential 10% penalty for early withdrawal, depending on your age. This tax penalty is over and above the interest that you were paying on the loan. Work with a qualified rollover specialist if considering rolling over your 401(k) with outstanding loans, and ensure that you implement the best strategy to rollover your 401(k) with minimal penalties.

3) Early withdrawal penalties for those under the age of 59½

Unless you are planning to retire at age 55, taking distributions from your 401(k) before age 59½ can be accompanied by additional taxes and penalties, thus reducing the available funds for your retirement. There are a few exceptions to the rule, including distribution upon death or disability of the plan participant, distribution due to a divorce decree or separation agreement or medical expenses representing more than 7.5% of your adjusted gross income. Your rollover specialist can help you avoid early withdrawal penalties with a proper transition and allocation of funds best suited to your financial goals.

4) Not properly allocating investment funds

You've been a diligent saver and set aside a portion of your salary each month since you began working. But even though that savings habit is good financial practice, improper allocation of invested dollars could put your savings and future income at risk. Not allocating properly is risky business, and your risk tolerance should be assessed based on your stage in life and financial goals. Those closer to retirement generally keep a more conservative portfolio, while those with a longer savings time frame can often be more aggressive. Determining your risk tolerance and comfort level is necessary to achieve optimal growth and, in the long run, protect your assets. A rollover specialist can conduct an evaluation of your portfolio's risk tolerance to help you increase the efficiency of your invested dollars with proper management, planning, and a rollover strategy.

5) Improper naming of beneficiaries

Leaving a legacy for loved ones is not always as easy as it sounds; the paperwork can be quite confusing, and one missed step could result in a loss of funds and difficulties for loved ones. Choosing a beneficiary for your 401(k) is not as easy as simply writing the person's name. Just because you want your niece to receive the funds, doesn't mean it will happen as planned. Oftentimes, the documents are filed incorrectly and 401(k) plans are considered marital assets. Thus the law states that if married, your spouse will automatically receive the distribution from your plan. The only way around this is to have a signed waiver. Naming a contingent beneficiary is another important step to insuring proper distribution after you pass. Single parents should pay particular attention to the beneficiary guidelines when choosing a minor as a beneficiary. Check with your retirement and rollover specialist about your beneficiary designations.

6) Rolling your 401(k) into an IRA before retirement

Despite the desire you may have to roll your 401(k) into an IRA, it isn't always the best option. If you are not ready to retire upon rollover, an IRA may not be the best option. When moving to another company, consider rolling over your 401(k) into the new company plan to take advantage of their fund matching, if available, along with any other benefits their 401(k) plan may offer. Employee-sponsored retirement plans such as this offer more flexibility for early withdrawal, loan opportunities, lower minimum balance requirements, and a higher allowance of pre-tax contributions. This combined with any company-matched funds will enable your savings to continue accumulating until retirement.

7) Rolling your 401(k) into an IRA when you have after-tax contributions

When rolling over your 401(k) into an IRA, it is important to make adjustments for any contributions that were made after tax. These non-qualified funds should be separated and rolled over into another savings vehicle, such as a CD, or taken as a lump sum distribution. If contributions made after tax are rolled over into an IRA, the invested money should be tracked continuously to ensure that when distributions are taken, the appropriate tax is applied. Distributions that include previously taxed dollars should only be assessed an income tax on the accrued interest. A proper transition of all of your 401(k) contributions will allow you to establish and maintain an easy and efficient retirement savings plan.

8) Choosing the wrong custodian for your Rollover IRA account

Making a decision on a new custodian can be difficult but, in the end, it is crucial to find a person who you can work with and trust to direct you in a way that serves your financial needs most appropriately. You have been putting aside money each month to ensure a financially secure retirement, so finding the right person to facilitate the growth, preservation, and distribution of that money is a decision that should not be taken lightly. Make sure that you choose a custodian that offers a broad selection of investment options, excellent customer service, and works with you based on results, not product sales. In retirement planning, one size does not fit all, so choosing a custodian that is open to customized diversification and knows what is available outside of stocks is an important player to have on your financial team.

9) Failing to create a road map to retirement

After years of accruing money in a company-sponsored retirement plan to allow you a comfortable retirement, rollover decisions should not be made hastily. It is important to know exactly what you expect from your retirement savings before determining the best rollover options for your 401(k). Mapping out your financial goals and needs for the 30 years you may spend in retirement is a step you cannot afford to skip. Defining your retirement goals is necessary before choosing the investments that will work best for you and tailoring your portfolio to garner optimum results. Lack of planning prior to a rollover can lead to improper allocation of investments, reduced return, and unnecessary increased risk. Knowing what you want and understanding what to expect from your portfolio is just another step to securing your future. With proper planning, you can achieve your retirement goals and ensure financial security for a lifetime.

10) Not working with a retirement distribution specialist

In today's chaotic market with a rising cost of living and medical expenses, not seeking the advice of someone with a comprehensive knowledge of the available options is a mistake that can lead to financial disaster. Your financial security in retirement affects you, your future, and your family. With a global market that continues to grow more and more complex each day, consumers cannot be expected to understand every financial product and option available. Finding a trusted advocate to help you choose the right products, plans, and processes to achieve all of your goals is essential to unlocking the door to a secure and comfortable retirement. Retirement specialists will work with you to reduce unnecessary taxes, maximize income, assess risk, and plan your estate. Your financial advocate will be able to educate you on your options, allowing you to develop realistic expectations of retirement. Be sure to choose a retirement specialists who wants success for you as much as you do, and thus maintains a working knowledge of investments and insurance products that fit your needs. Plus a professional analysis of your portfolio can uncover hidden money and significant savings.

Meeting with a qualified rollover and distribution specialist will help you avoid making these common mistakes. Assuring your accounts are correct today will give you great peace of mind for tomorrow.

Now, you have to use a custodial-approved legal document to accomplish this type of planning. It may now be more obvious that you just can't open an IRA and write down MGA or some kind of term on the application; it doesn't work that way. It has to be approved by the government, the IRS, and the custodial company you're with that's responsible to the IRS for your IRA. We call this Customized Beneficiary document for the explicit intent of helping you save taxes and making your IRA last for your heirs. This process of protecting your IRA is one that you should take seriously and seek professional guidance. To illustrate the seriousness, I've included the following information distributed at one of Ed Slott's advisors seminars that was hosted by a national Insurance Field Marketing Firm. This fits in perfectly with the number nine mistake listed above regarding beneficiaries.

IRA Custodial Documents:
10 Questions Advisors Must Ask

1. What is the "default option" when there is no beneficiary named?

By "default option," I mean the legal provision in the custodial agreement that stipulates what will happen to your IRA if you do not name a beneficiary or if the financial institution cannot locate the form (which could also happen, and often does), resulting in an unnamed beneficiary. If the agreement says the IRA goes to the estate, you know that's bad. You want a default option that says if no beneficiary is named, then your IRA goes first to your spouse; if no spouse, then to your children; and if no spouse or children, then to your estate. This will help to preserve the stretch option for your heirs if, for whatever reason, no beneficiary is named.

2. Are "per stirpes" beneficiary provisions accepted?

For an inherited IRA, the "per stirpes" provision describes how your IRA will pass if your beneficiary dies before you do. This is important to some IRA owners who may leave their IRA equally to three children, but want to make sure that if one of the children dies before you do, then that child's share passes to his or her children and not to the remaining siblings. Otherwise, the deceased child's family would be disinherited. Of course, if a beneficiary dies before you, then you can change the beneficiary form and correct the situation yourself. But what if you are incapacitated at that point and unable to make the change yourself, or forget to change your beneficiary form as too many people do? Then per stirpes is your safety valve. Some agreements will allow you to write it on the form yourself. For example, let's say you are leaving your IRA in equal shares to your three kids, one of whom is Mary Smith. You could simply write: "Mary Smith, per stirpes." This means if Mary Smith (your named beneficiary) dies before you do, then Mary's share of your IRA will pass to her children.

3. Is a customized beneficiary form accepted?

A customized beneficiary form replaces the traditional IRA beneficiary form. You create it with an attorney or financial advisor as a way of ensuring post-death control. It is as close as you can get to naming a trust as your IRA beneficiary without actually doing so. The problem with customized IRA beneficiary forms is that many Custodians will not accept them. They often will accept only their own forms. You should find out now before you go through the trouble and expense of customizing a beneficiary form with your attorney or advisor whether the Custodian will accept it. Even if a Custodian does accept it, another problem with a customized bene-

ficiary form is that as events in your life change and you want to go back and re-customize the form to reflect your new wishes, the process can get very expensive, like redoing a trust (or a Will) — in which case if you want this much post-death control, you are probably better off naming a trust as your IRA beneficiary in the first place.

4. Can the beneficiary name a beneficiary?

Why do you care if your beneficiary will be allowed to name a beneficiary? If your beneficiary has, say, a 40-year life expectancy when he or she inherits and dies prematurely 10 years later, there is still 30 years left on the stretch period, and the IRA will allow a successor beneficiary to stretch withdrawals over that 30 years — unless the Custodian refuses. In that case, the inherited IRA must go through probate court, subjecting your IRA to estate claims and contests, taxes, and other costs — likely killing the remaining stretch. The way to avoid all of this is to set your IRA up with a Custodian that agrees to allow your beneficiary to name a beneficiary. This way, if your beneficiary dies before the IRA is paid out, the named successor beneficiary will receive what's left and be able to continue the stretch based on the original beneficiary's remaining life expectancy at the time of death. If your IRA Custodian won't allow this, switch to one who will.

5. Can non-spouse beneficiaries move investments via a trustee-to-trustee transfer?

You certainly want to give your non-spouse beneficiaries the flexibility to change investment or custodians if they wish. For example, they may want to put the IRA in less conservative investments that may pay more, or move the IRA to another bank. In either case, they cannot just take the money out, then re-invest it or take it to another bank. That's called a rollover. The only alternative for them — other than accepting a lump sum check and getting hit with taxes — is to move the inherited IRA funds from one Custodian to another via what is called a trustee-to-trustee (or direct) transfer. The funds are untouched in the transition and safe from taxes. Make sure your IRA Custodian allows this; if not, pick another who does.

6. Are multiple beneficiaries and IRA splitting permitted?

Most institutions will let you open several IRAs and name different beneficiaries on each one, but what I'm talking about here is naming several beneficiaries on one IRA. It is important to know now if your Custodian will permit you to name multiple beneficiaries (your three children, for example) and allow them to split the IRA into their separate shares after you're gone so that each beneficiary can stretch distributions over his or her own life expectancy. If your IRA Custodian does not allow splitting, then your beneficiaries must all take distributions over the life expectancy of the oldest one. To put it another way, they must use the beneficiary with the shortest life expectancy to calculate post death withdrawals. If you name your three children and they are all around the same age, this won't make much of a difference. But if one beneficiary is 92-year-old Aunt Edna and the other is two-year-old granddaughter Samantha, the latter will be stuck using Aunt Edna's life expectancy for the stretch period.

7. Will a trust be accepted as beneficiary?

If you want to name a trust as your IRA beneficiary, make sure that your IRA Custodian will accept a trust to be utilized and agree to pay out the inherited IRA according to the terms of the trust. It would be a shame to go through the trouble, time, and expense of naming a trust as your IRA beneficiary only to have your beneficiaries find out too late after you are gone that your custodial agreement does not provide for trusts to be utilized.

8. Will your Power of Attorney form be accepted?

A Power of Attorney allows the person you designate to act in your place. Bestowing a POA can prove invaluable if, for health reasons, you are unable to act for yourself. Depending upon how much power you give the person you designate, he or she will be able to make investment decisions, execute IRA transactions, including transferring IRA funds, changing IRA beneficiaries on your IRA beneficiary form, making required IRA distributions, and so on. Obviously you would give this broad power only to a spouse, child or some other trusted family member or friend. It's good to have just in case. Be sure your custodial agreement will accept a POA form allowing you to appoint another person to act on your behalf to maintain all stretch options.

9. Is there a divorce provision?

Is the agreement silent on divorce or does it say how the Custodian will treat an ex-spouse who is not removed as beneficiary? Here's the situation. You go through a messy divorce and your property and other assets are split up. The divorce papers are signed; you even do a new will. Then you walk away, never to look back because you want to move on with your life. What happens if you never removed your ex-spouse as beneficiary on the IRA beneficiary form? While most Custodians are silent on the issue, some agreements do contain a provision that says a divorce or legal separation revokes the previous designation of a former spouse as beneficiary, unless the divorce decree stipulates otherwise. This provision is a way of making sure your ex-spouse doesn't inherit and get to stretch your IRA instead of your new spouse and children in case you split up. Of course, this is just a safety net since changing the beneficiary after a divorce should always be addressed, but often this is missed and a safety net could really come in handy.

10. Is there a simultaneous death provision?

How will your IRA Custodian handle things should you and your designated beneficiary (your spouse, for example) die at the same time? You'll want to be assured that your children (or whoever is next in line) will be named designated beneficiary so they can get the benefit of the stretch. Also, for estate planning purposes, if you and your spouse die together in a car accident or plane crash, it is important to know who is deemed to have predeceased the other.

If you have an IRA of $50,000 or more, you can get a free proposal on your IRA. Recently, we produced this IRA proposal for a 3.2 million dollar IRA. Just send me an email, and ask me how you can get it: info@semmax.com.

Once you have your free IRA proposal, here's what it'll tell you. It's going to tell you what your children are going to get and even what the grandchildren will get. How many of you remember the first and last names of your granddaughters? Made you think, didn't I? Okay. What if your granddaughter or grandson was receiving a check from you every month with your name on it 27 years from now? Do you think they'll remember your first and last name? They'll remember. Where's that check? It's a day late. Where is it?

We provided one retiree with his IRA report, and it shows his grandson, whose name is Jacob, in the year 2069 will be getting an $8,000 annual distribution from his grandfather's IRA. So this is what I was telling you. We plug in **your** numbers; it's a great thing to have. You should also have an assessment of your risk management completed, know whether or not you should have your money in the market and stock market at risk, and determine gift planning. What is the gift planning rule? How much? You know what my rule of thumb is? Gift the money while you're alive. It makes better tax sense, and it makes better sense when the kids can give you a hug and thank you in person. You can watch them enjoy it now before you are gone.

You'll also need to have an annual review. And finally, know that you don't have to keep your IRA with the broker, banker, annuity or planner that it's currently with now. You can reposition and rebalance your IRA 401(k) to another custodian and/or advisor by rolling it over to a new company without IRS penalties, no capital gains, and no taxes — if it's done correctly. Just remember that most brokers or financial planners don't want you to move it because they will not be able to manage it and charge their fees or commissions. As I said earlier, it's your money and you're the captain of your ship. If you see the IRA tax tsunami getting ready to hit, I suggest you make the changes to safety as soon as possible.

The Other Rider

Did you know that a sixteen-year-old outrode Paul Revere? It's true! Young Ludington lived on a farm in New York with a father who was a captain of the state militia.

On the night of April 27, 1777, a messenger arrived on the Ludington farm with the urgent news that the British, in a surprise attack from Long Island, had burned the city of Danbury, Connecticut, and were advancing on the countryside. Every farmer must be called out immediately. Because the senior Ludington had to stay for military duty, the sixteen-year-old volunteered for the job of riding and calling the farmers to fight.

Grabbing a big stick, the young Ludington leaped on a horse and galloped into the darkness. It was an all-night ride with pauses only long enough at each farm house to crash the stick against the door and shout a warning, "The British are coming! Get out and fight!" And they did. Ludington mustered up enough men to not only stop the British, but also send them running back to their boats in defeat. Ludington far outdid Paul Revere's famous ride. Paul only got about ten miles before the British at Lexington captured him. Ludington covered a staggering forty miles of hard riding.

It's interesting to note that one of America's first heroes was a sixteen-year-old girl named Sybil Ludington!

Chapter IX: Retirement Income Tsunami

~~~

Are You Still Using The Wrong Accounts To Create Tax-Favored, Safe Income?

Seniors so often use the wrong financial accounts to accomplish income planning. The typical bank CD holder is absolutely LOVED by the bank. The bank returns 1% interest on their $100,000 CD while, all the time, the bank loans that same $100,000 out for 4–7% or more in consumer or small business loans to the local community. Consequently, the CD holder gets a LOW return and then has to pay taxes on that return. Here is a sample retiree's Bank CD portfolio:

- $400,000 at 2% interest provides $8,000 of yearly income.
- This $8,000, whether the senior spends it or not, is recorded on line 8a of their tax return, resulting in an average NC state and Federal marginal tax of 30%.
- So $2,400 of the $8,000 the CD made is now returned to the IRS.

Using a tax-favored plan, the same $400,000 should result in $24,000 of income. However, this time even though more income is received only $1,200 shows up on line 8a of the tax return, resulting in the IRS getting a measly $36. Is this legal? Yes. Is this safe? Yes. Are their strings attached? Yes. Check with your advisor about the SIPS tax-favored financial income strategy. Why doesn't the bank tell me about this? Do you think the bank wants to have you move the money that they pay you 1% interest on and lose the opportunity gain their 7% profit? Banks are public, for-profit companies. They want to make money for their stockholders, so they are in business to take your money and make more money.

Peter "Coach Pete" D'Arruda has a syndicated radio show, *The Financial Safari*, which can be heard nationwide. Recently, Coach Pete interviewed 14 experienced financial advisors from around the nation. This team provided an insider look into the financial world and translated the complicated financial realm into something that is easy to understand, relatively speaking. I've included this in my book to help you make more informed choices as you put together your own financial roadmap to meet your own financial goals. The following is a reprint from Chapter 8 of Peter J. D'Arruda's book *Have You Been Talking to Financial Aliens?* (Used with permission.)

"True discovery consists not in finding new landscapes but in seeing the same landscapes with new eyes." — *Marcel Proust*

What do you tell someone who is looking for lifetime income using the assets they have?

As we age, more and more of our funds need to not only be in safe places, but also in places that guarantee a lifetime income. This is called income planning. An income plan, also known as a "Basket Strategy," can help ease people's worries about retirement income as well as market volatility. The basic theory of a "Basket Strategy" is to separate your money into four places, or baskets, each one with a specific purpose. One basket provides immediate income and three others grow to provide income down the road. At least one basket should be guaranteed income you cannot outlive, with the remaining assets passing to children, grandchildren, or charity. The main goal of a "Basket Strategy" is to provide a 15-year income stream from three baskets, and at the end of that 15-year period, the final basket still contains an income account with a value equal to or greater than the total amount used to start the "Basket Strategy." The final basket is always built with a guaranteed income withdrawal benefit to take the account holder the rest of the way. This helps establish a predictable and guaranteed yearly income. Income planning is unique and must be customized for each person depending on their risk tolerance, needs, and time frame in which the income is needed. The team answered this question like this:

Brad Zucker — "Like all of our clients, we are in agreement that future inflation will rise faster than the rate it has in the last ten years. Thus, it is important to have an income plan in place."

John Pollock — "I try to ascertain if where they want to be (the amount of monthly income they want), and where they are (current assets, plus retirement income streams) times the erosion of inflation (we use the hundred year average and a double digit calculation) is actually attainable. If not, we try to determine if they need to save more, get better returns, spend less, or work longer. If they do have enough, we use some strategies and tactics that minimize risk and maximize returns; these tools will help them hit their goals and protect them from making bad decisions, which would undermine their own stated objectives."

Lee Hyder, CSA — "I would have to ask these questions first: What are the current investments they plan to take lifetime income from? Are these investments in a guaranteed investment class? I know this sounds almost childish to say, but it needs to be said: You cannot guarantee income from a non-guaranteed account. Would it surprise anyone to learn that if the portfolio you were using for monthly income went down 40% that you would have to also reduce the income that you were taking from the account or jeopardize running out of money during retirement? If you are looking for guaranteed income, you first have to examine the underlying portfolio and the risk you are exposed to. For a true guaranteed retirement income, I would lean toward many of the latest products available today that have been specifically designed to create guaranteed retirement income."

Bob Grace, JD, CLU, ChFC — "There is only one asset available to provide lifetime income and that is a lifetime income benefit rider available on a fixed or variable annuity. The value of acquiring a fixed annuity is that the asset base is more likely to grow than a variable asset base. Also, the fees for income riders on fixed annuities are much less and the compound growth rate is much greater than on almost every variable annuity. A lifetime income benefit rider will absolutely guarantee that you can never ever run out of money, even if you live to 100, 110 or 120."

Eric Scott — "I like to ask a very important question of those who visit with me: 'What is more important to you if you happen to live to 100, your money or the income that currently comes from that money?' I always hear that it is a trick question, but it is not. Based on what may happen in the future with interest rates, the market, taxes, and inflation, if all you did was hope your money lasted, you could run out of money and income. After explaining that, I ask again: 'Is it your money or income that is most important to you?' Most people understand what I am asking then, and answer 'income.' We then share with them ways to guarantee their income for the rest of their lives, have control of their money and even if it runs out, they will not lose the income."

Mike Reese, CFP, CLU, ChFC — *"To have lifetime income from the assets a person already has, those assets absolutely, positively MUST be guaranteed. Their retirement income should not be affected based on what the stock market does or does not do."*

Joel Johnson, CFP — *"If someone is looking for lifetime income using the assets they have, I would tell them that the only institutions that can guarantee lifetime income are the government and insurance companies. If clients are comfortable moving away from guaranteed safety and income, then we will discuss preferred stocks, investment grade corporate bonds, real estate investment trusts, and alternative investments, such as gas and oil programs or equipment and leasing. The latter can be structured with a very high degree of safety, but not an absolute guarantee. Returns on these alternative investments can be 6% –12% or more."*

Bill Smith, RFC® — *"I would tell people looking for lifetime income that they must never risk the money they need to provide lifetime income, the necessities in life or the money they need to be able to go out and enjoy life. You should never, ever risk that money."*

Jeff Knoedl, RFC® — *"I tell my clients there is a way to receive a guaranteed income for life without losing control of the asset. Also, I mention that all plans are not the same. I see too many situations where someone's current financial person gave very bad advice about a supposed income plan. A few months ago, I met a prospective client who told me her broker did not disclose that she was required to wait ten years to begin the income payout. How is that an income plan when the nice lady was in need of immediate income? The only immediate aspect of this was the commission the broker earned!"*

Peter Richon — "Trying to maximize your guaranteed lifetime income can be a tender and emotional subject. People must be realistic. If you are used to living on $40,000 of after-tax income per year and want to retire at the age of 62 with a retirement nest egg of $200,000 in your 401(k) or IRA, how long will you expect that to last? If you are looking to guarantee a lifetime income, then you must have your money positioned where it can provide a consistent amount for however long you may live. For example, in a guaranteed income plan, 5% of $200,000 would produce $10,000 per year for however long the person lives. However, in income plans that are not guaranteed, fluctuations in account values due to market forces can affect their income dramatically if they plan to utilize a certain percentage of their assets each year. In the previous example, if the market drops the value of your account to $160,000, taking the same percentage will only net $8,000 in income. Also, for qualified accounts you must factor in taxes."

Christopher Sleight, Managing Director of Global Capital Private Capital — "I believe that if we can guarantee an income that will meet or exceed the income needs while still leaving a level of liquidity within their portfolios, it's some- thing we must examine. No one likes locking up their money but it beats the heck out of losing your life savings and having to go back to work at 70 years of age. My goal is always to give my clients choices — as long as those choices follow the investment philosophy for retirees: Preservation and Income needs first."

Bryan Philpott, RFC® — "We run a cash flow analysis first by finding out how much money they need from their investments after Social Security is taken out of expenses. Then we look to see what rate of return they will need to achieve that need. If they are taking more than 5% of their retirement funds, they are in survival zone. They may want to consider some type of annuity to guarantee an income stream."

Translation

We are all historians when it comes to the stock market. However, past performance can never guarantee future results. The last decade has taught us how fragile our money can be if it's not in the proper financial vehicle. Proper income strategies help establish peace of mind as well as minimize the risk of loss of retirement funds. Let's picture a water wheel. The first basket in the wheel is pouring out water (income). While this first basket is pouring out income, more baskets are filling up, preparing to pour water (income) once the first basket empties. This example shows the constant motion involved in income planning, so there is a consistent and predictable cash flow with no worries about account evaporation. Because everyone is different, however, it is important to have a financial coach problem-solve with you in order to help build, preserve, and transfer wealth with the goal of having all of the money you need, when you need it.

Speaking of income, hybrid income annuities are great tools to use for planning. Below is information from a booklet I recently wrote regarding hybrid income annuities — how they work and if they are right for you.

With so many Americans now entering retirement, the question that is on the minds of many is: "Will I have enough for retirement?"

Another question retirees are asking themselves is: "Will I outlive my money?" After all, statistics show that Americans are living longer. In 1900, the average life expectancy in the United States was 47. Today, it's 86!

Many seniors who have relied on well-meaning friends and relatives or perhaps on the advice of profit-motivated financial salespeople may have experienced significant losses in recent stock market corrections.

This is one reason why many retirees are turning to the safety and guaranteed incomes provided by annuities. We will examine some of the most comprehensive, de-tailed, and unbiased research that has been conducted on annuities by retirement advisory and research groups as well as respected financial experts. The findings presented here will allow you to make an informed decision based on numerical and statistical fact and will help answer your questions on how to ensure that your retirement can be adequately funded without negatively impacting your present lifestyle.

Our surveys indicate that most Americans want, if at all possible, to at least maintain the standard of living during retirement that they enjoyed before they retired. But a July 2010 study by the Employee Benefit Research Institute entitled *"What Are the Prospects You Will Run Short of Money in Retirement?"* found that in 10 short years, 64% of Americans in the lowest income levels will run out of money. Twenty-nine percent of people in the next highest income bracket will run out of money after 20 years. The EBRI study also found that after 20 years of retirement, 13% of people in the highest income bracket will be out of money.

The Perfect Storm

How to invest your life savings as you prepare for retirement was the topic recently addressed by the Wharton Financial Institutions Center. Professor Craig B. Merrill and Professor David F. Babbel, leading academics in retirement income planning, produced a paper in 2007 entitled *Investing Your Lump Sum at Retirement* that pointed out that retirees of this generation are facing a perfect storm, or a unique turbulent financial situation, hitting from all sides, comprised of an unfortunate convergence of simultaneous negative economic developments. They list these five forces currently at work, which are capable of destroying wealth:

1.   The decreasing levels and importance of Social Security Benefits

2.   The demise of defined benefit pensions

3.   The aging of the baby boomer generation

4.   The emergence of post boomers

5.   The increasing longevity of the American population

There is no way we can reverse those economic and social phenomena. But we can plan for them and account for them in our retirement strategy and, perhaps, placing a portion of our assets in an annuity may have the effect of defusing the time bomb.

Professors Merrill and Babbel, in explaining the benefits of annuities, said the following, "In the case of life annuities, the risk of outliving one's income is pooled among all annuity purchases, providing a kind of insurance against outliving one's assets."

Please note that these professors do not sell annuities. The Wharton Financial Institutions Center, more commonly referred to as the Wharton Institute, is one of the most prestigious business schools in America. So we can take their report at face value when they say that a life annuity is the only investment vehicle that allows its owners an income to "spend at the same rate, but be covered for as long as they live."

As to the affordability of annuities, Babbel and Merrill said, "Trying to replicate this advantage of a secure lifetime income, but without the risk-pooling of a life annuity, will cost you from 25% to 40% more money, because you would need to set aside enough money to last throughout your *entire possible* lifetime, instead of simply enough to last throughout your *expected* lifetime. Even at this higher cost, you cannot be sure that you will achieve a secure lifetime income because interest rates could change over the next 30–50 years while you are in retirement."

Recommendations of the Wharton Professors

So in the final analysis, what is the recommendation of these two professors? The following is a summary:

1. "You should begin by annuitizing enough of your assets so that you can provide for 100% of your minimum acceptable level of retirement income. Annuitization provides the only viable way to achieve this security without spending a lot more money."

2. "Next, our study shows that you will generally need to annuitize a significant portion of your remaining wealth, while investing the balance in stocks, fixed income securities, and money markets."

a) "You will want to make provisions for any extraordinary expenses, such as uncovered health costs and institutional care. These gaps in coverage can be purchased through supplemental health and long-term care insurance or, perhaps, from a rider to a life annuity that increases the payments beyond a certain age."

b) "You will want to make provisions for your heirs, but balance these provisions against your own desire to live above your minimum acceptable living standard."

c) "Our study found, as have most other studies, that the greater the tolerance you have for financial risk, the higher the proportion of your excess assets (i.e., assets not needed to provide for your minimum acceptable standard of living) could be placed in stock or other risky investments."

d) "Remember, these generalizations depend on the size of the bequest you wish to leave, as well as a host of other financial assumptions."

Lastly, and probably the most profound of all their recommendations, the professors state the following: "Finally, we suggest that annuities be purchased only from the most financially sound insurance providers. You will be able to sleep a lot better."

I heartily agree with this conclusion by the Wharton Institute's researchers, which is why my company only works with the most financially sound insurance companies and offers institutionally money managed accounts.

Income for Life

As mentioned earlier, people are living longer. That's good! But it also creates a different set of challenges regarding income planning. What happens if you outlive your money? This is why the concept of making plans to have an income stream that is (a) sufficient for your needs, and (b) guaranteed to last as long as you do, is gaining in popularity among the latest crop of retirees.

According to the Social Security Administration, a 65-year-old male will live to age 81 and a 65-year-old female will reach 86 years of age. So when planning for retirement, this projected longevity needs to be taken into account. Insurance companies, because they deal in the science of actuarial statistics, are keenly aware of this. They are also keenly aware of the rising public demand for financial vehicles that will enable retirees to accommodate this new longevity in their retirement planning. In the last decade, many companies have introduced to the financial planning market contracts that will provide generous returns, safety, and income for life... *without annuitizing*!

Why is that important? When an annuity is annuitized, the client opts to receive payments for a designated period of time, perhaps even for life.

That's called "annuitizing" the contract. But when this option is taken, the annuitant loses control of the account. If the annuitant dies, the payments cease, naturally, because the contract has been fulfilled. What if the annuitant dies early and there is money remaining in the account that has not been paid out. Do the annuitant's heirs receive that account balance? No. Once the contract is annuitized, the insurance company keeps any money that is left in the account.

While there are times when annuitizing an annuity contract may be desirable (using a tax-favored bucket system for time-triggered income planning, for example), in general we do not recommend it, especially now that the addition of "income riders" has made it possible to receive a guaranteed lifetime income stream without having to annuitize. In the past, when an annuity was annuitized and the client lost control of their money, it was in exchange for the guarantee of receiving regular income payments from the insurance company. If the annuitant's goal was to provide a lifetime income, then it could be compared to your betting that you would live a long time and the insurance company betting that you would die early. You felt safe and secure knowing that your "paycheck" would be there every month. But if you die early you lose.

While annuities like those mentioned above still exist and still continue to be sold by some insurance salespeople, a new generation of income annuities is, I feel, much more desirable and have made the old-style annuities, for the most part, obsolete. These "income riders" that have become so desirable among this generation of retirees are "additions" (thus the term "rider") to the annuity contract that can be purchased at a fee so nominal as to be negligible. These options were introduced relatively recently and have had an enormous impact on the financial world. With these riders, the owner is allowed to receive an income stream for life, but still maintain full control of the account. If, for example, an unexpected need arises, he may withdraw the money to care for it. In many cases, the contract can be structured so that if the annuitant dies while the income is being paid out, the income stream can continue to the surviving spouse. Regardless, any money remaining in the account does not go to the insurance company, but is passed on to the annuitant's designated beneficiaries.

How Income Riders Work

To provide this feature, insurance companies have to work with a formula. The payout amount for income riders is determined by a factor based on the annuitant's age and the income account value.

It is important to note that the INCOME ACCOUNT VALUE is used to calculate income. It is not the same as the actual ACCOUNT VALUE. Although based on the initial deposit into the annuity contract, these are two separate columns within the annuity and they grow at different rates.

The INCOME ACCOUNT usually has a crediting method applied to it by the insurance company. It will grow by anywhere from 4–8%, that is, as long as the income is not taken. Once the income is triggered, the growth in these accounts typically stops.

So, naturally, like a planted garden, it produces the best results if we let it grow and harvest it when it reaches its target growth. Since the INCOME ACCOUNT is growing every year that the income is deferred, the longer you wait to turn it on, the higher the income payout will be.

Which Income Rider Is Best?

After the first insurance company introduced a guaranteed lifetime income rider to their Fixed and Fixed Indexed Annuity, most other major annuity companies were quick to follow with a design of their own. Not all income riders work the same, and I believe it's important to make an informed decision in this regard. Here are nine questions to ask before selecting an income rider:

1. How is the growth rate of the income account calculated? Some products may offer a higher growth rate percentage, but use simple interest rather than compound interest. Other products may limit the accumulation period to a set number of years, while others may offer the ability to restart the accumulation period. We recommend matching the product to your specific needs. If, for example, you plan on taking income in year 8, a product that limits the accumulation period to 10 years is not a disadvantage. If you plan on starting the income at a point beyond the 10 years, then you obviously want a product that doesn't limit the accumulation period.

2. What are the charges for the rider?

Charges for the rider vary anywhere from .20% to potentially as high as 1.50%. Since they are generally below a full percentage point, these charges are usually referred to in terms of "percentage points." As a general rule, these charges are deducted from the actual account value, not the income account value, which reduces the amount available upon surrender. It's also important to determine if the charges are calculated using the income account value or the actual account value. Most products calculate the charge using the income account value which may result in higher charges, assuming the income account grows at a faster pace than the actual account value. While the charge for the rider is small, it is, nonetheless, a good idea to find out whether it can be increased, at what point this could occur, and by how much. Most companies have a maximum for this charge, and some companies guarantee that it cannot change once the contract is issued.

3. What causes the growth of the income account to stop? With most income riders, the income account grows at its prescribed rate as long as the income payments are not commenced. Then, once the income payout begins, the income account stops growing. (This does not generally affect the continued growth potential of the actual account.) But what happens if you make a withdrawal prior to starting income?

Some products penalize this type of withdrawal by stopping growth in the income account for that year. Others don't.

4. What is the impact of an "excess" withdrawal on the income account value?

Let's assume you have started taking income under the rider and an emergency occurs and you need to make an additional withdrawal in excess of the income available under the rider. As a general rule, companies will reduce the income account proportionately. This means that the same percentage will be deducted from each account, not the same dollar amount. This is called a "pro rata" withdrawal. Other companies deduct the withdrawal on a "dollar for dollar" basis. But keep in mind, either way this will mean that the lifetime pay out amount will be lower.

5. How should you plan for RMDs?

Required Minimum Distributions are required by the IRS on qualified accounts, such as IRAs, beginning at age 70½. If RMDs are required prior to income commencing under the rider, some contracts will treat these as an "excess" withdrawal and reduce the income account proportionately. A few products may stop the growth of the income account once RMDs start. If this is a factor, consider another source of funds to satisfy the RMD until you are ready to trigger your income. Ask your registered financial advisor for details on how this can be done.

For these reasons, I suggest you consider another source of funds to support RMDs until you are ready to start income under the rider. Once income under the rider starts, it's usually sufficient to satisfy the RMD. That's because the income is calculated on the higher income account value and the RMD would be calculated on the lower actual account value.

6. How are the income payout rates calculated?

It's important to review the payout rates offered under the rider. While most companies offer joint payout rates, some companies reduce the payout factor by only .50% for a joint payout. Still others reduce the payout rate by 1%. Also, some companies offer a graduated payout rate that increases every year, while others increase the rate every five or 10 years. So a 67-year-old may have a payout rate of 4.5% with one company, 5.0% with another, and 5.2% with still another. One other thing to watch for — some companies only allow a joint payout if both spouses are named as owners and annuitants. This doesn't work for IRAs since they require a single owner.

7. What are the death benefit options if death occurs before income starts?

With some companies, the income account is not available as a death benefit and with some companies it is. Some companies allow for the income account value, which is usually larger, to be passed on to the beneficiary or beneficiaries as long as it is taken over a five-year period. The other option is that the beneficiary or beneficiaries may take the actual account value, which is usually smaller, as a lump sum. These details are usually spelled out clearly in the company's brochure and in the actual annuity contract itself. If the surviving spouse is the sole beneficiary, the tax rules allow the spouse to continue the base annuity contract. However, the ability of the spouse to continue the rider varies by company. You have to ask whether the spouse can restart the accumulation period and whether the lifetime income guarantee provisions continue to apply.

8. What are the death benefit options if death occurs after income starts?

Generally, the income account is not available as a death benefit so the beneficiary would be limited to the actual account value. One of the companies I often work with will pay the income account value to the beneficiary over five years provided the actual account value is still positive. If the spouse is the beneficiary, the options depend upon whether a joint payout was elected at the time income commenced under the rider. If so, income continues to the spouse for his or her lifetime. If the joint payout option was not elected at the time the income was started, some contracts allow the spouse to continue income until the income account value is exhausted (no lifetime guarantee).

9. Can the rider be attached to a traditional fixed annuity?

While most sales of income riders today involve Fixed Indexed Annuity products, some companies do allow the rider to be attached to a Traditional Fixed Annuity. While the sale of Fixed INDEXED Annuities is outpacing the Traditional Fixed Annuities, the latter can be an excellent choice in some circumstances, as they are both simple and predictable.

The chart below shows how an annuity account such as this would perform as compared to the same amount invested in the stock market. Note that the S&P 500 stock market index has been volatile over the past 10 years. Investing directly in that index would have lost the investor $19,169, whereas the INCOME ACCOUNT value and the ACCOUNT VALUE of the annuity would have increased. In this illustration, the INCOME ACCOUNT value has been increasing at an annual rate of 8.2% compounding. The ACCOUNT VALUE increased during positive years on the index; during negative years, the value remained level.

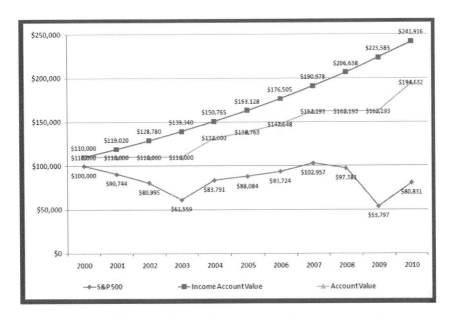

End of Year	Age	Income Account Value	Withdrawal Percentage	Income	Confinement Benefit
Issue	70	$110,000	6.00%	$6,600	N/A
1	71	$119,020	6.10%	$7,260	N/A
2	72	$128,780	6.20%	$7,984	$15,969
3	73	$139,340	6.30%	$8,778	$17,557
4	74	$150,765	6.40%	$9,649	$19,298
5	75	$163,128	6.50%	$10,603	$21,207
6	76	$176,505	6.60%	$11,649	$23,299
7	77	$190,978	6.70%	$12,796	$25,591
8	78	$206,638	6.80%	$14,051	$28,103
9	79	$223,583	6.90%	$15,427	$30,854
10	80	$241,916	7.00%	$16,934	$33,868
11	81	$261,754	7.10%	$18,585	$37,169
12	82	$283,217	7.20%	$20,392	$40,783
13	83	$306,441	7.30%	$22,370	$44,740
14	84	$331,569	7.40%	$24,536	$49,072
15	85	$358,758	7.50%	$26,907	$53,814

Please note that the calculations shown here assume a guaranteed interest rate of 8.2% on the Accumulation Period Withdrawal Payment Base and that the payments have not yet begun. Any additional withdrawals taken may reduce the Guaranteed Annual Withdrawal Payment. The calculations shown here are realistic projections, but are not guaranteed; and they assume that no changes to the policy are made and reflect no fees. Tax implications are not shown, and it is advisable to consult a tax professional for any tax-related questions.

Just as a sidecar is attached to a motorcycle, Lifetime Income Riders are attached to Fixed Annuities and Fixed Indexed Annuities, with the newer INDEXED annuity being the most popular "chassis" choice. These INDEXED annuities are designed to give you the positive returns of an INDEX, such as the S&P or the Dow, up to a point, while still guaranteeing you that you won't lose money in a year when there are negative returns. They are sometimes called "Hybrid" annuities because they are a combination of the most desirable features on an annuity, such as safety, guaranteed lifetime income option, etc., and an earnings potential tied to, but not directly invested in, the stock market.

Goldilocks and the Three Bears

Although hardly a fairytale, indexed annuities might by illustrated by borrowing from the plot of Goldilocks and the Three Bears. This is because they are not too cold; that is, they are not too low yielding in the case of the traditional fixed annuities. And they are not too hot; that is, they are not at risk in the market place like most variable annuities. But they are "just right" in the respect that they are perfect for investors who are looking for something in between: something with complete safety, but with the potential of market-like returns. You might say, the "best of both worlds."

With an income rider added, they are sometimes referred to as Hybrid Income Annuities, and they have been surging in popularity because they can supply what amounts to a pension for retirees at a time when more and more corporations are cutting pensions from their benefit packages. Adding to their popularity is the fact that these pension-plan-like features give you the ability to better control your money. By control, we mean that you can get your money and start receiving payments when you want to receive them. You also have the ability to turn on and turn off your income at will.

A select few of these Hybrid Income Annuities not only offer you an income for life but offer an ever-increasing income for life. I believe this is important because, it appears that inflation, while perhaps relatively tame right now, is not going away, and we need to plan with this reality in view. The possibility of ever-increasing income for life can be accomplished through the use of inflation riders and other methods. It is true that typically these retirement income planning vehicles do not allow for any alteration in the terms of the income stream once that income stream is turned on. But in SOME contracts, a provision for inflation is built in, and with OTHERS an inflation rider can be purchased for protection in this regard.

There is no one-size-fits-all approach, so clients are urged to make these decisions with the assistance of a registered financial advisor after an individual case assessment.

One of the greatest concerns in income planning is preparing for the unknown when it comes to health deterioration in older years. To deal with this, many insurance companies offer what are known as "confinement benefit riders" that can be purchased at a nominal fee. Other annuity contracts have these features built in. Again, these options should be fully explored to determine if they are suitable for your individual situation.

How a Fixed Indexed Annuity Works

Fixed Indexed Annuities were introduced at a time when rates for the traditional fixed annuity were coming down from their 1980s highs, and variable annuities were under a lot of scrutiny for their lack of transparency and high expenses. Indexed annuities were a breath of fresh air for investors who still appreciated the unique features of annuities, but wanted the potential for greater gains that the stock market, when on a good run, could provide.

They have often been called a "fusion" of the characteristics of fixed annuities and those of variable annuities, but with the complete safety that has become so much in demand with recent market disappointments. The fact that they hold the potential for growth-type returns is appealing to investors who seek returns that are more exciting than the fixed yield of fixed annuities and CDs, but are still concerned with the preservation of their assets now that they face retirement.

The Moving Parts of a Fixed Indexed Annuity

One of the most dynamic moving parts of the Fixed Indexed Annuity is the "lock-in/reset" feature. It is particularly useful when it comes to income planning. This simply means that when there is a growth, that growth is locked in, and the annuity's account value can never go below that point again. It is important to choose an annuity that locks in increases in value as often as possible. This annuity lock-in feature is often referred to as ratcheting. If you have ever seen the way a ratchet works, a gear with teeth turns and there is a noticeable click when the gear teeth are impacted by a cog device, which prevents the gear from going backward. When an annuity locks in increases (interest credits) or "ratchets," it goes without saying that it is advantageous to the owner for this to happen as often as possible.

Let's say you have two different annuities. One locks in increases every year and the other locks in increases every two years. It stands to reason that the longer it takes to lock in increases, the higher the probability of losing those gains due to market volatility. If your annuity ratchets and resets every year, your increases will lock-in every year when the market goes up. What happens in a down year? You will not lose money. You are insulated from any losses. Your annuity can only move upward, not backward. That should make a good case for at least an ANNUAL

Say, for example, that in the first year, the S&P market index shows a 15% increase. Then in the second year, there is a 16% drop. If your annuity ratchets up every two years, you would show no increase for this two-year period. With a one-year ratchet, however, you would have locked in those increases for the first year and you would have lost not one dime of your annuity's account value during the second year!

The most commonly used index is the S&P 500, which is representative of the 500 most actively traded stocks and leans toward larger companies. Other indices used are the Dow Jones Industrial Average and the NASDAQ 100, just to name a few.

If you read or listen to the popular media, you might get the impression that the Dow Jones Industrial Average, usually called "The Dow," is the pulse of the market. But that is not necessarily the case. The Dow is the oldest and most widely known index, but it's a mistake to consider it the market barometer. Why? The Dow currently has only 30 or so stocks, and each of these stocks represents one of the most influential companies in the United States. But the Dow is price weighted, which means if a stock's price changes by $1, it has the same effect on the index regardless of the percent change for the stock.

In other words, a $1 change for a $30 stock has the same effect as a $1 change for a $60 stock. The calculation of the Dow takes into account numerous stock splits over the years. By adjusting the math, it is possible to keep a historically viable index meaningful. The Dow stocks represent about one-quarter of the value of the total market, so in that sense, it is a factor — and big changes indicate investor confidence in stocks. However, it does not represent small or mid-size companies at all.

Perhaps the reason why the S&P 500 is the most frequently used index by financial professionals as a representative of the market is because it covers about 70% of the market's total value. So in those terms, it is much closer to representing the true market than the Dow. The S&P 500 is a market capitalization, or "market cap" weighted index, as are almost all of the major indexes. What does that mean? Weighting by market cap gives more importance to larger companies. So changes in Microsoft stock, for example, will have a greater impact than almost any other stock in the index. Even though the S&P 500 is weighted toward larger companies, it is a more accurate gauge of the broader market than the Dow is and, even though some of the talking heads on TV may emphasize the Dow, you will get a clearer picture of the market by focusing your attention on the S&P 500.

Ultimately, however, when it comes to choosing a strategy within the contract, it is the client who gets to make the selection among the choices available as to which index to use as a matrix for growth. Some insurance companies only offer the S&P. Others will allow a mixture of these indices and assign a percentage to each.

Crediting Strategies

Once you make that selection, you then get to select what "crediting strategy" you want to use. From my vantage point, which is based on research and experience, I have found that the two most successful and popular are (a) Annual Point to Point and (b) Monthly Point to Point.

(A) **ANNUAL POINT TO POINT:** This crediting strategy allows for annual resets as described earlier, and it compounds. There are caps to this strategy, however. Pick the point on the calendar when you began and pick the point on the calendar when the year ends. The DIFFERENCE is your growth factor up to the cap. In this hypothetical example below, the S&P 500 starting value was 1,000. Then it gains 24.70%. The investment only gains 8.00% because of the cap, which is the trade-off for the security and safety offered by these contracts. Caps are adjusted each year and float with market and interest rate conditions.

Month	Jan	Feb	Mar	Apr	May	Jun	Jul	Aug	Sep	Oct	Nov	Dec	Total Return	Actual Return
S&P 500	1,053	1,031	1,044	1,118	1,104	1,123	1,144	1,157	1,194	1,209	1,222	1,247		
Gain	5.30%		1.23%	7.10%		1.70%	1.90%	1.10%	3.17%	1.30%	1.10%	2.03%	= 24.70%	= 8.00%
Loss		-2.10%			-1.20%									

(B) **MONTHLY POINT TO POINT:** When market conditions are steadily on the rise, this can be a very good crediting meth-

133

od. When the market goes steadily up, your account goes up with it. However, a word of caution… a bad month or two could reduce or eliminate gains in the current year. These strategies employ a monthly cap. Below is an example of this crediting strategy using a 2.5% monthly cap with a maximum 30% annual gain (2.5% x 12 months). The sum of the gains and losses will determine the percent credited to the account.

Month	Jan	Feb	Mar	Apr	May	Jun	Jul	Aug	Sep	Oct	Nov	Dec	
S&P 500	5.30%	-2.10%	1.23%	7.10%	-1.20%	1.70%	1.90%	1.10%	3.17%	1.30%	1.10%	2.03%	= 14.56%
Positive	2.50%		1.23%	2.50%		1.70%	1.90%	1.10%	2.50%	1.30%	1.10%	2.03%	
Negative		-2.10%			-1.20%								

As you can see, both of these crediting strategies are based on the same annual S&P returns. But in this specific example, the annual point to point cap rate during this one year led to a lower overall return than the monthly point to point.

If this appears to be a bit confusing, don't despair! Spread out over time, our experience has been that the strategies you choose will level out and be approximately the same. Just as it is impossible to time the market when you are buying and selling stocks, it is impossible to tell how the market will behave by keeping a vigilant eye on a market index.

It is noteworthy that, for your safety and protection, index annuities do not directly participate in equity, bonds or other security investments. Rather, your annuity is credited with an interest rate based on the percentage gain in a stock market or bond index. And while Indexed annuities are not insured by the FDIC, they have other protections — the merits and characteristics of which we will discuss later.

Also, when comparing the numbers in the above illustrations, remember that, while possible, gains of 24.7% are very rare! But with these types of annuities, you don't need to have the stock market rise anywhere near as much as the illustration portrays in order to benefit. Your indexed annuity should benefit you during almost any year in which the stock market goes up.

On average, over time, the stock market tends to rise about 10% per year. Extrapolated to the month, that's less than 1% per month, on average over time. Ibbotson Associates, a well-known and well regarded research firm, has reported that from 1925 to 2004, small stocks returned on average 12.7% per year and large stocks returned on average 10.4% per year.

Stock market returns differ every year, of course. But Bill Gross of PIMCO, who is a very highly respected investment manager, believes that both stock and bond returns are likely to be below normal in the next few years. Gross has written extensively about what his firm calls the "new normal," contending that it may not be realistic for us to assume that stock market returns will continue to rise at the average rate of 10% per year. But the consensus among most financial professionals is that, spread out over a 15-year or even a 20-year period of time, the returns will be much the same. Regardless, you can rest assured that during those years in which the market does rise, your account should increase in value as well.

The Annual Point to Point and the Monthly Point to Point are not the only crediting methods available to you. There are several other crediting methods that your registered financial advisor will be happy to explain to you, as well as provide you with your options as they pertain to your individual needs, desires, wishes, and tolerances. There is, as I stated before, no one-size-fits-all when it comes to these matters. Remember, too, that no one can precisely predict what the stock market will do tomorrow, next month or next year. For this reason, you may wish to diversify your crediting methods by splitting your investment into two annuities, using the Annual Point to Point crediting method in one while at the same time using the Monthly Point to Point crediting method in the other.

To illustrate, if you place $400,000 into two annuities, employ the Annual Point to Point crediting method in one and the Monthly Point to Point crediting method in the other. That way, if the stock market has one of those very high return years, the $200,000 in the Monthly Point to Point crediting method could do extremely well.

Meanwhile, you still had a very nice gain in the other account, although not as much. But if the market has an average gain then the Annual Point to Point would give you higher returns.

Using this diversified approach alleviates the challenge of trying to guess how the stock market will behave over the next year. No matter what the stock market does, as long as it rises in value, you should enjoy an increase in value. And, if it falls, you will not lose any money — all of your principal and gains from prior years will be protected!

How Safe Is Your Annuity?

"How SAFE is my money if I put it into an annuity?" you may ask.

Answer: You cannot lose any of your principal as long as you do not over withdraw your capital early during the surrender penalty. In the early years of your annuity, there is usually a surrender charge which is somewhat similar to the early withdrawal fee on a CD. But like CDs, once the surrender charge period is over, then you can usually withdraw as much of your money as you want to without penalty. With annuities, the surrender period can be anywhere from 3 to 16 years, 10 years being the most commonly used in Fixed INDEXED annuities.

Insurance companies are cognizant of the fact that emergencies arise and most companies will allow you to withdraw 10% of your account value annually without penalty. You do not have to have a reason. It's your money. Just ask for it. If you need to withdraw more than 10% and it is within the surrender penalty period, simply tack on the surrender penalty to the amount withdrawn. The insurance carrier will do the math for you and accommodate your request. Obviously, you would not want to place money you need for the daily expenses of life or for foreseeable necessary expenses, such as an automobile purchase or home purchase, into an annuity.

One of the primary safety features of an annuity is that, no matter how much the stock market declines in any given year, you cannot lose money. You cannot say that about mutual funds, variable annuities or 401(k) plans that do not have a principal guarantee. Variable annuities may sometimes come with a principal guarantee but these guarantees are not free. They come in the form of a rider, which comes with an expensive price tag. The principal guarantee is built into a Fixed Index Annuity with no fees.

How Safe Is The Insurance Company?

If you have money in a bank, it is insured by the Federal Deposit Insurance Corporation (FDIC) for up to $250,000. If you have an annuity with an insurance company, the FDIC doesn't enter the picture because you aren't dealing with a bank. But with the annuity, you have not one, but at least five layers of protection for your money. Some of these protection layers are mandated by the government and some are placed there by the insurance companies themselves and are self-regulatory. Nonetheless, these layers of protection are all for the purpose of keeping your money safe from loss due to default or negligence.

First, you have the assets of the insurance company itself backing up your annuity. This is one reason why reputable insurance companies, those whose accounts are audited and the results published on a regular basis, are proud to show their numbers to you. This lets you know they are solid and can pay all claims presented to them.

Know also that, when it comes to the security of your investment, insurance companies are some of the most highly regulated enterprises in America. They are subject to strict capital reserve requirements that are much higher than the capital reserve requirements for banks. Because of this, insurance companies are conservative when it comes to investing their profits, using only the most highly rated investments available — the bulk of the capital invested in U.S. government bonds. What could be safer than an investment backed by the full faith and credit of the United States government?

A much smaller portion of their assets is invested in conservative A-rated investment real estate, such as large office buildings rented by Fortune 500 companies. When you travel to any major city in America, you will see skyscrapers and other large buildings owned by insurance companies. In many cases, these Class A properties have either no mortgage or a very small mortgage, adding further to their safety.

Insurance companies also own corporate bonds in the biggest, safest corporations in the world. These bonds make regular interest payments to the insurance companies.

Protected From Creditors

By law, the assets of insurance company policyholders cannot be attacked by creditors of the insurance company. The assets of policy holders (your assets in an annuity) are held in segregated accounts that are beyond the reach of plaintiffs and attorneys.

Even if an insurance company is sued and loses the lawsuit, the plaintiff cannot go after the money of policyholders! In other words, lawyers and plaintiffs cannot go after the money you have deposited in your annuity. This should bring you great peace of mind as to the safety of these vehicles.

Strong Reserves

Which institutions are safer, banks or insurance companies? Insurance companies are safer!

Banks are allowed to use a great deal of leverage compared to insurance companies. This is one of the factors that makes them riskier. Historically, there have been many bank failures in the United States, while insurance company failures are a rarity. For example, if a bank takes in $10 million in deposits from customers, it might make $90 million in loans. If only $10 million of those loans go bad, the bank could exhaust its reserves and have essentially no capital on hand to back up the deposits of its customers. As we have seen with the real estate bust of 2007 and 2008, many banks suffered losses on their loans and required government bailout by taxpayers to remain solvent.

This is in stark contrast to insurance companies. While banks are required to have a DIME in reserve for every DOLLAR they have at risk, an insurance company is required by law to have a DOLLAR in reserves for every DOLLAR it has at risk — meaning every dollar it has that is obligated through the insurance and annuity contracts, it has on the books. This should be very reassuring if you own an annuity, since YOU are the policyholder and the money is promised to YOU!

Surplus Capital

Just like some fiscally conservative companies like to have more in their operating account than other companies, some insurance companies do not only have just a dollar in reserves for every dollar promised to policyholders. They have more. This is called having surplus capital.

Traditionally, throughout the years, it has been acknowledged that while all manner of other companies around may fall into financial trouble, insurance companies are set apart from such difficulty. This is true, but few understand the reasons why.

It is well known that in 2008, when Bear Sterns, Lehman Brothers, and Wachovia were requesting and receiving bailout money, one of the insurance giants, AIG, known as a conglomerate also experienced financial difficulty and accepted bail-out funds. What is not as well-known is the fact that the actual insurance division of the conglomerate remained financially sound and was never in any danger. The moneys of the conglomerate and the insurance companies within it could not mix.

Both independent analysts and other officials agree that insurance companies are in no danger of going the way of the extinct banks. In order to maintain their charters of operation, insurance companies must comply with state audits, which ensure that they are fully capable of maintaining these funds in sufficient amounts.

Guaranty Associations

Guaranty Associations were created by state legislatures to protect life, annuity, and health insurance policyholders and beneficiaries of an insolvent insurance company. All insurance companies licensed to write life insurance or annuities in a state are required, as a condition of doing business in the state, to be members of the guaranty association. If a member company becomes insolvent, money to continue coverage or pay claims is obtained through assessments of other insurance companies writing the same kinds of insurance as the insolvent company.

Please know that I feel that the existence of state guaranty associations should not be a factor in selecting an annuity. If you want to research what state guaranty associations are, you can do so using Google or your favorite search engine. When you enter the words "state guaranty association" on Google, you get thousands of websites that contain explanations of this safety provision.

While most retirees know about how the FDIC guarantees a minimum amount of bank deposits, few retirees know about how state guaranty associations stand as a bulwark of additional safety of their money, if it is in an annuity.

A unique advantage of the legal reserve system is that if one company is purchased or merged into another, there is no change whatsoever in the policy benefits or premiums. This way, the insurance company has a public responsibility to respect both the letter and the spirit of laws and regulations so the interests of their policyholders are always protected.

The purpose of state guaranty associations is to provide a mechanism for the prompt payment of covered claims of an insolvent insurer. (To date, no one has ever lost a penny of their principal in a fixed index annuity, nor has anyone in America ever failed to receive the full death benefit on a life insurance claim). This safeguard exists so that a catastrophic financial loss to certain contract and policyholders may be avoided. These guaranty associations make assessments to obtain the funds to pay claims if an insurer becomes insolvent.

So in the rare instance of an insurance company's reserves falling short, it goes into what is called "receivership." Should that occur, the remaining insurance companies in the state legal reserve pool must assume the liabilities and obligations of the now-defunct insurer. The amount of the defunct insurer's liability they are required to accept is based on the amount of insurance and annuities the healthy company has issued in that state. If one company has issued 10% of all insurance and annuities in that state, then they must accept 10% of any bankrupt insurer's obligations for the state.

Legal Reserve System

The insurance industry has gone to great lengths to assure the safety of annuity investments and to establish consumer confidence. An insurance company must be able to handle the unexpected, hence the institution of the Legal Reserve System. It is this organization that specifies that the insurance companies must maintain the appropriate amount of money kept in reserve. This solvency ratio can be likened to a client saving cash for a rainy day. How the reserve amount is calculated varies from state to state, and, as with all insurance matters, it involves adequately predicting and balancing risk.

Reinsurance

The definition of reinsurance is insurance purchased by an insurer. In many states, the Department of Insurance requires insurance companies to reinsure one another before they can offer their products in that state.

From a global perspective, Swiss Re is one of the world's leading rein-surers and the world's largest life and health reinsurer. A global expert in managing capital and risk, Swiss Re's objective is to anticipate, identify, and understand industry developments that shape the future risk landscape. Reinsurance is just an extra level of protection whereby a multi-billion dollar insurance firm guarantees and backs up a percent-age of the reserves of the client insurance company.

Holding Companies

Many insurance companies, while having full credentials in the United States, are not domiciled in the United States. Rather, several insurance carriers with North American headquarters located in the United States are part of a larger parent company. These larger parent companies have such deep pockets that the risk of a company failure becomes practically non-existent on its face. There are numerous examples, but let's look at two: Allianz Life Insurance Company and Aviva Life and Annuity.

Allianz Life Insurance Company's parent company is Allianz SE, which is headquartered in Germany. Allianz SE has more than 75 mil-lion customers in about 70 countries, employing 150,000 people worldwide. Allianz SE has generated more than $64 billion dollars in Indexed Annuity sales, and is the fourteenth largest corporation in the world and the third largest money manager on the planet. Allianz's sol-vency ratio is 161% (meaning that for every dollar on deposit, they have $1.61 in reserve — vastly different from the banking industry, where reserves are always less than deposits, hence the need for FDIC).

Aviva PLC is the fifth largest insurance group in the world with $573.8 billion in funds under management, 50 million customers, and 54,000 employees worldwide. Aviva has been delivering on its promises for more than 300 years, since 1696. Over the years, Aviva has insured Sir Winston Churchill, Queen Victoria, and turned down Napoleon Bonaparte. The rest is history. Deep pockets mean more safety for you.

The five pillars of safety for insurance companies are:

- Strict regulatory investment practices
- State guaranty funds
- Legal reserve system
- Reinsurance
- Holding companies

At this point, you may think that all of these layers of protection are excessive. Yet this is exactly what has kept the vast majority of insurance companies safe, sound, and solvent for the past several hundred years.

Ratings

Insurance companies are given grades by independent ratings organizations which monitor their stability and performance. The AM Best Company, which was founded in 1899, is probably the oldest and most widely recognized of these rating agencies. Others include Standard & Poor's, Moody's, and Fitch.

The ratings are in an alphabetical range from A++ to E. The majority of insurance companies have an alphabetical rating of A- (Excellent) or better by AM Best. There are a few companies that fall within the B++ category, but are still considered to be excellent by AM Best. A carrier with an alphabetical rating of B or less is considered by AM Best to be vulnerable. E is the final category they offer, and a carrier with that rating is under Regulatory Supervision.

Interestingly, until recently AIG had a Best Rating of A+. Along with other carriers, they have seen AM Best review and/or change their rating depending on what was happening with that company. AIG currently has a Best Rating of A, still considered to be very strong.

How Secure Are Corporate Retirement Plans?

It used to be that retiring with a pension from work was commonplace. *Not so much anymore.* Charlie Morris, author of *The Century Foundation* report, Apart at the Seams: The Collapse of Private Pension and Health Care Protections *says this about private pensions*: "To the Depression Era generation entering the workforce after World War II, one of the secrets of the good life was to catch on with 'a big company with a pension'."

Although fewer than half of private sector workers ever had a de- fined benefit pension, it was one of the trademark features of the American dream — a defined benefit pension, promising a set monthly payment for the rest of your life, and usually your spouse's life, so long as you put in the service time.

The first realization that pension promises were not ironclad may have come when the Studebaker Company folded in 1963 and de- faulted on its pension obligations. Congress eventually responded with the Employee Retirement Income Security Act (ERISA) of 1974. ERISA established financing and accounting standards for defined benefit pensions and created the federal Pension Benefit Guarantee Corporation (PBGC) to insure private defined benefit pension commitments.

The modern portfolio management industry is, to a great extent, a creature of ERISA's requirement that companies set aside assets to fund their future pension liabilities. If the actuarially determined present value of pension liabilities exceeds that of pension fund assets, the shortfall is subtracted from the company's net worth as if it were a debt. As of mid-2005, private companies have amassed $1.8 trillion in assets to support their defined benefit pension obligations, against future liabilities valued at about $2.2 trillion.

Pension funds initially concentrated their investments in high-grade bond portfolios, but as the stock market recovered through the 1980s, funds gradually shifted to higher-yielding stocks, in the hope that higher returns would allow reductions in annual contributions. During the 1990s market boom, stock returns were so high that many plans became overfunded, and pension funds be-came an important driver of company earnings. When the markets reversed after 2000, pension fund underperformance hammered profits at the same time as falling operating earnings reduced companies' ability to increase plan contributions. Just as important, although not widely understood, the steady fall in interest rates after 2001 greatly ratcheted up the book value of future pension liabilities.

The negative swing in corporate pension fund positions has been roughly $750 billion since 1999 — from a $300 billion surplus to an estimated $450 billion deficit as of mid-2005. Analysts at Credit Suisse/First Boston (CSFB) recently published a list of 20 major companies with pension liabilities that equal or exceed the company's market value. The list includes Delta Airlines (which has since declared bankruptcy), with pension obligations 13 times higher than its market value; General Motors, 4.7 times higher; Ford, 2.7 times higher; Lucent, 1.9 times higher; and U.S. Steel, 1.4 times higher. Mounting deficits at the PBGC are creating the potential for a federal bailout on the scale of the 1980s Savings and Loan crisis. (Technically, the PBGC, which is supposed to be self-financing through fees and insurance premiums, has no legal call on the federal purse, but political pressure for a federal response could be overwhelming.)

A number of proposals are being floated to shore-up defined benefit pension funding and accounting, but most would require companies to report higher levels of debt and lower profits. More likely, companies will accelerate the process of extracting themselves from their pension obligations. One path is the strategic bankruptcy. Shedding pension obligations has become practically a standardized financial engineering tool in the hands of private equity buyout managers — in steel companies, auto parts companies, and, more recently, a string of airline bankruptcies.

Collectively, it appears that United, Delta, and Northwestern Airlines, and the auto parts maker Delphi will be relieved of some $32 billion in pension liabilities through the bankruptcy process. (The companies on that list have not yet officially requested a PBGC takeover, but that seems inevitable.) Less dramatic alternatives include terminating a plan or closing it to new employees, or converting it to a "cash balance" plan. Even financially healthy companies, like IBM, have been taking the cash balance route; at least one-third of employees in nominally "defined benefit" pension plans have been converted to the cash balance format.

In short, the days when defined benefit pensions were a major support of American retirement systems are over. Currently, only about 20 percent of private sector workers participate in defined benefit pensions, and that number will drop to the vanishing point over the next 10 years or so. Overall, defined benefit coverage is higher because almost all federal employees and up to 90% of state and local government employees are members of defined benefit plans. Analysts have estimated, however, that the unfunded liabilities of state and local defined benefit plans are even higher than in the private sector.

Pension fund payments have become the fastest-growing items in many jurisdictions, squeezing out education and other essential spending. State issues of tens of billions of "pension obligation bonds" to take advantage of rising markets in the late 1990s have only worsened the problem. The phasing in of private-sector-like accounting rules for state and local governments starting in the late 1990s is forcing accurate disclosure, although their initial effects have been masked by superb market returns — indeed, many jurisdictions fattened benefits.

"Smoothing" provisions have also blunted the stated impact of market underperformance and falling discount rates, but the scale of the liability overhang cannot be suppressed much longer.

For many decades, it was thought that a pension from a large Fortune 500 company would guarantee a comfortable retirement. With the bankruptcy of General Motors, Chrysler, airlines (United, Delta, Northwest, US Airways, etc.), many big banks (Lehman Brothers, Bear Stearns, Washington Mutual, etc.), the bankruptcy of major retail chains (K-Mart, Circuit City, Borders Books & Music, Radio Shack, etc.) and many more companies, everyone has learned that having a pension from a big company is no guarantee that you will have a comfortable retirement.

The purpose of this information is to educate you on what has happened and what is happening now with corporate and government pensions. All of the information contained here is completely factual. Unfortunately, many retirees have suffered losses and have had to reduce their standards of living in retirement be-cause they were not fully informed of these important changes that are now taking place.

Through education, I hope to be able to assist you in avoiding any such losses.

Some long-term employees and executives of the big companies mentioned above, and of many other companies, have seen their pension income significantly reduced. In some cases, they are receiving only 10 cents or 20 cents of every dollar of income that was promised to them.

The Pension Benefit Guaranty Corporation

A record-breaking number of failed pension programs have been turned over to the government-run Pension Benefit Guaranty Corporation (PBGC). Many may think that, because it is a government entity, the PBGC is required to pay the benefits promised to retirees in the original pension plan. But this is not the case.

147

Here are some facts, of which few retirees and pre-retirees are aware. Regardless of how much you were promised in your pension plan, if you are age 60, the maximum monthly pension that the PBGC pays would only be $2,925.

Many retirees who thought their retirement was guaranteed and that the dollar amount of their pension was locked in have had to alter their lifestyle dramatically to compensate for the shortfall.

What about small and mid-sized companies? They have fared even worse. Many small companies either have no pension plan because they simply cannot afford it or have a 401(k) program, but do not match funds. These retirement programs have lost hundreds of billions of dollars in the recent stock market crashes of 2000 to 2002 and 2008.

Many 401(k) plans are totally exposed to stock market volatility and risk. You truly have no guarantee of a safe, secure retirement if you have a 401(k) plan. The best you can do is to elect the safest options and diversify. The truth is that most Americans have saved very little for retirement. This is also why the very mention of the word "retirement" can cause instant anxiety and fear. It is little wonder that prescriptions for anti-anxiety medication have proliferated so much in the last decade.

A Possible Solution

It goes without saying that I want to help as many people as possible enjoy retirement security. Based on the research I have conducted and all of the research reviewed from many other sources, the exciting secure hybrid income annuities discussed earlier may be the right solution for many who are serious about planning their retirement.

Why? Because hybrid income annuities offer a high level of guaranteed income benefits and a high level of safety. Regardless of what the stock market does, and regardless of what your employer does and no matter what your pension plan or 401(k) does or doesn't do, when you own this income annuity as part of your retirement portfolio, you will be assured that your money will last as long as you do.

What about Government Employees?

One reason government pensions were considered to be the "crème de la crème" in pension programs was because they always went up. When the market crashed and private citizens saw their retirement programs lose money, government employees and retirees sailed right through, getting every dime they were promised. But that was then, and this is now.

Lately, many government employees who thought they had a totally safe retirement program are now learning otherwise. Retirement plan contributions are being cut in one state after another. Cost of living adjustments, which at one time were viewed as an entitlement, are being significantly reduced and, in some cases, suspended. A nationwide movement to reduce pensions promised to current employees is gaining momentum.

Consider the fact that in 1999 in California, Governor Gray Davis doubled the pensions of all state workers. In addition, the Governor made these changes retroactive so that *whatever you were promised in previous years was doubled in size*! But then, when people in cities and states across the country began to discern that these generous government pensions were about to threaten the financial health of their economies, protests ensued and the cutbacks followed.

What should you do if you think that any of the above may affect you and your retirement? I highly recommend that you take steps to develop an alternative income stream now. The longer you wait, the more difficult it may be to significantly increase your income in retirement.

What If I Get Sick?

Some seniors *falsely believe* that if their money is invested in annuities, they might not be able to pay for needed health care. In the Wharton Report, Professors Babbel and Merrill point out that this is not necessarily the case. Medicare pays many of the health care costs of retirees. In addition, supplemental health insurance can be purchased, which covers gaps in Medicare coverage. Then there is the eventuality that some may need care in a confinement facility, such as a nursing home.

One of the outstanding features in some of the hybrid income annuities we have discussed here is what is termed a "confinement doubler," which provides that if the income is triggered, and the recipient is subsequently confined to a nursing home, the income doubles. So if the annuitant is receiving, for example, an income of $30,000 per year from the lifetime income account of his annuity, that amount would double to $60,000 for as long as the recipient is confined to a nursing home.

Other annuities offer riders that cover a variety of contingencies that may involve confinement health care or extended long-term care.

Most policies use activities of daily living (ADLs) to determine if someone qualifies for these benefits under the contract. For example, if the annuitant cannot perform two of the following six ADLs, then he or she qualifies for the additional benefits:

- Dressing
- Bathing
- Eating
- Walking
- Taking medication
- Getting in and out of beds or chairs

The authors of the Wharton Report also explain that, "Life annuities are now available that will increase monthly payments by up to 400%

when the annuitant reaches a specific age (e.g., 85 years of age). The annuitant can choose an age when the need for institutional care begins to become more likely, and select the desired level of increase in payments. While annuities with this feature cost more than regular annuities that provide level payments throughout life, they can be well worth the extra cost."

Professors Babbel and Merrill show that there are other innovative life annuities that will allow you to withdraw a certain amount of money each year — or when you need it — with no penalties.

As I mentioned earlier, when it comes to annuities, there is no one-size-fits-all solution. Each person is different and so are the circumstances of each individual and each couple. Your registered financial advisor should be willing to listen to you and your situation, and by doing so, they will be able to find the best and most appropriate solution for your concerns.

Rule of Gold

James was born in Hamilton, Missouri. He was one of twelve children raised in poverty on a farm. His father worked the land six days a week and on Sunday, he preached in a small church for no pay. James got his first job in a general store and saved enough money to finally purchase his own butcher shop. To retain the town's leading hotel as a customer, he was expected to buy a bottle of liquor for the head cook each week. But James didn't smoke or drink and he wouldn't bribe the cook, so the hotel didn't buy its meat from his shop. His butcher business failed. Later in life, he often said, "I lost everything I had, but I learned never to compromise." His real career began when in Kemmerer, Wyoming, when he opened the Golden Rule store. Those were the days when everyone bought on credit and paid high prices. He tried a different formula: cash and lower prices to attract more sales. It worked. He changed the name of his stores as he expanded, but the Golden Rule was still his motto. By 1927, he had 750 retail stores in forty-five states. Managers were allowed to buy an interest in their stores, and profits were shared with employees. James believed that Christian ethics and hard work would succeed in business. And he left 1,700 stores scattered all across America with his name on the front door to prove it: J.C. Penney.

Chapter X: 28 Retirement Risks

Now that we have discussed the various financial tsunamis that can dramatically impact your retirement, I want to share with you the following Global Financial Private Capital checklist, which details 28 specific risks you should be aware of as you approach retirement. In the words of the famous American golfer, Fred Couples, "When you're prepared, you're more confident. When you have a strategy, you're more comfortable." One of the best ways to help you prepare for retirement is to be educated about factors and risks that can affect your retirement. Possessing knowledge of such risks will help you create a strategy that minimizes exposure to these risks and provides a sense of comfort as you approach your retirement years.

28 Retirement Risks Checklist

1. **Longevity Risk** — Outliving retirement resources by living longer than planned

2. **Excess Withdrawal Risk (Portfolio Failure Risk)** — When depletion of retirement assets through poorly planned systematic withdrawals lead to the premature exhaustion of retirement resources

3. **Inflation Risk (Purchasing Power Risk)** — When the price of goods and services increases in such a way as to impede the client's ability to maintain his/her desired standard of living

4. **Long-term Care Risk** — When dementia and/or physical impediments restrict a person from performing the activities of daily living and may require him/her to outlay significant resources for custodial or medical care

5. **Incapacity Risk** — When deteriorating mental or physical health prevent a retiree from being able to execute sound judgment in managing his/her financial affairs and/or may become unable to conduct his/her financial affairs

6. **Health Care Expense Risk** — Lack of adequate medical insurance

7. **Investment Risk** — Losing money in the financial markets

8. **Asset Allocation Risk** — Losing money in the financial markets due to inadequate diversification

9. **Market Risk** — Events cause all stock market prices to fall

10. **Sequence of Returns Risk** — Receiving low or negative returns in the early years of retirement, which lead to a long-term negative effect on the ability of the retirement portfolio to provide needed income

11. **Reinvestment Risk** — When higher-yielding, fixed income investments mature and the client may be forced to reinvest that principal in a lower-yield fixed income investment

12. **Forced Retirement Risk** — When work ends prematurely because of poor health, caregiving responsibilities, dismissal by the employer, lack of job satisfaction or other reasons

13. **Business Continuity Risk** — When the employing business closes and the client is unable to amass the appropriate amount of retirement resources

14. **Public Policy Change Risk** — An unanticipated transition in government programs, such as Medicare and/or Social Security, that were embedded in the retirement planning process to the point where they will not provide sufficient protection during retirement

15. **Tax Risk** — Significant tax increases or elimination of tax benefits

16. **Loss of Spouse Risk** — Planning and financial hardships that arise upon the death of the first spouse

17. **Unexpected Financial Responsibility Risk** — When the client acquires additional unanticipated expenses during the course of retirement

18. **Liquidity Risk** — The inability to have assets available to financially support unanticipated cash flow needs

19. **Legacy Risk** — The inability to meet the philanthropic and/or bequest goals set by the client

20. **Financial Elder Abuse Risk** — An advisor or family member preys on the frailty of the client, recommends unwise strategies or investments or embezzles assets from the client

21. **Reemployment Risk** — The inability to supplement retirement income with part-time employment due to tight job markets, poor health, and/or caregiving responsibilities

22. **Home Maintenance Risk** — The inability or unwillingness of clients to continue household chores and activities that they once handled themselves, which may require financial resources to pay for these outsourced activities

23. **Timing Risk (Point-in-Time Risk)** — Considers the variations in sequences of actual events beginning with different time periods

24. **High Debt Service Risk** — Clients retiring with significant mortgage, student loan, and/or consumer debt that may erode the resources needed for retirement spending

25. **Procrastination Risk** — Clients started saving for retirement too late

26. **Retirement Saving Opportunity Risk** — Working for an employer that did not provide a retirement plan

27. **Inadequate Resource Risk** — Clients have not saved enough to provide adequate retirement income

28. **Unrealistic Expectation Risk** — Client makes poor choices because he/she was not properly educated or remained unaware of the consequences of insufficient retirement income planning

GLOBAL FINANCIAL
Private Capital
COMPREHENSIVE WEALTH MANAGEMENT

Chapter XI: Mutual Funds?

PART I

Why Most Retirees Won't Be Caught Dead With Mutual Funds

Does my title sound a little strong? I'm strongly against the use of mutual funds. Unfortunately, many investors who own mutual funds in their portfolio are not informed as to the cost and risk that comes with owning most mutual funds. This is an important topic of discussion that you may never have had with your current advisor. Just as with any other investment vehicle, mutual funds internally have costs and risks. Additionally, the nature of how they work increases your cost and risk. Ultimately, how a typical financial advisor or broker uses mutual funds can increase your risk and cost. Fund managers have very specific investment policy statements that they are contractually obligated to follow; they are handcuffed to that policy, even if it's to your disadvantage. For example, if a bond fund is to be *long bonds* (buying bonds) and interest rates go up (which is bad for bonds), they still must buy bonds.

If you have saved at least several hundred thousand dollars for retirement, then you have earned the right to institutional money management (the land free of expensive mutual funds). Mutual funds were made so people like my young adult daughter just starting out with 100 dollars a month could start their investment savings and still be diversified. It was never designed to be the inexpensive, long-term way to save. For example, if 12 different stocks would help her be diversified and each stock costs $100, then buying 1 share of each stock each month would take her 12 months to be diversified. So mutual fund companies were created to buy those 12 shares immediately with $100 from 12 investors and let her have 1/12th share in the fund. For this opportunity, she must pay extra.

Making a decision on a specific investment is not financial planning. You don't just weigh that individual decision based upon the associated costs, risks, and past returns. That's like trying to drive down the road looking in the rear view mirror. Eventually, you're going to crash. Did your portfolio crash in 2008? That may have been the strategy that got you to retirement.

However, in our volatile, ever-changing new-world economy, you don't just need help with specific investments; you need a total financial strategy to get you through retirement. Remember all of those "investments" must pay you retirement paychecks for the next 25 to 30 years of retirement. If you are taking a *paycheck* and the fund manager is taking a *paycheck* and the fee's coming out for management is another *paycheck* and the 'turn over' costs is another *paycheck* and 'Mr. Market' loses value, that's another *paycheck* coming out of your savings for retirement. All I can say is that there seems to be too many hands in the retirement cookie jar. Don't forget other *paychecks* associated with retirement: taxes, inflation, and health care!

The following articles from major publications, research companies, and insightful industry leaders prove the cost and expenses found in mutual funds and how they impact savings for retirement. Warning: read on and you will never look at a mutual fund the same.

Mutual funds as recently discussed by:

The New York Times

MnRNINGSTAR®

THE WALL STREET JOURNAL.

Reprinted from

The New York Times

Opinion

The Mutual Fund Merry-Go-Round

By DAVID F. SWENSEN

David F. Swensen is the chief investment officer at Yale University and the author of "Unconventional Success: A Fundamental Approach to Personal Investment."

New Haven.

AS stock prices have gyrated wildly, many investors have behaved in a perverse fashion, selling low after having bought high. Individual investors bear some responsibility for ill-advised responses to the ups and downs in the market, but they are not the only ones to blame. For decades, the mutual fund industry, which manages more than $13 trillion for 90 million Americans, has employed market volatility to produce profits for itself far more reliably than it has produced returns for its investors.

Too often, investors believe that mutual funds provide a safe haven, placing a misguided trust in brokers, advisers and fund managers. In fact, the industry has a history of delivering inferior results to investors, and its regulators do not provide effective oversight.

The companies that manage for-profit mutual funds face a fundamental conflict between producing profits for their owners and generating superior returns for their investors. In general, these companies spend lavishly on marketing campaigns, gather copious amounts of assets — and invest poorly. For decades, investors suffered below-market returns even as mutual fund management company owners enjoyed market-beating results. Profits trumped the duty to serve investors.

Mutual fund companies, retail brokers and financial advisers aggressively market funds awarded four stars and five stars by Morningstar, the Chicago-based arbiter of investment performance. But the rating system merely identifies funds that performed well in the past; it provides no help in finding future winners. Nevertheless, investors respond to industry come-ons and load up on the most "stellar" offerings.

In 2010, investors redeemed $152 billion from one-star, two-star and three-star funds and placed $304 billion in four-star and five-star funds. In the crisis-scarred year of 2008, even as investors withdrew $174 billion from one-star, two-star and three-star funds, they added $47 billion to four-star and five-star funds. Year in and year out, flows to four-star and five-star funds prove remarkably resilient and overshadow flows to the three bottom categories.

This churning of investor portfolios hurts investor returns. First, brokers and advisers use the pointless buying and selling to increase and to justify their all-too-rich compensation. Second, the mutual fund industry uses the star-rating system to encourage performance-chasing (selling funds that performed poorly and buying funds that performed well). In other words, investors sell low and buy high.

Ill-advised buying and selling of funds costs the investing public a substantial sum. In 2010, Morningstar found that if mutual fund investors in 2000, as a whole, had simply bought and held their funds for 10 years, their investment outcomes would have improved by an average of 1.6 percentage points per year. That 1.6 percent may not sound like much, but it adds up to tens of billions of dollars per year. Another Morningstar study, in 2005, examined 10 years of returns for 17 categories of stock funds. In each category, the actual returns — after taking into account the ill-timed buying and selling — fell short of the returns that were advertised to the public. More stable funds performed better; more volatile funds performed worse.

Highly volatile technology funds, for example, generated annual returns that were a stunning 13.4 percent below the reported results, as a direct result of monumentally mistimed buying and selling. Holders of less volatile conservative allocation funds suffered only a 0.3 percent annual deficit.

Even while the investing public suffers from exposure to funds with volatile performance, the mutual fund industry benefits. With a volatile set of offerings, the fund companies will always have some (temporarily) strong performers that rise to the top and earn the four or five stars needed for marketing to a gullible public. Of course, the volatility cuts both ways, ensuring that erstwhile top performers fall to the bottom and end up with one star or two stars. From a business perspective, however, all is not lost, as a number of one-star and two-star funds, with sufficiently volatile strategies, will rise phoenix-like from the ashes and join the exalted ranks of four- and five-star funds.

Why isn't there more of an outcry? Investors naively trust their brokers and advisers. Most understand too little about

The Mutual Fund Merry-Go-Round

By DAVID F. SWENSEN

Davis F. Swensen is the chief investment officer at Yale University and the author *of Unconventional Success: A Fundamental Approach to Personal Investment.* New Haven.

As stock prices have gyrated wildly, many investors have behaved in a perverse fashion, selling low after having bought high. Individual investors bear some responsibility for ill-advised responses to the ups and downs in the market, but they are not the only ones to blame. For decades, the mutual fund industry, which manages more than $13 trillion for 90 million Americans, has employed market volatility to produce profits for itself far more reliably than it has produced returns for its investors.

Too often, investors believe that mutual funds provide a safe haven, placing a misguided trust in brokers, advisers, and fund managers. In fact, the industry has a history of delivering inferior results to investors, and its regulators do not provide effective oversight.

The companies that manage for-profit mutual funds face a fundamental conflict between producing profits for their owners and generating superior returns for their investors. In general, these companies spend lavishly on marketing campaigns, gather copious amounts of assets, and invest poorly. For decades, investors suffered below-market returns even as mutual fund management company owners enjoyed market-beating results. Profits trumped the duty to serve investors.

Mutual fund companies, retail brokers, and financial advisers aggressively market funds awarded four stars and five stars by Morningstar, the Chicago-based arbiter of investment performance. But the rating system merely identifies funds that performed well in the past; it provides no help in finding future winners. Nevertheless, investors respond to industry come-ons and load up on the most "stellar" offerings.

In 2010, investors redeemed $152 billion from one-star, two-star and three-star funds and placed $304 billion in four-star and five-star funds. In the crisis-scarred year of 2008, even as investors withdrew $174 billion from one-star, two-star, and three-star funds, they added $47 billion to four-star and five-star funds. Year in and year out, flows to four-star and five-star funds prove remarkably resilient and overshadow flows to the three bottom categories.

This churning of investor portfolios hurts investor returns. First, brokers and advisers use the pointless buying and selling to increase and justify their all-too-rich compensation. Second, the mutual fund industry uses the star rating system to encourage performance-chasing (selling funds that performed poorly and buying funds that performed well). In other words, investors sell low and buy high.

Ill-advised buying and selling of funds costs the investing public a substantial sum. In 2010, Morningstar found that if mutual fund investors in 2000, as a whole, had simply bought and held their funds for 10 years, their investment outcomes would have improved by an average of 1.6 percentage points per year. That 1.6 percent may not sound like much, but it adds ups to tens of billions of dollars per year. Another Morningstar study, in 2005, examined 10 years of returns for 17 categories of stock funds. In each category, the actual returns — after taking into account the ill-timed buying and selling — fell short of the returns that were advertised to the public. More stable funds performed better; more volatile funds performed worse.

Highly volatile technology funds, for example, generated annual returns that were a stunning 13.4 percent below the reported results, as a direct result of monumentally mistimed buying and selling. Holders of less volatile conservative allocation funds suffered only a 0.3 percent annual deficit.

Even while the investing public suffers from exposure to funds with volatile performance, the mutual fund industry benefits. With a volatile set of offerings, the fund companies will always have some (temporarily) strong performers that rise to the top and earn the four or five stars needed for marketing to a gullible public. Of course, the volatility cuts both ways, ensuring that erstwhile top performers fall to the bottom and end up with one star or two stars. From a business perspective, howev-

er, all is not lost, as a number of one-star and two-star funds, with sufficiently volatile strategies, will rise phoenix-like from the ashes and join
the exalted ranks of four- and five-star funds.

Why isn't there more of an outcry? Investors naively trust their brokers
and advisers. Most understand too little about financial markets to
make informed decisions, intervene too frequently in counterproductive
ways, and gather too little information about portfolio holdings to eval-
uate results. Investors like to believe they are doing well, even when
they are not.

Meanwhile, the mutual fund industry shouts through a mega-phone,
making campaign contributions to influence politicians and lobbying to
avoid regulation. Without any offsetting pressure from the investing
public, Wall Street crushes Main Street.

What should be done? First, individual investors should take control of
their financial destinies, educate themselves, avoid sales pitches and
invest in a well-diversified portfolio of low-cost index funds, like those
offered by Vanguard, which operates on a not-for-profit basis. (Even
Morningstar concludes, in a remarkably frank study, that low costs do a
better job of predicting superior performance than do the firm's own
five-star ratings.) Such a strategy reduces the fees paid to the parasitic
mutual fund industry, leaving more money in the hands of the investing
public.

Second, the Securities and Exchange Commission should employ its
considerable regulatory and enforcement powers to encourage individual investors to embrace low-cost index funds and shun the broker-
driven churning of high-cost actively managed funds.

The SEC should think outside of the box in policing the behavior of the
mutual fund industry. What about a requirement that every mutual fund
offering be accompanied by an index-fund alternative, with the burden
of proof on the vendor to justify the sale of the high-cost product? Fund
companies, brokers and advisers would have to list all fees associated

165

with the fund offering, along with a description of the impact on expected returns. Over time, mutual fund purveyors would have to provide a head-to-head comparison of the recommended fund and the index fund alternative (including the impact of taxes), demonstrating as clearly as possible the long-term superiority of low-cost, tax-efficient index funds.

Third, the SEC should hold the mutual fund industry to a "fiduciary standard," one that puts clients' interests first. Currently, retail brokers operate under a weaker standard. As it carriers out the Dodd-Frank reform act that became law last year, the SEC must insist that brokers act as fiduciaries, not merely as agents who offer "suitable" investments. For all players in the mutual fund industry — brokers, advisers, and fund managers — strong fiduciary standards and investor-oriented regulatory oversight would subordinate the pecuniary interests of the fund purveyors to the interests of the individual investors that the industry purports to serve.

For two decades, laissez-faire attitudes toward financial markets allowed the rich and powerful to take advantage of those less well-off. In the mutual fund world, the hands-off approach must be abandoned in favor of aggressive, intelligent regulation.

This is serious business. The financial security of millions of Americans hangs in the balance.

Are There Hidden Fees in Your Mutual Fund?

By Christine Benz | 10-27-09 | 06:00 AM | E-mail Article

I'm often surprised that many investors--even those who are quite savvy--aren't aware that a mutual fund's expense ratio doesn't encompass all of the costs associated with owning a fund. A host of other charges, ranging from a fund's brokerage charges to tax costs, can reduce your bottom line just as surely as your expense ratio will.

Take brokerage commissions. Your manager has to pay these costs when he or she buys or sells stocks and bonds for the portfolio, but fund companies don't have to include these costs when calculating fund expense ratios. You'd expect funds' trading costs to be lower than what you or I would pay to execute a trade; after all, funds are typically trading large numbers of shares, so they should be able to negotiate volume discounts, right? Well, yes and no. Unfortunately for fund shareholders, some fund shops have paid more than they've needed to for trades because they received research and other goodies in exchange for paying higher commissions. And under a practice called "directed brokerage," which regulators banned in 2004, some fund shops paid inflated trading commissions in exchange for having their funds placed on that brokerage firm's "preferred list."

Funds also face so-called market-impact costs. That means that if your manager is trying to buy or sell a big block of a given stock, there's a chance that the fund will have to accept a less advantageous price for that security than if he or she were buying or selling fewer shares. For example, say your manager is trying to buy 1 million shares of a certain small-company stock. If only 100,000 shares of that stock typically change hands each day, that means it will take your fund manager a minimum of 10 days to complete your fund's trade--and that's assuming your manager is gobbling up all of the shares that traded on those 10 days. In the meantime, the stock could get more and more expensive, reducing the amount of money that your manager can make on it.

So if these costs aren't included in a fund's expense ratio, how can you try to keep track of them and limit them? We have a couple of suggestions. To keep fund trading costs from dragging on your bottom line, we'd urge you to focus on those funds that simply don't trade much. Index mutual funds and exchange-traded funds, especially those that focus on large-company stocks, generally limit their trading costs, because they simply mirror the holdings in a given market benchmark. You could also look for those actively managed funds with low turnover rates, an indication that their managers like to buy their holdings and hang on. As a general rule of thumb, a fund with a turnover rate of 25% or less, indicating that the manager completely makes over the portfolio every four years, will have lower trading costs than one with a turnover rate of 100%.

What about limiting market-impact costs--the risk that your manager will obtain a less-than-advantageous price for your fund's securities? A couple of different characteristics tend to put a fund at a greater risk for racking up those hidden costs. First, because high-turnover funds trade frequently, it only stands to reason that they run a greater risk of affecting securities' prices when they buy and sell.

And funds that traffic in small-company stocks, which invariably have fewer outstanding shares than large-company stocks, could also see market-impact costs erode their returns. Finally, market-impact costs will tend to be a bigger problem for funds with large asset bases than for tiny, nimble funds, simply because the manager of the big fund has to step up and buy or sell a greater number of the outstanding shares of a given security than does the manager of a tiny fund. We're not saying that you should automatically dismiss a fund simply because it has a large asset base, high turnover, or focuses on small-company stocks. But if you're considering a fund that has more than one of these risk factors, you would do well

---

Are There Hidden Fees in Your Mutual Fund?
By Christine Benz | 10-27-09 | 06:00 AM | E-mail Article

I'm often surprised that many investors--even those who are quite savvy--aren't aware that a mutual fund's expense ratio doesn't encompass all of the costs associated with owning a fund. A host of other charges, ranging from a fund's brokerage charges to tax costs, can reduce your bottom line just as surely as your expense ratio will.

Take brokerage commissions. Your manager has to pay these costs when he or she buys or sells stocks and bonds for the portfolio, but fund companies don't have to include these costs when calculating fund expense ratios. You'd expect funds' trading costs to be lower than what you or I would pay to execute a trade; after all, funds are typically trading large numbers of shares, so they should be able to negotiate volume discounts, right? Well, yes and no. Unfortunately for fund shareholders, some fund shops have paid more than they've needed to for trades because they received research and other goodies in exchange for paying higher commissions. And under a practice called "directed brokerage," which regulators banned in 2004, some fund shops paid inflated trading commissions in exchange for having their funds placed on that brokerage firm's "preferred list."

Funds also face so-called market-impact costs. That means that if your manager is trying to buy or sell a big block of a given stock, there's a chance that the fund will have to accept a less advantageous price for that security than if he or she were buying or selling fewer shares. For example, say your manager is trying to buy 1 million shares of a certain small-company stock. If only 100,000 shares of that stock typically change hands each day, that means it will take your fund manager a minimum of 10 days to complete your fund's trade--and that's assuming your manager is gobbling up all of the shares that traded on those 10 days. In the meantime, the stock could get more and more expensive, reducing the amount of money that your manager can make in it.

So if these costs aren't included in a fund's expense ratio, how can you try to keep track of them and limit them? We have a couple of suggestions. To keep fund trading costs from dragging on your bottom line, we'd urge you to focus on those funds that simply don't trade much. Index mutual funds and exchange-traded funds, especially those that focus on large-company stocks, generally limit their trading costs, because they simply mirror the holdings in a given market benchmark. You could also look for those actively managed funds with low turnover rates, an indication that their managers like to buy their holdings and hang on. As a general rule of thumb, a fund with a turnover rate of 25% or less, indicating that the manager completely makes over the portfolio every four years, will have lower trading costs than one with a turnover rate of 100%.

What about limiting market-impact costs--the risk that your manager will obtain a less-than-advantageous price for your fund's securities? A couple of different characteristics tend to put a fund at a greater risk for racking up these hidden costs. First, because high-turnover funds trade frequently, it only stands to reason that they run a greater risk of affecting securities' prices when they buy and sell.

And funds that traffic in small-company stocks, which invariably have fewer outstanding shares than large-company stocks, could also see market-impact costs erode their returns. Finally, market-impact costs will tend to be a bigger problem for funds with large asset bases than for tiny, nimble funds, simply because the manager of the big fund has to step up and buy or sell a greater number of the outstanding shares of a given security than does the manager of a tiny fund. We're not saying that you should automatically dismiss a fund simply because it has a large as-set base, high turnover, or focuses on small-company stocks. But if you're considering a fund that has more than one of these risk factors, you would do well to consider whether market-impact costs could eventually drag on your own bottom line.

Reference: This is an excerpt from the second edition of The Morningstar Guide to Mutual Funds: 5 -Star Strategies for Success.

Christine Benz is Morningstar's director of personal finance and author of 30-Minute Money Solutions: A Step-by-Step Guide to Managing Your Finances and the Morningstar Guide to Mutual Funds: 5-Star Strategies for Success.

http://news.morningstar.com/articlenet/HtmlTemplate/PrintArticle.htm?time=1042964

THE WALL STREET JOURNAL.

2010-03-01   (copyright)

The Hidden Costs of Mutual Funds; Portfolio managers can rack up steep expenses buying and selling securities, but that burden isn't reflected in a fund's standard expense ratio

BY ANNA PRIOR

How much does it cost you to own a mutual fund? Probably a lot more than you think.

In selecting mutual funds, most investors know to check the expense ratio, the standard measure of how costly a fund is to own. U.S.-stock funds pay an average of 1.31% of assets each year to the portfolio manager and for other operating expenses, according to Morningstar Inc.

But that's not the real bottom line. There are other costs, not reported in the expense ratio, related to the buying and selling of securities in the portfolio, and those expenses can make a fund two or three times as costly as advertised.

"These trading and transaction costs are very real," says Stephen Horan, head of professional education content and private wealth at CFA Institute, a nonprofit association of investment professionals. "While it's very important to look at that expense ratio, it's just not going to capture" all of the costs, Mr. Horan says.

One reason trading costs go unreported is their complexity, which leaves the fund companies in disagreement about exactly how to calculate those costs. Trying to quantify a fund's trading expenses can look at as easy as performing brain surgery.

Fund firms on the whole aren't clamoring to disclose more information about these costs. The Securities and Exchange Commission seems to revisit this issue every several years without much happening. And investors are left trying to piece something together from snippets of information disclosed in a prospectus or other materials.

"The average investor can't really even begin to get a strong grasp on these additional costs, says Richard Kopcke, an economist at the Center for Retirement Research at Boston College who co-wrote a recent study about fees and trading costs of mutual funds in 401(k) plans. "There's just not enough information. Not even close."

Even experts come up with some very different estimates. Mr. Kopcke's study looked at the 100 largest U.S.-stock funds held in defined-contribution plans as of December 2007 and found trading costs for the funds that averaged from 0.11% of assets annually in the quintile with the lowest costs, to 1.99% of assets in the quintile with the highest costs, with a median of 0.56%.

A study updated last year of thousands of U.S.-stock funds put the average trading costs at 1.44% of total assets, with an average of 0.14% in the bottom quintile and 2.96% in the top. Expenses are one of the most important things investors can look at, says study co-author Richard Evans, an assistant professor of finance at the University of Virginia's Darden School. "We find that our estimates of trading costs" are an important predictor of performance. While "some trading actually adds value," Mr. Evans says, high trading costs overall tend to have a negative impact on performance. On average, $1 in trading costs decreased net assets by 46 cents in this study.

Mr. Horan, meanwhile, estimates that trading costs for stock funds total 2% to 3% of assets annually, though conservative estimates place them closer to 1%, he says.

Identifying Costs

What exactly are these costs? There are four main components: brokerage commissions, bid-ask spreads, opportunity costs and market-impact costs.

The brokerage commissions a fund pays to buy or sell securities are the simplest piece to understand. The SEC requires three years of brokerage costs in dollars to be disclosed in a fund's statement of additional information. Putnam Investments, for example, reported commissions of $21.5 million for its Putnam Voyager fund for the fiscal year ended last July 31. Doing some math, that was equal to 0.69% of the fund's $3.12 billion in assets on July 31, on top of a reported expense ratio of 1.26%. A Putnam spokeswoman notes that the fund outperformed its benchmark by 17.1 percentage points, net of fees and expenses, for that period. Commissions for that period were also higher than normal, due to a new manager and volatile environment, she says.

A few fund groups, including Brandywine Funds and Selected Funds, do the math for investors by quoting their commissions costs as a percentage of assets.

But the SEC doesn't require commissions to be factored into expense ratios. The commissions only tell part of the story and so could be misleading, the SEC explained to Congress in a 2003 memo, and the agency has not revised this position.

Commissions typically make up less than half of a fund's total trading costs, says Mr. Horan. The other three components are much harder to quantify.

Bid-ask spreads deal with the difference between the lowest price at which a seller is willing to sell a security and the highest price a buyer is willing to pay. The gap between them usually associated with thinly traded securities is the spread. At any given moment, for example, a security may have a bid price of $98 and an asking price of $100. Say a fund bought that security for $100,

The Hidden Costs of Mutual Funds: Portfolio managers can rack up steep expenses buying and selling securities, but that burden isn't reflected in a fund's standard expense ratio

BY ANNA PRIOR

How much does it cost you to own a mutual fund? Probably a lot more than you think.

In selecting mutual funds, most investors know to check the expense ratio, the standard measure of how costly a fund is to own. U.S. stock funds pay an average of 1.31% of assets each year to the portfolio manager and for other operating expenses, according to Morningstar Inc.

But that's not the real bottom line. There are other costs, not reported in the expense ratio, related to the buying and selling of securities in the portfolio, and those expenses can make a fund two or three times as costly as advertised.

"These trading and transaction costs are very real," says Stephen Horan, head of professional education content and private wealth at CFA Institute, a nonprofit association of investment professionals. "While it's very important to look at that expense ratio, it's just not going to capture" all of the costs, Mr. Horan says.

One reason trading costs go unreported is their complexity, which leaves the fund companies in disagreement about exactly how to calculate those costs. Trying to quantify a fund's trading expenses can be about as easy as performing brain surgery.

Fund firms on the whole aren't clamoring to disclose more information about these costs. The Securities and Exchange Commission seems to revisit this issue every several years without much happening. And investors are left trying to piece something together from snippets of information disclosed in a prospectus or other materials.

"The average investor can't really even begin" to get a strong grasp on these additional costs, says Richard Kopcke, an economist at the Center for Retirement Research at Boston College who co-wrote a recent study about fees and trading costs of mutual funds in 40l(k) plans. "There's just not enough information. Not even close."

Even experts come up with some very different estimates. Mr. Kopcke's study looked at the 100 largest U.S. stock funds held in defined-contribution plans as of December 2007 and found trading costs for the funds that averaged from 0.11% of assets annually in the quintile with the lowest costs, to 1.99% of assets in the quintile with the highest costs, with a median of 0.66%.

A study updated last year of thousands of U.S. stock funds put the average trading costs at 1.44% of total assets, with an average of 0.14% in the bottom quintile and 2.96% in the top. Expenses are one of the most important things investors can look at, says study co-author Richard Evans, an assistant professor of finance at the University of Virginia's Darden School. "We find that our estimates of trading costs" are an important predictor of performance. While "some trading actually adds value," Mr. Evans says, high trading costs overall tend to have a negative impact on performance. On average, $1 in trading costs decreased net assets by 46 cents in this study.

Mr. Horan, meanwhile, estimates that trading costs for stock funds total 2% to 3% of assets annually, though conservative estimates place them closer to 1%, he says.

Identifying Costs

What exactly are these costs?

There are four main components: brokerage commissions, bid-ask spreads, opportunity costs, and market-impact costs.

The brokerage commissions a fund pays to buy or sell securities are the simplest piece to understand. The SEC requires three years of brokerage costs in dollars to be disclosed in a fund's statement of additional information. Putnam Investments, for example, reported commissions of $21.5 million for its Putnam Voyager fund for the fiscal year ended last July 31. Doing some math, that was equal to 0.69% of the fund's $3.12 billion in assets on July 31, on top of a reported expense ratio of 1.26%. A Putnam spokeswoman notes that the fund outperformed its benchmark by 17.1 percentage points, net of fees and expenses, for that period. Commissions for that period were also higher than normal, due to a new manager and volatile environment, she says.

A few fund groups, including Brandywine Funds and Selected Funds, do the math for investors by quoting their commissions costs as a percentage of assets.

But the SEC doesn't require commissions to be factored into expense ratios. The commissions only tell part of the story and so could be misleading, the SEC explained to Congress in a 2003 memo, and the agency has not revised this position.

Commissions typically make up less than half of a fund's total trading costs, says Mr. Horan. The other three components are much harder to quantify.

Bid-ask spreads deal with the difference between the lowest price at which a seller is willing to sell a security and the highest price a buyer is willing to pay. The gap between them usually associated with thinly traded securities is the spread. At any given moment, for example, a security may have a bid price of $96 and an asking price of $100. Say a fund bought that security for $100, and the security's value later rises. If the fund decides to sell the security when the asking price is $110 and the spread has stayed the same, the fund will only receive $106. The spread thus cost the seller $4. Over time, spreads can be a significant cost for a fund that does a lot of trading in less-liquid holdings, such as very small stocks.

Market-impact costs, and the resulting opportunity costs, are often the largest component of trading costs as much as 10 times brokerage commissions, says Mr. Horan. These costs occur when a large trade say, unloading a big stake in a thinly traded stock changes the price of a security before the trade is completed. Similarly, opportunity costs are when the impact of a trade inhibits a fund manager from filling an order on his or her desired terms, resulting in either a less-favorable price or fewer shares purchased or sold, says Steven Stone, a partner and head of the investment management practice group at law firm Morgan, Lewis & Bockius.

Funds do factor these costs into their returns, just like the costs stated in the standard expense ratios. So why should investors try to quantify these costs? Because the higher the costs are, the more value the manager will need to add in his or her security selection and trading decisions to make the investment worthwhile compared with, say, a passive index fund. And when the costs are not all broken out for investors to see, it's harder for investors to tell where that performance bar lies.

When a fund has high trading costs, that's "a higher hurdle to clear when coupled with the expense ratio," says Russel Kinnel, director of fund research at Morningstar Inc.

Debating Disclosure

Trading costs other than commissions aren't required to be disclosed by funds. Trying to include all trading costs in the expense ratio, the SEC told Congress in 2003, could produce a number that is "not comparable because it would be based on estimates and assumptions that would vary from fund to fund." Last week, an SEC spokesman said: "We continue to analyze portfolio transaction costs as the agency focuses on enhancing disclosure to retail investors."

At the fund industry's Investment Company Institute trade group, Chief Economist Brian Reid said "mutual funds work hard to quantify their total transaction costs." But there isn't an "agreed-upon methodology on how to quantify implicit transaction costs, such as market-impact costs." Thus, he says, "requiring funds to disclose total trading costs would not provide adequate means for investors to compare trading costs across funds and could result in investor confusion."

In addition, quoting estimates in a prospectus can get into dicey territory, says Mr. Stone, the lawyer. "A mutual fund has to stand by information in its prospectus. Factual information should be clearly and objectively established and confirmable," he says.

But Mr. Kinnel of Morningstar says that investors are "really entitled to that information," and that some methodology should be developed. Not having a standard "doesn't mean it's not worth doing and not worth coming up with one," he says.

For the past several years, Morningstar has been trying to develop a "trading cost ratio" to complement the standard expense ratio; there's no date or timeline yet for when the project might be completed.

Meanwhile, "a lot of fund companies pay trading-cost consultants to estimate their trading costs," says Mr. Kinnel, so it would be a "piece of cake" for those companies to make these estimates known to investors.

Not so fast, says Gus Sauter, managing director and chief investment officer at Vanguard Group. "While many of the larger firms might attempt to do these calculations," making it mandatory would be almost impossibly difficult for midsize and small investment managers that can't afford consultants, he says.

'Turnover' Clue

While you can't find a fund's total trading-related costs, you can get a clue from a standard and imperfect measure of how much trading the fund is doing, called "turnover." Turnover, expressed as a percentage, shows at what rate stocks in the fund have been replaced. A stock fund that sold half its stocks and replaced them with an equal value in new stocks would have turnover of 50%. But in an extreme case, say there's a fund that's getting a lot of new money coming in from investors and it doesn't have to sell anything to generate cash. The turnover rate would be 0%, even if the fund has been buying stocks, because it didn't sell anything.

The SEC voted last year to require fund companies to disclose one year of turnover in the front of a prospectus, in the summary, in addition to the previously required five years of turnover disclosed in the financial highlights section sometimes found near the back of the document.

Turnover of more than 100% can indicate trading costs may be on the high side, Mr. Kinnel says. In a Morningstar list of the 200 largest U.S. stock funds, the funds with the highest turnover ratios were CGM Focus, a 504%, and American Century Equity Income, at 296%. Of the 32 funds that had turnover above 100%, 11 were from Fidelity Investments, topped by Fidelity Advisor Mid Cap, at 244%. Officials of CGM Focus's management firm, Capital Growth Management LP, did not respond to requests for comment.

American Century Investments product manager Shawn Connor says the Equity Income fund managers may buy and sell the same securities repeatedly when they believe them to be undervalued or overvalued. The company has sought to lower trading costs by using electronic trading systems and other means to lessen market impact, Mr. Connor says.

Fidelity spokesman Vincent Loporchio says "there may be any number of factors impacting turnover during a given period, and turnover can vary over time. As we have many large funds, it's not surprising that we would show up frequently on a list like this."

Two other factors to consider in gauging a fund's trading costs are size and style. Small funds usually aren't big enough to move markets, Mr. Horan says. An exception is when the fund trades in a low-volume segment, such as for small stocks or a thinly traded international market. Large funds, too, incur higher trading costs when they delve into less-liquid areas such as small or microcap stocks.

Style comes into play in terms of bid-ask spreads, says Mr. Horan. "Aggressive growth funds tend to have higher spreads [which increase costs], while income funds tend to have lower spreads," due to the types of securities in which they invest.

Copyright by the Wall Street Journal

Are Mutual Funds for Poor People?

This headline is sure to raise some eyebrows. But this is the type of question that floats around in my head when I have idle time.

The basis of my inquiry is propagated from my experience of working with high-net worth clients that have been taught that mutual funds are the right investment tool for creating/preserving wealth. *But are they?* And, if not, *who are mutual funds appropriate for?*

The first open-ended mutual fund was invented in 1924 with the creation of the Massachusetts Investors Trust. It's understandable that you and I take the concept of mutual funds for granted be-cause we grew up with them. But in the U.S., this was a relatively new concept of pooling investors' money into a collective "basket" to purchase investment instruments like stocks, bonds, and the like. Over the last 80+ years, the mutual fund industry grew like wildfire mostly because it was the easy investment of choice in many 401(k)s in conjunction with the bull markets of the 80s and 90s. Wall Street cheered all the way to the bank as the industry grew from $27 billion in 1929 to a whopping $11.8 trillion in 2010 (according to the Investment Company Institute). This is a BIG industry with DEEP pockets, so it begs the question… do you think the mutual fund industry has VESTED interests in keeping your money invested in mutual funds?

So, What's Desirable about Mutual Funds?

1. Professional investment management for investors of all sizes (as low as $1,000 minimum investments)
2. Daily liquidity
3. Diversification
4. Easily Accessible and Widely Available

BUT, What's the Catch?

1. Fees, Fees, Fees – There can be up to 15 different layers of hidden fees
2. Lack of transparency – Can you find out what your fund is really invested in?
3. Lack of control and tax efficiency
4. No opportunity to customize or tailor to your unique situation

5. No predictable income
6. Overlap (holding the same investments in different mutual funds, losing the power of diversification)

Anything Else?

The most flagrant abuse of mutual funds, in my opinion, is when a broker/advisor charges you a "management fee" to pick "the best" mutual funds, further lowering your return and compounding your losses. One of the all-time favorite mutual funds that brokers/ advisors sell is Pimco Total Return C. The core fee of this fund is 1.65% (the expense ratio); but, of course, there are other hidden fees as well like 12b-1 fees, sales fees, tax consequences, etc. If an advisor charges 1% to pick "the best" funds, the real fee is closer to 3% per year. See the hypothetical illustration below:

Growth of $300,000 in PPTCX from 2005 - 2010

	Fund Return	Return After Fund Fees	Return After Fund Fees + 1% Advisor Fee
2005	$304,920	$302,400	$299,400
2006	$313,274	$307,480	$301,435
2007	$337,616	$327,159	$317,771
2008	$349,567	$331,444	$318,698
2009	$393,192	$366,345	$349,070
2010	$422,879	$385,725	$364,045

($37,154 lost to fund fees or 30% of gains)
($58,833 lost to fund & advisor fees or 48% of gains)

(data compiled by morningstar.com)

So, did the advisor earn his keep of $21,679 for picking the right fund? Maybe. Maybe not. I'm curious, if one of the benefits of mutual funds is professional investment management, why would you need to hire another financial professional to manage the professional fund managers? Is this duplication of effort worth the $21,679? Or worse, just a lazy way to manage money?

So, maybe mutual funds aren't for poor people after all? Was I being too harsh when I titled this blog post? I think when you boil it all down, mutual funds have their place – for unsophisticated investors struggling to save for retirement. But, if you've done a good job accumulating retirement savings and you want to:

1. Preserve your wealth

2. Pay less money in fees

3. Have more control

4. Create retirement income

5. Have a custom, tailored solution

… then you need to look outside of the mutual fund world and upgrade your approach to investing.

Securities offered through Kalos Capital, Inc., Member FINRA, SIPC. Investment Advisory Services offered through Kilos Management, Inc., 3780 Mansell Rd. Suite 150, Alpharetta, GA 30022, (678) 356-1100. Russell & Company is not an affiliate or subsidiary of Kalos Capital, Inc. or Kalos Management, Inc. The opinions in the preceding commentary are as of the date of publication and are subject to change. Information has been obtained from third-party sources we consider reliable, but we do not guarantee the facts cited are accurate or complete. This material is not intended to be relied upon as a forecast or investment advice regarding a particular investment or the markets in general, nor is it intended to predict or depict performance of any slots online investment. Past performance is no guarantee of future results.

Reference: Rob Report, The Straight Scoop About Your Retirement blog post by Rob Russell dated January 12, 2012.

Robert Russell is a frequent contributor to CNBC, Fox Business, The Wall Street Journal, Reuters, International Business Times, and Smart money. He also co-hosts "Retirement Rescue Radio" on AM1290 and 95.7fm WHIO.

http://blog.rescueyourretirementradio.com/2012/01/12/are-mutual-funds-for-poor-people/

These articles were probably very eye-opening for most of you. When I meet with potential clients and do a cost and risk analysis of their portfolio, many cannot believe the amount of hidden expenses. I think related mutual fund expenses, such as an advisor's management fee just to pick a mutual fund with another manager who must pick the stocks, is like paying your friend at church $100 to have him pick your neighbor to mow your lawn for $60. Then your neighbor uses your mower to mow and asks your wife for $10 for gas money when he's done!

Let me give you a real-life example from an experience I had with a client. Jane wanted us to analyze her portfolio and give her a second opinion. Her portfolio of $900,000 was primarily in mutual funds managed by another advisor. What we discovered was after 5 years, her annualized return was negative nearly three percent. She pays 2.65% for her mutual funds and 1.5% for the advisor's management fee. That's a total fee of 4.15% which equaled over $37,000 annually.

What's worse for Jane is that, although she described herself as a conservative investor, her portfolio is set up by her broker to be managed moderately *aggressive*! If the market went through another decline like it did in 2008, she stands to lose nearly 48% of her savings for retirement, a loss of more than $430,000. These powerful numbers show why mutual funds may not be appropriate in saving for retirement.

PART II

Why Mutual Funds? Why Now?

I hope to accomplish two goals in providing you with this research information from Global Financial Private Capital. The first is to educate investors on mutual funds and how the mutual fund industry works. I am a big believer that it never hurts to know a little bit more about one's current situation. The second goal is to provide a less-biased look than those portrayed in the regular investment industry propaganda; ideally to present the good things and the bad about mutual funds, as well as to dig a little bit deeper into the fine print that investors should know before they make a decision to put their savings to work in these vehicles.

When I started my first job, I was encouraged by my parents to save and invest for the future. I contributed to my company's tax-deferred savings plan (which featured mutual funds) and even started investing outside in mutual funds on my own. Over the years, as the money started to accumulate and I opened my own practice managing assets for clients, it became clear to me that if I was going to act as a Fiduciary for others I would have to raise my level of education about the investments I was recommending. So I started asking questions and collecting research. It quickly be-came clear to me that there were many paths available to investors and that "one path for all" would not be the very best we could do. The Fiduciary standard dictates that we be knowledgeable, promote full disclosure, and do what is in the very best interests for our clients.

One of the most shocking things about this research is that some of it is so simple and straightforward. It was amazing to me that much of this knowledge is not taught every day to teenagers at high school and college levels. Given that so many people have historically used mutual funds to begin their lifelong savings journey, one would think this would be part of a basic adult learning curriculum. Yet somehow many of us are not schooled in these topics and are supposed to just "pick things up" along the way. The purpose of the following information is to help change this situation.

I am giving this brief summary to you. The information in it is extremely valuable and may save you a great deal of money.

GLOBAL FINANCIAL

Private Capital

COMPREHENSIVE WEALTH MANAGEMENT

A Close-Up Look at the Mutual Fund Industry
8 Things You May Not Know About Mutual Funds
(that can hurt you!)

MUTUAL FUNDS
The Good, the Bad, and the Fine Print

At first, the mutual fund was a beautiful concept. Any investor, of any net worth, could invest and gain access to professional portfolio management. It meant the person on the street could save and build hope for the future. Times have changed. Maybe your investment habits should, too.

Let us share some information that might help you grow your wealth. We're going to take you behind the scenes of one of the largest industries in the world — mutual funds — and show you how that industry affects investors. We would like to share some information with you to provide additional transparency about the mutual fund industry that today's financial media may not regularly report. Let's take a look at the good and the bad in mutual funds, and then provide you with some ideas of what you can do to improve how you invest. Our goal is that you become better informed — and, hopefully, wealthier over time.

What Is a Mutual Fund?

Since their inception in 1924, open-end mutual funds have been a fast-growing, profitable industry. At the time of the Great Crash in 1929, 19 mutual funds existed.[1] At year-end 2011, there were more than 8,600 — approximately three times the number of companies that trade on the New York Stock Exchange.[2] Most of this growth has occurred over the past 20 years.[3] Almost one-half of all U.S. households (52 million) have investments in mutual funds.[4]

A mutual fund is a professionally managed collective investment that gathers money from many individual investors to purchase securities. Theoretically, by having access to a larger pool of money, the company is able to create a diversified basket of investments that can be accessed by many small, unrelated investors.

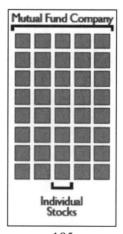

185

Investments in a mutual fund may not be limited to just stocks. Some mutual funds invest in bonds, commodities, real estate, currencies, art, precious metals, and more (or any combination of these). An investor can find a mutual fund company that will specialize in just about any asset class or mix imaginable.

The mutual fund structure provides several advantages:

- Easy access to lots of different securities. Instead of having to research and buy possibly hundreds of stocks and pay commissions on each, an investor can buy shares of this pooled company.
- Easy access for small investors. As long as an investor has enough money to buy a minimum number of shares, they can be an owner.
- Easy liquidity. Shares can easily be bought and sold at the end of each business day.
- Access to professional wisdom. Mutual funds typically hire experienced people to manage these companies.

Doesn't the investor profit most from mutual funds?

Unfortunately, it's not that simple.

At the end of 2009, the more than 7,600 mutual funds of all types in the United States had combined assets of $11.1 trillion. The Investment company Institute, a national trade association of investment companies in the U.S., reports that mutual fund assets were $23.6 trillion worldwide on the same date. In an industry this size, the net profits are huge — estimated at $75.7 billion.[5]

Three groups can profit from mutual funds:

1. The companies that create these funds. For the most part, the investment firms that create mutual funds make money from the fees they charge to manage and administer them.

2. The brokers that sell shares of mutual funds to their clients and de-generate commissions and fees.

3. The investors that buy shares (provided the investments actually make money).

As we move forward in this paper, we will see that companies and brokers almost always make money from mutual funds. Unfortunately, such is not always the case for investors.

Every dollar of expense that your mutual fund incurs is a dollar that you don't get to keep. Mutual funds can incur many expenses, only some of which are revealed in the fund's prospectus.

Mutual funds support an enormous industry and all elements take their cut.

On the periphery of the companies that create and manage mutual funds, a whole industry has sprouted that provides information and services to investors.

- Custodians to hold the funds
- Sales and wholesaling organizations to distribute and market funds
- Law firms specializing in mutual funds
- Accounting and reporting firms
- Mutual fund ratings services
- Mutual fund newsletters

A river of money flows through the mutual fund industry, supporting hundreds of thousands of jobs and creating substantial profits for the companies involved. When any industry becomes this well entrenched in an economy and the profits are as large as they are, it invites not only greater efficiencies but also potentially ruinous competition in the long run.

Educated investors and U.S. government regulators are starting to take a hard look at the industry and what goes on behind the scenes of mutual funds. Stick with us for the rest of this paper as we outline eight of the problems and inequities we have identified for investors and how they can use this information to help themselves.

Eight things you may not know about Mutual Funds (that can hurt you!)

1. Expenses can be much higher than you think.

An investor's goal is to keep as many dollars as possible; and to do that, investors must keep expenses as low as possible and total returns as high as possible. Two types of expenses work against an investor's goals: stated and unstated. Together they produce a formidable obstacle for growing wealth.

Stated Costs	Unstated Costs
Administrative fees	Trading costs
Management fees	Commissions
Marketing fees	Market impact costs
Loads	Taxes

When all expenses are added to the stated costs in a fund's prospectus, an investor may feel like a racehorse with a 350- pound jockey on its back.

Stated expenses are listed in a mutual fund's prospectus. Most investors know to check the expense ratio of a fund to determine the stated costs. According to the Investment Company Institute, the average expense ratio in an equity mutual fund is 1.4 percent per year. Remember that this is the average — many are substantially higher (especially in smaller funds, where there are fewer investors to share those costs). The higher the expense ratio, the less the investor stands to gain. Unstated expenses are more difficult to quantify and not required by law to be disclosed (yet). Like an iceberg, the stated costs visible above the waterline may dwarf the unstated costs that lie below. Let's look at those unstated expenses.

Trading Costs

Found in all securities transactions, these can really magnify the expenses in large, active funds. Also known in the industry as the bid/offer spread, trading costs are buried in the internal workings of each fund. Trading costs are the difference between the price a buyer is willing to pay for a security and the price at which the seller is willing to sell. Each time a mutual fund manager buys and sells securities, the fund incurs small trading costs. The greater the trading activity, the higher the trading costs for the fund and its shareholders. A 2009 study of thousands of U.S. equity mutual funds discovered that trading costs investors, on average, **1.44 percent**.[6]

Transaction Commissions

These are almost impossible to avoid because there is a cost to process any trade order. Even large mutual funds are not exempt from these fees. Because the trade sizes are usually larger, most mutual funds operate in a very low commission structure (pennies per share), but the costs are always there. Again, the more active a fund is, the more potentially negative the impact on fund owners. Although relatively simple to quantify, the SEC does not require these costs to be stated in the expense ratios of mutual funds.

Market Impact Costs

This is potentially one of the greatest costs to shareholders. There are concessions in price to which all institutional investors are subject when they execute larger trades. When funds execute these trades, it can move the price of a security higher (for buying) or lower (for selling) in the marketplace because of their sheer size and liquidity conditions. For example, when an individual sells 200 shares of Apple stock in the market, the price of the stock will barely move. If a large fund manager sells 200,000 shares, it could move the share price significantly lower.

The relative burden of these market impact costs on a mutual fund portfolio can be estimated, given the total size of its portfolio, the number of issues, the median market capitalization of the issues in which the fund specializes and the fund turnover rate.[7]

Taxes

Tax implications for mutual fund investors are so important that we've given the subject its own section. Learn about tax inefficiencies in Section 2.

Why aren't these trading costs reported by the mutual funds?

Trading costs are typically not reported by mutual funds mainly because calculating a precise number is difficult, and there is no standard method of doing it; so most companies will not report these costs until they are mandated to. It is not, however, difficult to calculate rough estimates of what unstated expenses actually cost shareholders. The key for an astute investor is to look at a measure called *turnover*, which funds do disclose, and which can be used to estimate transaction costs. Stephan Horan of the CFA Institute (a non-profit professional organization) estimates this cost to be 1% to 3% annually for equity funds.[8]

How could these costs affect the average investor?

A 55-year-old with $250,000 in a savings plan begins to generate income at age 70. If he earns an average of 5 percent over 15 years, his nest egg will grow to $519,732. If he is charged just 2 percent annually by his mutual funds, the same $250,000 will be worth only $389,492 — a difference of $130,240 of his retirement funds.

Remember, the impact of fund expenses reduces the compounding effect forever. The impact of high fees gets even more frustrating once the investor begins taking withdrawals from his funds. If he takes an annual income at age 70 of 5 percent to maintain his life- style, the fees result in an actual drain of 7 percent (40 percent more than his required income). As this impact causes his nest egg to shrink further, it requires larger and larger distributions to maintain the same lifestyle. The potential web of fees above should give investors a reason to pause and reevaluate when they choose a *retail* mutual fund path.

High investment expenses compounded over several decades can be a very big deal for an individual investor.

2. Mutual funds can be tax inefficient.

When someone buys a share of a publicly traded mutual fund, he or she is buying a share of an existing company that owns many individual investments — each with its own pre-existing tax liabilities. Whether or not that person ever sells those shares, he or she is responsible for a proportional share of the existing tax liabilities. The way mutual fund accounting works, a fund must pay out at least 90 percent of any investment income earned and 98 percent of any realized capital gains. The internal trading activity of the fund manager and fund inflows and outflows affect all shareholders, even though they may have personally performed no trading during the year.

If a fund has assets that have appreciated over time, and they sell them during the current tax year, it could create a situation where a new investor buying shares could inherit the tax liability of existing holdings. For example, an investor purchases 10 shares of an equity mutual fund for $10 per share (total investment of $100). Shortly thereafter, the mutual fund passes through a $2 per share short-term capital gain that has built up during the previous 12 months. If we assume that the shareholder simply reinvests all dividends and capital gains, here is what happens:

Starting value	$100	10 x $10
Capital gain	$20	$2 per share
New share price	$8	$10 minus $2 capital gain distribution to shareholders
Capital gain reinvested	$20 ÷ $8 per share	2.5 shares purchased
Ending value	$100	12.5 x $8

The only difference is that the shareholder now has an unexpected tax liability. Assuming the $20 short-term capital gains distribution is taxed at 25 percent, he or she has a $5 tax liability that reduces the value of the investment to $95. Direct owners of stocks are allowed to defer taxation on the appreciated value of their stock shares, while mutual fund shareholders may be forced to pay taxes yearly, even if they don't sell any of their own mutual fund shares!

How about losses? When a fund experiences net realized losses during the year, it does not have the ability to pass along these losses to the shareholder to offset against ordinary income up to $3,000 (as the shareholder would if he or she had purchased individual investments).

The inability to control their own taxes can frustrate investors and create a serious headwind for investment performance.

"If investors simply bought and held their funds in 2000, they would have been better off by 1.6 percent annually by 2010."

– 2010 Morningstar Study reported in New York Times article 'The Mutual Fund Merry-go-round' (2011)

3. Mutual fund performance provides mixed results.

Many mutual fund companies face a conflict between providing maximum performance for investors and generating profits for themselves. If you read a typical issue of *Barron's* or *Money Magazine*, it is clear that mutual fund companies spend gargantuan sums on advertising and promoting their funds to gather assets. Many pay brokers handsome incentives to get them to favor their products as a solution for clients. As noted above, all of the fees, costs, and ancillary expenses associated with running a mutual fund work in direct conflict with maximizing returns to investors.

It is no mystery that most mutual funds have a difficult time providing above-average returns. The majority of funds have a goal to *beat the market*. That normally means they are charged with the task of outperforming a given benchmark index, such as the S&P 500 Index, the Dow Jones Industrial Average or the Barclays Aggregate Bond Index, etc. If a mutual fund is faced with an expense hurdle of several percentage points, it is extremely difficult for most managers to keep pace with any benchmark index. Only a minority of fund managers are able to beat their benchmarks — and that minority is constantly changing.

Survival of the Fittest

One thing inherently wrong with the statistics commonly quoted by the mutual fund industry is that the sample of funds used includes only those funds that are still active. Each year, hundreds of mutual funds close their doors and either cash is returned to investors or funds are merged together. The main cause of this is poor performance (causing investors to abandon the fund). When a fund closes, it is no longer included in the studies. This leads us to believe that the percentage of fund managers underperforming their benchmarks is even higher than stated.

"In Mid-2012, 73.24 percent of active domestic stock mutual funds were unable to beat the benchmark S&P 1500 composite index over the trailing three-year period."

- U.S. News and World Report article 'Index Funds Still Beat Most Managers' 10/12/2012

Chasing Stars and Comets

Mutual fund companies focus their efforts on promoting funds that are awarded four- or five-star ratings from Morningstar (a Chicago-based ratings firm). Unfortunately, these ratings identify only those funds that have performed well in the past, but provide little help finding those that will do well in future.

According to a study done by the Vanguard group, they found that a given rating offers little information about expected future relative performance; in fact, the analysis reveals that higher- rated funds are no more likely to outperform a given benchmark than lower-rated funds.[9]

In addition, most individual investors also follow the latest star ratings. Knowing the above facts, investors continue to pour money into four- and five-star funds year after year, chasing past performance. Chasing performance is not unlike chasing shooting stars and comets. In a tribute to the effectiveness of advertising, almost 90 percent of new mutual fund money inflows go to these historically top-performing funds. This behavior often results in selling poor-performing funds when they are low and buying better ones when they are high.

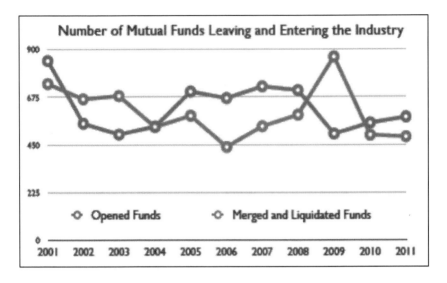

Each year, hundreds of mutual funds close their doors or merge together.

Poorly timed selling and buying activity like this takes its toll on investor performance over time. A 2010 Morningstar study stated that if investors simply bought and held their mutual funds in the year 2000 (without the selling and buying activity), they would have been better off by 1.5 percent annually. (It should be noted that past performance is not a determinant of future returns).[10]

The study also found that investors tend to do worse when they participate in this type of activity with funds that are more volatile (equity funds). Human nature is partially to blame for this. When the markets experience a large downward swing, people tend to panic and sell their investments that are down the most (selling low). On the contrary, when equity markets surge, investors tend to jump in at just the wrong time (buying high). Those that hold less volatile, more diversified funds tend to weather these storms better.

The question investors should ask themselves is, why would I pay more for advice than I have to?

Too much cash, too little interest

Another reason that many mutual funds may underperform over the long-term is that they typically hold significant amounts of cash. Mutual funds are constantly receiving new money contributions and requests for redemptions. When new money is received into the fund, there is often a delay before the money is allocated to securities purchases. If the market is rising, this works to the detriment of the shareholder. At the same time, funds must hold a certain amount of cash to meet end-of-day redemptions. Especially in a low interest rate environment, cash earns virtually no interest and no dividends and works against performance for shareholders.

4. Share classes exist to compensate intermediaries.

Investors are generally unfamiliar with the jargon that surrounds mutual funds. Funds tend to have several share class options that could impact investor returns. These include (but are not limited to):

A Shares – Also called front-end load shares, this share class can charge a sales commission at the time of purchase. For example, if you invest $100 into the Mutual Fund that has a 5% sales load, only $95 is actually invested inside the fund. The commission goes to pay your stockbroker.

B Shares – Also referred to as back-end load shares, these shares charge no commission up front. The broker receives compensation through a combination of higher marketing fees (12b-1 fees) and contingent deferred sales charges (CDSCs), charged if you sell your shares before six to seven years. B shares typically have higher expense ratios during this period.

C Shares – There is typically no front-end sales load on these shares. However, normally a 1 percent CDSC is charged against the customer's holdings if these shares are sold during the first year. A higher 12b-1 fee will continue to be charged against the portfolio until the shares convert to other share classes as stated in the prospectus.

The whole share class system exists as a way to get various intermediaries compensated. The fact that mutual funds arc sold by securities brokers means that the funds must charge higher loads and commissions to provide a broker's compensation. It's not uncommon for funds to have many different share classes. Investors have the choice of which type of fund they like, or they can seek out other vehicles that can carry potentially lower expenses that may benefit them over the long term. An option is to work with a fee-based advisor who is compensated based on an agreed-upon annual advisory fee for their guidance, no matter which investments they recommend.

5. Loss of talented managers hurts mutual funds.

Historically, mutual fund companies have attracted well-trained, smart, talented people to manage their funds for them. One of the goals of a fund manager is to provide superior investment performance to investors. Because of the high cost structure, large fund size, strict investment prospectus guidelines, and tax inefficiency in mutual funds, it has become difficult for talented managers to deliver above-average performance. An investment manager may have a great investment idea but find that the mutual fund is so large or has so many restrictions that the strategy is impossible to implement.

Many talented managers are defecting to the hedge-fund industry, which now manages more than $2 trillion and is growing rapidly. The compensation in hedge funds is often significantly higher and the structure allows more freedom to invest "outside the box." While mutual funds and hedge funds are very different investment vehicles and carry very different levels of risk, the mutual fund structure is now at a disadvantage because it is subject to SEC rules and is highly regulated by federal law.

Hedge funds are likely to remain at the head of the new frontier and continue to drain talented managers from the mutual fund industry.

6. Misleading ads and limited disclosure create confusion.

You can open almost any financial publication and see an advertisement for a mutual fund that has a catchy name, a smiling face, a graph with arrows pointing higher or maybe some stars. These ads could lead an investor to make a wrong turn. Unfortunately, it is up to a mutual fund buyer to figure out exactly what he is investing in. This usually involves a significant amount of time perusing an outdated prospectus.

Fund names can be confusing. The Securities and Exchange Commission (SEC) requires that funds have at least 80 percent of assets in the particular type of investment implied in their names. How the remaining assets are invested depends on the fund manager. A fund with a name like The United States Income Fund sounds like it would be composed mostly of fixed-income investments, when in fact it may have only 20 percent of its assets allocated there, with the remainder in income-generating stocks. Is it safe or risky? What is in a growth fund? Is it small cap stocks, international stocks, emerging market stocks, commodities? These questions need careful research.

Additionally, information released to the public is often limited, delayed, and outdated. Mutual funds are required to release accurate information on a quarterly basis. It is virtually impossible to know what happens in the interim. If asked, most investors would probably prefer to use a more transparent vehicle where they know exactly where they have invested each of their hard-earned dollars at any given time.

7. A bond mutual fund is not a bond.

If you purchase a 20-year bond, its price sensitivity to changes in interest rates declines as the bond moves closer to maturity (i.e., the older the bond gets, the less interest rate changes affect your principal). If you buy a bond fund that has an average maturity of 20 years, you're dealing with a different animal. The bond fund does not have a maturity date. Quite often, the fund maintains a fixed average maturity that does not decline over time. If you are a conservative investor that has adequate assets and your desire is to maintain a fixed stream of interest payments, an individual bond may serve your purposes better than a bond fund. It is up to the individual investor to take on the risks appropriate to his or her situation.

Moreover, a bond mutual fund may use leverage to increase its yield, or to pay for internal fees and commissions. This leverage may serve to magnify the holder's principal risk.

It is up to the consumer to dig into the documents to see how the river of money flows. Or, consumers can seek out cleaner waters in other investment vehicles.

8. The murky river of money flows deep.

Let's determine where more of the money goes by talking about soft-dollar payments and shelf-space payments.

Soft-dollar payments are the payments made by the mutual fund companies to brokerage houses. The reason they are called "soft" dollars is that, rather than pay brokerages in cold, hard cash, mutual fund companies direct trading activity to certain brokerages, generating commissions for them. This enables mutual fund companies to pass along the cost of services, like research and software to the fund's shareholders, and it can be a tremendous profit center for brokerage firms. FINRA, the Financial Industry Regulatory Authority (formerly NASD, the National Association of Securities Dealers), has brought numerous actions where the direction of soft-dollar payments has been linked to the sales volume of a particular mutual fund's shares by a brokerage firm.

Shelf-space payments are akin to what happens in supermarkets when competing brands of cereal pay for prime shelf space so their products will be displayed at eye level for consumers. In the mutual fund industry, companies often provide revenue-sharing arrangements with brokerage firms in exchange for the brokerage recommending a specific fund to clients. This is an obvious conflict of interest and not necessarily in the client's best interests.

Such arrangements, also called *pay to play*, have been particularly prevalent in 401(k) plans that primarily use mutual funds. According to the General Accounting Office, any company that administers a 401(k) plan "may also be receiving compensation from mutual fund companies for recommending their fund. As a result, participants may have more limited investment options and pay higher fees than they otherwise would."[11]

These activities result in billions of dollars changing hands. Does it sound unfair? Mutual funds are required to disclose these activities in their prospectuses, but consumers need to read the documents thoroughly to become aware of such practices.

Graduate to SMAs

We've shown you what concerns us about today's mutual funds. We admit they can be a good way for small investors to begin their savings plan and build a critical mass of assets. But once you start to accumulate significant assets, you have access to potentially more efficient investment options.

If you are in this situation, we encourage you to consider institutional separately managed accounts (SMAs) held by a reputable custodian. An SMA is a portfolio of assets under the management of a professional investment firm. In the U.S., these firms are called registered investment advisors, or RIAs.

Like mutual funds, SMAs provide access to professional money management and diversification. At the same time, they provide the following benefits:

Potentially lower overall expenses

Compared to mutual funds, many of the costs of ownership, such as marketing fees and tax costs, may be lower in the SMA structure.

Tax efficiency

Since an SMA is composed of individual securities with an individual cost basis, your institutional manager can use this information to control the amount and timing of gains and losses. He can employ strategies, such as tax-loss harvesting, to reduce the overall tax drag on your portfolio.

Customization

Because your institutional investment manager is choosing individual securities, you can choose not to invest in certain companies or certain sectors of the market. Virtually any investment requirement can be satisfied. Because you will be working with an investment advisory representative (IAR), the concepts of shelf space, soft dollars, and commissions will become less important. Your IAR will help you design the best portfolio possible, tailored to your needs — rather than one that is just "okay."

Control the maturity of your bond portfolio

Especially today, when interest rates are near historic lows, it may be more important to control the overall maturity (or duration) of your fixed-income portfolio, as well as have the ability to adjust quickly as market conditions change. SMAs can help you achieve that.

Transparency

The owner of an SMA can see everything that happens, including trading costs and any other deductions from their principal investment.

A tested and effective investment strategy

SMAs have been around since the 1970s. They were developed to accommodate larger clients who needed to meet specific objectives that did not fit the mutual fund structure. Technological changes have made it possible for investors to access SMAs with as little as $25,000. As of 2012, there is more than $2.7 trillion invested in SMAs in the U.S., and the amount is growing. Given the advantages of SMAs, it is likely that money will continue to flow away from mutual funds into these vehicles.

> *Like mutual funds, SMAs provide access to professional money management and diversification.*

Make more from your investments.

You've read what we know about mutual fund performance. Take a moment to consider whether the following statements apply to you:

- ☐ I want to know what my portfolio is costing me each year to own.

- ☐ I want to know exactly which investments I own inside o f my portfolio.

☐ I want a clearer idea of my portfolio risks.

☐ I want to have access to institutional management on a wholesale, rather than retail, basis.

If you agree with any of the above, contact Semmax Financial Group for an unbiased analysis of your situation.

How can you learn the real cost of your fund?

Submit your mutual fund portfolio to Semmax Financial Group at (336) 856-0080 for a customized appraisal analysis. We will show you the true, total cost.

1 A Brief History of the Mutual Fund, Investopedia.com
2 Ibid.
3 2012 Investment Company Factbook, The Investment Company Institute
4 Ibid.
5 Statistical Abstract of the United States 2012, U.S. Census Bureau
6 The Hidden Costs of Mutual Funds, Wall Street Journal, 3/1/2010
7 Mutual Fund Efficiency and Performance, Dow Publishing Company, 2007
8 The Hidden Cost of Mutual Funds, Wall Street Journal, 3/1/10
9 Mutual Fund Ratings and Future Performance, Vanguard Research, 06/2010
10 Bad Timing Eats Away at Investor Returns, Morningstar, February, 2010
11 Report #GAO-07-530T, General Accounting Office, March, 2007

PART III

I believe there is a better way for high net worth families to have their savings for retirement looked after. I have included an expose on what a truly managed account with an institutional manager should look like. Notice that it's not so much about how much you make during your retirement and pre-retirement years... it's more about how much you don't lose.

GLOBAL FINANCIAL
Private Capital
COMPREHENSIVE WEALTH MANAGEMENT

The Potential Benefits of DIAS compared to Traditional Investment Portfolios

1. Comprehensive Diversification

Comprehensive Diversification means increasing the number of non-correlating asset classes, investment sectors and regions within a portfolio with the aim of risk reduction.

Diversification seeks to combine investments with different characteristics:

- Risks contained in one investment are balanced by other investment assets that move in different cycles or respond to different market factors.
- Returns can be increased by gaining exposure to markets and asset classes with greater potential for gain as leadership rotates from one segment of the market to another.

Comprehensive Diversification cannot guarantee to eliminate the possibility of loss of capital; it can dramatically reduce the probability of excessive portfolio value declines and periodically generate additional returns. In this way, smoother, less volatile investment performance may result.

a. Comprehensive Diversification – Asset Classes

The vast majority of retail investment portfolios contain a percentage of diversification between just two asset classes: Bonds and Stocks. This is not Comprehensive Diversification.

These retail 'portfolios' are then selected and titled according to a client's risk profile. For example: 80% Bonds, 20% Stocks = Conservative Portfolio, and 20% Bonds, 80% Stocks = Aggressive Portfolio.

Most tried and tested investment philosophies agree that risk can be reduced by combining different asset classes, each with their own specific factors which often dictate returns.

The DIAS management team aims to understand these factors, the information that drives them and their correlation, thereby producing a portfolio constructed and adjusted to maintain risk-adjusted returns.

So why stick with just two asset classes?

Modern diversification techniques, such as that employed within DIAS portfolios, incorporates diversification across more than two asset classes, thereby spreading the susceptibility of the portfolios to sudden and dramatic declines in any one asset class.

Asset Class Diversification Example: When Bonds look expensive, why not move some of the bond exposure to other asset classes with similar income and risk features?

Comprehensive Diversification – Geographical Region

For perfectly sound historical reasons, most traditional retail portfolios are heavily weighted toward U.S. holdings. While this remains a valid strategy, other regions of the world are becoming increasingly attractive for investors.

The factors which dictate investment success in non-U.S. markets are not necessarily the same as those in the U.S.; thus, a measure of risk reduction by understanding these factors may be achieved.

Geographical diversification can therefore offer similar benefits as those described under asset class diversification above.

Geographical Region Diversification Example: When the prospects for growth in Emerging Markets1 are clearly greater than the prospects back home, why not expose some of the portfolio to those regions, providing you understand the fundamental price determinants?

b. Comprehensive Diversification – Sectors

The traditional practice of selecting a number of the 'best' funds and managers results in the client owning many individual bond and stock positions and being exposed to the sector allocation views of each manager. However, there is little or no coordination between these sector preferences and individual holdings which may, at best, create a zero-sum cancelling effect between different portfolio weightings. At worst, it may leverage risk by concentrating investment allocation to individual sectors.

If a client invests in 10 Mutual Funds, each of which contains 30 positions or more, there's a lot of coordination required.

The DIAS management believes additional investment returns may be possible by 'tilting' their allocations toward attractive sectors and away from unattractive sectors. DIAS portfolios coordinate the Sector Diversification decision for the client and Financial Advisor.

Moreover, risk may be reduced by holding investments which move in opposite directions.

c. How does Comprehensive Diversification fit with the Risk Tolerance?

Comprehensive Diversification within DIAS uses asset classes and regions with similar volatility, income, and capital gain features to those traditionally associated with a client's risk tolerance.

Investing in 'different' asset classes and regions is not necessarily a riskier activity than concentrating on U.S. Stocks and Bonds. It should, however, be practiced with expertise and caution.

2. Active Portfolio Management

The vast majority of retail portfolios are based on Fixed Target Allocations and the principle of 'buy and hold.' The ideal allocation of assets is set according to a client's risk tolerance and rarely changes. Although this can make for a volatile ride, there is faith in 'things' working out over the 'long term.'

One possible reason for this is that changing allocations across a diversified portfolio of managers — all with 30 or more holdings and minimum investments — can be time consuming, costly, and detract from returns.

Another explanation may be many advisors within large financial distribution systems do not have the capability to perform this level of analysis.

Studies suggest that investment returns are determined by the allocation of assets in 90% or more of cases.2 However, we live in increasingly dynamic times. Assumptions that worked yesterday may not work tomorrow.

DIAS Dynamically adjusts asset allocations depending on the direction of markets, as suggested by the experience of the Investment Team and the research data analyzed. The aim is to reduce exposure to those asset classes and regions which may present an increasing probability of capital loss and relocate the capital to places with a better potential for capital appreciation or income with lower risk.

The Callan Periodic Table of Investment Returns (Annual Returns for key Indices Ranked in order of Performance)[3]:

1995	1996	1997	1998	1999	2000	2001	2002	2003	2004	2005	2006	2007	2008	2009
S&P/Citi 500 Growth 38.13%	S&P/Citi 500 Growth 23.97%	S&P/Citi 500 Growth 36.52%	S&P/Citi 500 Growth 42.16%	Russell 2000 Growth 43.09%	Russell 2000 Value 22.83%	Russell 2000 Value 14.02%	BC Agg 10.26%	Russell 2000 Growth 48.54%	Russell 2000 Value 22.25%	MSCI EAFE 13.54%	MSCI EAFE 26.34%	MSCI EAFE 11.17%	BC Agg 5.24%	Russell 2000 Growth 34.47%
S&P 500 37.58%	S&P 500 22.96%	S&P 500 33.36%	S&P 500 28.58%	S&P/Citi 500 Growth 28.24%	BC Agg 11.63%	BC Agg 8.43%	Russell 2000 Value -11.43%	Russell 2000 47.25%	MSCI EAFE 20.25%	S&P/Citi 500 Value 5.82%	Russell 2000 Value 23.48%	S&P/Citi 500 Growth 9.13%	Russell 2000 Value -28.92%	MSCI EAFE 31.78%
S&P/Citi 500 Value 36.99%	S&P/Citi 500 Value 22.00%	Russell 2000 Value 31.78%	MSCI EAFE 20.00%	MSCI EAFE 26.96%	S&P/Citi 500 Value 6.08%	Russell 2000 2.49%	MSCI EAFE -15.94%	Russell 2000 Value 46.03%	Russell 2000 18.33%	S&P 500 4.91%	S&P/Citi 500 Value 20.81%	Russell 2000 Growth 7.05%	Russell 2000 -33.79%	S&P/Citi 500 Growth 31.57%
Russell 2000 Growth 31.04%	Russell 2000 Value 21.37%	S&P/Citi 500 Value 29.98%	S&P/Citi 500 Value 14.69%	Russell 2000 21.26%	Russell 2000 -3.02%	Russell 2000 Growth -9.23%	Russell 2000 -20.48%	MSCI EAFE 38.59%	S&P/Citi 500 Value 15.71%	Russell 2000 Value 4.71%	Russell 2000 18.37%	BC Agg 6.97%	S&P/Citi 500 Growth -34.92%	Russell 2000 27.17%
Russell 2000 28.45%	Russell 2000 16.49%	Russell 2000 22.36%	BC Agg 8.70%	S&P 500 21.04%	S&P 500 -9.11%	S&P/Citi 500 Value -11.71%	S&P/Citi 500 Value -20.85%	S&P/Citi 500 Value 31.79%	Russell 2000 Growth 14.31%	Russell 2000 4.55%	S&P 500 15.79%	S&P 500 5.49%	S&P 500 -37.00%	S&P 500 26.47%
Russell 2000 Value 25.75%	Russell 2000 Growth 11.26%	Russell 2000 Growth 12.95%	Russell 2000 Growth 1.23%	S&P/Citi 500 Value 12.73%	MSCI EAFE -14.17%	S&P 500 -11.89%	S&P 500 -22.10%	S&P 500 28.68%	S&P 500 10.88%	Russell 2000 Growth 4.15%	Russell 2000 Growth 13.35%	S&P/Citi 500 Value 1.99%	Russell 2000 Growth -38.54%	S&P/Citi 500 Value 21.17%
BC Agg 18.46%	MSCI EAFE 6.05%	BC Agg 9.64%	Russell 2000 -2.55%	BC Agg -0.82%	S&P/Citi 500 Growth -22.08%	S&P/Citi 500 Growth -12.73%	S&P/Citi 500 Growth -23.59%	S&P/Citi 500 Growth 25.66%	S&P/Citi 500 Growth 6.13%	S&P/Citi 500 Growth 4.00%	S&P/Citi 500 Growth 11.01%	Russell 2000 -1.57%	S&P/Citi 500 Value -39.22%	Russell 2000 Value 20.58%
MSCI EAFE 11.21%	BC Agg 3.64%	MSCI EAFE 1.78%	Russell 2000 Value -6.45%	Russell 2000 Value -1.49%	Russell 2000 Growth -22.43%	MSCI EAFE -21.44%	Russell 2000 Growth -30.26%	BC Agg 4.10%	BC Agg 4.34%	BC Agg 2.43%	BC Agg 4.33%	Russell 2000 Value -9.78%	MSCI EAFE -43.38%	BC Agg 5.93%

Too many investors spend their time fighting the last war; DIAS aims to prepare for the next war.

a. How Does Active Diversification Fit With The Risk Tolerance?

Active Diversification within DIAS does not involve dramatic changes in asset allocation percentages. It aims to 'tilt the odds' in the client's favor by adjusting allocations within stated tolerances, which fit within the general risk tolerance of a client.

b. Is Active Diversification 'Market Timing?'

No. DIAS attempts to actively avoid those asset classes with a higher potential for capital loss. It is not seeking excessive returns by 'being in the right asset class.' Moreover, the DIAS management team is not looking to make 'home run bets' in search of market performance; they are looking for singles and doubles to tilt the odds in the investor's favor.

Many studies pit Active Management against Passive (Buy-and-Hold) Management. The long-term track record of the DIAS management team shows a positive return during a decade where buy and hold produced nothing.[4]

More importantly, DIAS does not focus on outperforming a given index or benchmark over time. Those who say buying and holding the S&P 500 over time will give better results are missing the point. The point is most investors want a smoother ride; they want to avoid the precipitous drops of 2008 and, in many cases, they want income that they can spend.

c. Portfolio Rebalancing

Many traditional portfolios feature a practice called Portfolio Rebalancing: the periodic or scheduled buying and selling of holdings because they have strayed from fixed target allocations as prices vary over a period of time. For example, if bonds are 80% of the portfolio and depreciate by 10% when the rest of the portfolio does not change in price, a traditional rebalance would buy more bonds to bring the allocation back to 80%.

This activity adds little value to the investor; it does add cost. What if bonds look poised to rise 10%? Why sell an asset just because the rules say so?

DIAS does not indulge in the arbitrary rebalancing of portfolios. Portfolios are continually reviewed to ensure they are positioned in line with client goals and the investment team's prevailing view of markets.

3. Focus on Allocation, Not Managers

Traditionally, retail advisors perform investment allocation decisions on behalf of clients, in many cases focusing on selecting the 'best managers or funds.' Not only is this in direct contravention of the commonly accepted belief that the asset class or region you are invested in is 90% or more of the investment return determinant, but many studies prove that selecting managers based on historical returns does not work.

The DIAS Investment Committee focuses virtually all of its efforts on the right allocation, totally ignoring the selection of the 'best managers' by investing directly in a security; in the majority of cases, this is an Exchange Traded Fund (ETF).

Studies show that 95% of all investor dollars flowing into Mutual Funds are invested in to four- and five-star Morningstar-rated Funds; investors favor those managers with excellent short-term performance. However, a portfolio which continually adjusts to only hold five-star Funds returned 6.9% between 1994 and 2004 — just over half of the 11% return of the general Stock Market Index.[5]

To use a real estate analogy, DIAS spends most of its time researching neighborhoods to check if they look safe before selecting an average house in that neighborhood. Most traditional managers search for the houses that look better than nearby houses, irrespective of neighborhood quality. Where would you prefer to live?

To grind the point in, 90% of all managers fail to beat their respective index.[6] Or as Jim Cramer puts it: "managed funds fail to beat the market 80 percent to 90 percent of the time."[7] Studies always differ, but most agree: paying a Mutual Fund manager to beat an index is rarely successful. Why not ask the manager to find the better asset classes to invest in and use an ETF, which doesn't need to pay a manager?

4. Flexibility

Traditional Fund managers are limited by the legal constraints contained in the Fund's Prospectus. While this is valuable in preventing managers exposing clients to excessive risk, it can restrict the manager's ability to avoid risk or generate returns. Limits are set on the amount and type of investments that can be bought, which is great for limiting surprises and covering the liability of the investment manager. But is this really the best way to manage money? Do you want to force your stock manager to never go below 95% invested long in stocks?

Mutual Fund managers must invest in the areas their prospectus tells them, and in the percentages specified, irrespective of their belief in market direction.

DIAS managers operate within guideline allocation tolerances allowing more flexibility to match the client's needs and adjust portfolio allocations to changing market risks.

The concept of Core & Explore available to Advisors using DIAS provides for further flexibility in meeting client goals.

5. The Value of Value

One of the main investment philosophies of DIAS is to identify asset classes and sectors that provide value to the investor — typically areas which temporarily trade below their fair market value or what they are really worth. This is generally accepted to provide a less volatile investment strategy than seeking assets which have a high probability of growth.

The Value Discipline can also be applied across many asset classes, including Fixed Income and Commodities.

In our opinion, the best way to provide an investment edge is to invest in areas that are underappreciated... a technique we call Attention Arbitrage. The fact that most investment professionals focus on stock selection provides DIAS with an attractive Attention Arbitrage Opportunity to find undervalued asset classes and regions. For example, we can invest in areas which are traditionally barred from large investment portfolio managers due to arbitrary 'large company' rules and limits. These rules are usually driven by large company inflexibility, not compliance or risk reduction.

6. The Increasing Importance of ETFs

ETFs, which were in their infancy in the 1990s, offer cost, taxation, and flexibility advantages over mutual funds for retail investors and portfolio managers, alike.

In addition to these advantages, their widespread use within DIAS portfolios allows the Investment Team to focus on asset allocation by providing the return profile of an asset class or region within a single security, instead of having to select 30 or 40 holdings traditionally held within mutual funds in the hope that all of this cost and activity beats the index after costs.

When a DIAS allocation change is required, an ETF can be bought or sold immediately, providing the investment managers with the level of flexibility required to keep portfolios aligned to market changes. In fact, we test each investment for the liquidity to enable immediate sale at market prices.

ETFs are not without their risks and detractors, though. The DIAS Investment Team researches the liquidity, market capitalization and correlation of all ETFs prior to investment. For example, leveraged ETFs, which promise a multiple of the returns of a specific index, are rarely employed.

7. Bigger May Not Be Better

Traditionally, retail investors have favored large, well known investment management companies and teams.

This may no longer be the ideal way to run investment portfolios:

- Most employees on a large team perform research and analysis on individual companies, organizations, and the securities they issue. However, 90% of the investment decision can be attributed to the allocation of capital to sectors and regions, not specific stock selection. Seeing the wood for the trees is important; surrounding yourself with trees makes this more difficult.

- Large teams, and their focus on stock selection, are difficult to manage to maintain focus. Everyone wants their stock suggestion to be included in the portfolio, and personal preferences may creep in.

- Large companies that manage many billions of assets generally aim to closely follow the returns and volatility of a stated index (benchmark), sometimes called 'closet indexing.' The manager is indifferent to dramatic declines in that index because they are judged relative to it. But what value is this to a retail investor? If you lose 30% of your investment, are you happy with the comment: "But all stocks are down."? Is this adding value and worth paying for?

- Traditionally, the smartest people worked for the largest companies who provided good salaries and job security in return. That paradigm has been demolished. Today, the smartest, most independent thinkers tend to form their own businesses.

- Twenty years ago, information was scarce and expensive. It also required a 'cast of thousands' to manually collect and analyze. In today's 'Information Age,' technology has made research data ubiquitous and low cost. This favors smaller, more flexible operations above larger, highly structured companies. Furthermore, computerization is making increasingly sophisticated analysis systems available to all and not just the biggest enterprises.

DIAS is managed by a small dedicated team of investment and financial professionals accessing real-time information and utilizing advanced trading and research tools. The managers are highly experienced and have involvement in the ownership.

NOTE: Past performance is not indicative of future results. This article is not intended as investment advice or an investment recommendation; it is solely the opinion of our investment managers at the time of writing. Nothing in this article should be construed as a solicitation to buy or sell securities.

Reference: Global Financial Capital "Why DIAS?" Report dated March 2010

1 Investments in Emerging Markets may feature greater volatility and risk than those in developed markets. Investments in non-U.S. markets may be subject to additional currency taxation, geopolitical, and liquidity risks.

2 Ibbotson, Sungard et al

3 The Callan Periodic Table is available at www.callan.com

4 S&P500 Total Return - 1999 to 2009

5 Yesterday's Winners, Tomorrows Losers – The Little Book of Common Sense Investing – John C. Bogle 2007.

6 John Bogle on Investing: The First 50 Years by John C. Bogle and Paul A. Volcker (Sept. 2000)

7 Jim Cramer's book "Stay Mad for Life"

Chapter XII: Exchange Traded Funds (ETFs)

~~~

E very week on my radio program, The Financial Safari, we like to bring in a special guest to help us determine what's happening in the financial world. My co-host, Peter "Coach Pete" D'Arruda, recently interviewed a featured guest, Tom Lydon, who started ETF Trends, an online source for news stories that focus on educating investors regarding specific offerings, current market trends, sectors, economies, and sentiment about the various ETF markets. The interview highlighted information about ETFs.

Coach Pete: This week, we have a very special guest. He's joining us from Orange County, California. His name is Tom Lydon, and he's written a book that got on my radar screen... and I wanted to have him on because of it. But he also does a lot of other fascinating things. The book title is The ETF Trend Following Playbook: Profiting from Trends in Bull or Bear Markets with Exchange Traded Funds. Tom, welcome to the show.

Tom: Thanks Pete, it's great to be with you.

Coach Pete: Yeah, now let's talk about ETFs. I mean, this is a phrase that draws cold sweats in people when they hear that a lot of times because, even people that are supposedly in the know, Tom, people don't understand what an ETF is. So for our audience, can you take us from square one? Tell us what an

ETF is and then, square two, tell us why they are a good part of a portfolio many times.

Tom: *Absolutely Pete. And for a somewhat confusing name and even complicated acronym, it really is a simple product. The whole idea about an Exchange Traded Fund, it IS a mutual fund. It's a form of a mutual fund, but 99.9% of them are indexed-based. The advantage here is you're following an underlying index, you know what the constituents of that underlying index are and you don't need to pay a manager. So the expense ratios are just a fraction of what you're paying in an actively managed mutual fund. It's very tax-efficient and, more importantly, it's liquid, so you could actually buy one in the morning and sell it in the afternoon as opposed to a mutual fund where your buying and selling is executed at that night's closing price. So we've seen a huge adoption in the ETF area, there's $1.4 trillion in ETFs and more than 1,400 ETFs available today. We've come a long way from just the S&P 500 ETF (SPY) — the first one that started 20 years ago.*

Coach Pete: *Yeah, and still see a lot of confusion out there when people are trying to make their investment decisions. Either they try to do it themselves where they try to pick individual stocks or get some of the magazines and start reading about mutual funds to invest in ETFs. That's not the right strategy a lot of times, is it?*

Tom: *Well, you're right. If you looked at the average investor portfolio, most of it is chock-full of actively managed mutual funds and seven out of 10 actively managed mutual funds over time have underperformed their benchmark, and they've got big expense ratios. If all you did was replicate that asset allocation with ETFs within the same asset classes, two things would happen. Number one, you'd align with the benchmark because they* *really are indexes that meet those benchmarks. And number two, you'd probably save yourself over 1% in annual expenses because the expense ratios are so low It would just, overnight, clean up your portfolio, make it so much more transparent and liquid, and you'd be aligned with what your overall goals are.*

Coach Pete: *The 21 years up in the financial world, when someone asks me what a mutual fund is, what we've always said is, "it's a basket of stocks in a device called a mutual fund." But that's also what an ETF is, isn't it?*

Tom: *It is, but you know exactly what it is every day. With a mutual fund, mutual fund disclosure only has to happen every 90 days and, many times, once you finally get that report, that portfolio manager has already made some changes and you don't know really what's going on. Now some fund managers are great and they've done an excellent job over an extended period of time. And I'm not here to say a lot of bad things about the fund industry be-cause it is fantastic. But there's a new player in town in the form of ETFs and a lot of folks are looking at them saying, "I'm comfortable with them. They're inexpensive and I know exactly what I'm invested in." And now with the choices, it's tremendous. And as you look to the future, just some simple areas like alternative investing in areas like commodities or energy or agriculture or metals, or currencies, it gives you very instant access where you don't necessarily have that in mutual funds. And then we've also got some challenges down the road regarding fixed income. We will be facing higher interest rates and most investors know that with higher yields, you can actually lose money in the bonds that invest in those fixed income securities, so there are areas to protect yourself there as well.*

Coach Pete: *Is it easier to zero in on various asset classes using an ETF as opposed to a mutual fund?*

Tom: *Absolutely. I mean, you can get as specific as Asian technology stocks or small cap Latin American stocks. There's plenty in there to keep people busy and on our website, ETFtrends.com. We write 12 to 15 stories a day about different aspects of the ETF marketplace — areas that we see that are doing well and maybe some areas to avoid.*

Coach Pete: *Folks, we're talking to Tom Lydon. He's the author of The ETF Trend Following Playbook: Profiting from Trends in Bull or Bear Markets with Exchange Traded Funds. Tom, question to you, I know you write about, you write various articles, 12 or more a day on this world of ETFs. Why are people so scared of ETFs? I talk to people every day, and I think they're getting influenced by what they hear from people peddling mutual funds many times. But they're scared of ETFs because they don't really know about them. Is that the reason, you think?*

Tom: *I think, Pete, you hit the nail on the head. It's not that they're scared; they're looking for more information and looking for more education and, absolutely, people that are peddling mutual funds don't like talking about ETFs because they're disruptive. And the other thing is, because ETFs don't have a big expense ratio, there are not people out there peddling ETFs. The only time you hear about ETFs is if you happen to be on a financial radio show or on CNBC and maybe hear some ads, this and that. But, they basically sell themselves for all of the right reasons be-cause, I think, of the benefits. Back in the early 2000s, we began shifting our asset management clients from mutual funds to ETFs for these same reasons. We liked the choices, we liked the low expenses, we liked the liquidity, we liked the fact that we knew every day what these funds were invested in. But now with over 1,400 different ETFs, and every day there are hundreds that are going up and hundreds that are going down,* *it's almost too much for the average investor. So I think the advice is, as you probably continue to talk about, keep it simple. Don't go out of your comfort zone. Make sure you look under the hood in any case of buying an ETF or a mutual fund. Start with your main asset allocation program and if you happen to be moving outside of your comfort level, there surely are a lot of choices and there are a lot of free tools that are available out there. In addition to what we provide on ETF trends, there are many, many sites where you can get some great research information. But take it one step at a time.*

Coach Pete: *You know the enemy of dirty tricks is transparency, and that's what I like about ETFs, for the most part. Now there's good and bad in everything, but the transparent nature of ETFs, as well as the lower expense ratio many times, and the less money you share with other people, the more that stays in your account, right Tom?*

Tom: *Well, that's it! Ultimately, if ETFs ever make it to 401(k) plans, you think about the average employee and the expenses that they pay in the 401(k) plan. If they could save 1% a year in expenses, what that would mean to their retirement in 20 or 30 or 40 years, from being a so-so retirement to a great retirement. And that's something that we try to push every day.*

Coach Pete: *Well speaking of 401(k)s, in your experience with dealing with them and analyzing them, if you had to put a percentage on the number or the amount of hidden fees in the 401(k), I talk to people all the time that say, "Hey, my 401(k) is not like one of those you talk about on the radio. I only have a $25 fee per quarter. It shows it right on my statement." Tom, that's the tip of the iceberg, isn't it?*

Tom: *Well, absolutely. When you peel back the onion a few layers and you see all the expenses in running the 401(k)s, the 12-b1 fees that the person is selling the 401(k) to your company gets, it just adds up. And ultimately, there's not enough disclosure. And, you know, you and I could go on for hours about this. But, hopefully we're seeing Congress is on this. They're mandating better disclosure, better performance, and disclosure as well, and ultimately the government really does want what's best for the average investor and the average employee. I think we're gradually getting there, but not quickly enough.*

Coach Pete: *I was talking to someone in the office the other day and I said, "How long have I been talking about those hidden fees in 401(k)s?" and he said, "For as long as I've been employed here." And he's been here seven years. Tom, it's not coming fast enough. Hopefully the government will do something and hopefully people will get educated on the ETF world because there are a lot of hidden gems there. Again, educate yourselves, folks. Tom, what's your blog, one more time?*

Tom: *It's ETFtrends.com. And feel free to send me an email if you have any questions.*

Coach Pete: *Tom, as always, it's been great having you on the Financial Safari, and I hope to have you on again in the future.*

Tom: *Pete thanks. I really enjoyed it.*

Chapter XIII: 10 Things to Know About Income Planning

10 Things You Need to Know About Planning Your Retirement Income

Historically, the United States had three strong legs of the retirement stool: a well-funded Social Security system, substantial corporate pensions with retiree health benefits, and a strong personal savings rate. Unfortunately, the booming population coming of retirement age has changed all of that. Now, the responsibility for providing for retirement income has largely shifted away from the government and employers to individuals.

State and local government pension plans are typically underfunded, cutting back on benefits and raising retirement ages. In the private sector, only 42% of Fortune 1000 companies still maintain a defined benefit plan in which participants continue to accrue retirement benefits.[1] As for retiree health plans, the percentage of large employers that sponsor them has dropped from 46% in 1991 to just 8% today.[2]

We now have a proliferation of employer-sponsored, defined contribution plans that take the form of 401(k), 403(b), and 457 plans. These plans are an excellent way to save, but we are only now witnessing the first wave of 401(k) retirees who will live off of this type of savings. It remains to be seen whether defined contribution plans will be adequate for anticipated longer lives.

There are many variables involved in creating an income plan for today's retirees. Here are 10 things you need to know when working with an advisor to devise your personal income plan for retirement.

#1: PLAN FOR A LONG LIFE

In 1935, when the Social Security Act was passed, 65-year-old beneficiaries received payouts for an average of 12 to 15 years.[3] Now, however, a couple aged 65 has an 85% chance that at least one of them will live past age 85, which means providing for 20 years or more of income once you qualify for Social Security benefits.[4] The Social Security system wasn't built to sustain that long of a retirement, particularly not for 76 million Baby Boomers.

Average Life Expectancies

Those longevity statistics are quoted as averages for both men and women, but keep in mind that men weigh the average down, since women in modern times outlive men by about five to six years. Not only are women more likely to live longer than men, but they also appear to be a factor in helping men live longer, too. On average, married men tend to live many years longer than single men.[5]

#2: HEALTH CARE EXPENSES WILL INCREASE

Just because we are living longer doesn't mean we're going to be healthy throughout our longer lives. In fact, the more active you are now, the more likely you'll need a hip or knee replacement in your senior years. Not to mention that the longer you live, the more likely you'll experience chronic health conditions, such as diabetes, arthritis, and heart disease.

While some credit goes to more active, health-conscious, smoke-free lifestyles, it may be safe to say that today's seniors owe more to prescription drugs and medical advances for lengthening their lifespan. And as we all know, health care costs money — lots of it. In fact, Fidelity Investments found in its most recent Retiree Health Care Costs Estimate study that a 65-year-old couple retiring this year with Medicare coverage will need about $240,000 to pay for medical expenses throughout retirement, excluding nursing home care.[6]

In 2011, 74% of American employees had not considered a plan to cover health care expenses in retirement.[7] This is a key component of any well-conceived retirement plan, as health care expenses typically increase to represent a significant portion of a retiree's income. When creating a retirement income plan, it's important to consider that a couple's retirement assets may be diminished by the health care costs for the spouse who dies first. While you may end up spending less on things like travel and entertainment than when you first retire, be advised that medical and long-term care in your later years may require even more income.

One of the 10 things you should know is that seniors spend nearly as much money on health care services and prescription drugs as they do on food.[8]

#3: YOU'LL NEED A HOUSING PLAN (OR TWO)
As you are well aware, home values across the entire country have dropped in the last few years — in some areas, significantly. According to the Case/Shiller Index, which tracks U.S. housing values, home prices have traditionally followed a slow, but steady incline. The upward spike we experienced from 2005 to 2007 was quite the anomaly, and not one we're likely to see again in the Baby Boomer lifespan.[9]

This may impact you in several ways. Perhaps your home no longer provides as great a backup retirement income plan as you may have anticipated. Or, perhaps you've considered relocating to a senior community, but have delayed that move to sell your home when prices recover.

It's not likely we'll return to the over-valued housing bubble of 2006 anytime soon. Even though it feels like we've experienced a tremendous drop in value, consider what your home was worth back around 2003-2004. At the national level, we've not only returned to those levels but are, in fact, near where they would be had prices simply continued their slow, steady climb without the spike.[9]

Looking ahead, the rate of house appreciation is likely to revert closer to the long-term norms (pre-2006) of 0.75 to 1% per year over the rate of inflation — not double digit annual increases.[10] In today's environment, taking on a modest mortgage and paying it off before retirement is the goal. At that time, and based on individual situations, you may have the option to downsize your residence or use the equity to help fund your retirement income via a reverse mortgage. You can also stay in your home until you pass away and let its equity serve as an inheritance for your heirs.

Housing Away from Home
Plenty of elderly individuals who live independently in their own home may do so indefinitely. But realistically, you should be prepared with a back-up plan. If you've ever been laid up for a significant amount of time due to injury or illness, you know what it's like to need assistance. As we age, it takes even longer to recover; even an acute health condition may take months of home health assistance for recovery.

In-home professional health services offer a variety of fee-based options provided by home health aides, in-home physical or occupational therapists, nutritionists, and nurses. But these services can be quite expensive. Many seniors will spend an unexpectedly great amount of money living at home and paying for a mortgage or rent, utilities, maintenance, groceries, home care, and transportation.

While senior living communities run the gamut of care from independent living to assisted living, rehabilitative care, memory care, and complete 24-hour skilled nursing and long-term care, they can also be quite expensive. Consider the possibility that one spouse may suffer a stroke or some other debilitating condition that requires full-time nursing care, while the other spouse continues to live in the family home. Preparing for two housing situations is more than many retirees plan for, and as a result, this scenario can deplete retirement income sources.

It's good to have a contingency plan in place, such as a long-term care policy or an annuity that offers long-term care benefits — in the basic contract or through optional riders — to ensure that such a change in your housing situation doesn't drain your income resources.

Relying on Family for Assisted Living
Today, 78% of seniors who need long-term care depend exclusively on family and friends.[11] However, family caregivers shoulder a heavy burden when caring for elderly parents, which can lead to significant health issues for caregivers themselves.

The average caregiver tends to be a woman in her forties who spends more than 20 hours a week providing care for a senior family member and also works a full or part-time job.

She is at risk for high levels of stress, frustration, anxiety, exhaustion, anger, depression, increased use of alcohol or other substances, reduced immune response, poor physical health, and chronic conditions.

Furthermore, long-term care giving also can have significant financial consequences for a family caregiver, such as time off of work, which can subsequently lead to a loss of income, reduced retirement plan contributions, and lower Social Security benefits.

#4: PLAN FOR LONG-TERM CARE ASSISTANCE

With a longer life comes the greater likelihood of needing assisted living or long-term care. According to the Genworth 2011 Cost of Care Survey, assisted living averages $39,000 a year and nursing homes average more than $70,000 a year per person.[12] For a couple, this kind of care could cost far more than their annual house-hold income during their highest earning years.

Medicare pays for acute care, not long-term residency. Medicaid pays for long-term care but requires that you "spend down" your assets before coverage kicks in. Many of today's seniors who have not prepared adequately may have to move in with their adult children. In fact, one quarter of Baby Boomers already have an aging parent living with them.[13] Consider the impact of longer lifetimes in just one household, with potentially two generations of seniors cohabitating.

Individuals who delay buying long-term coverage are typically considered high risk, and can expect to be denied coverage or charged sky-high premiums. A policy that pays out $100 a day for three years would cost an average 55-year-old $709 in annual premiums. That same policy would cost a typical 65-year-old $1,342.[14]

One of the 10 things you should know is that the sooner you start thinking, researching, preparing, and structuring your long-term care plan, the more time and choices you'll have to meet your personal needs and desires.

The Cost of Long-Term Care[15]

Homemaker Service (Licensed): $18/hour Home Health Aide Services (Licensed): $19/hour Adult Day Health Care: $60/day

- Assisted Living Facility (One bedroom/single occupancy): $3,261/month
- Nursing Home (Semi-private room): $193/day

- Nursing Home (Private room): $213/day
- Continuing Care Retirement Community (CCRC) (a senior community with assisted and/or LTC available): $20,000–$500,000 entrance fee $500–$3,500/monthly fee

#5: INFLATION MAY MATTER MORE IN THE FUTURE

Inflation is measured a little differently when you retire because you spend money proportionally on different things. Unfortunately, retirees tend to spend more money on the things that experience a higher rate of inflation. For instance, health care, which has an inflation rate of about 8% — currently two to three times greater than the overall inflation rate.[16]

As you can see in the accompanying graph, older Americans devote a substantially larger share of their total budgets to medical care and housing, which is why these categories receive a higher weighting in the Consumer Price Index-Elderly (CPI-E).

Even without the higher inflation rate on certain expenses, you still have to account for the fact that many things cost more over time when planning for retirement income in the future. Not only do the basic necessities for living increase in price over time, but inflation decreases the value of long-term savings and investment returns. No matter how much income you plan on having when you retire, you'll need more as time goes on.

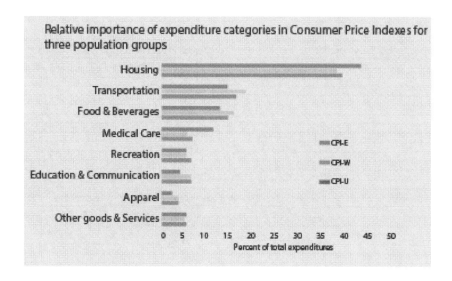

Relative importance of expenditure categories in Consumer Price Indexes for three population groups

The Rule of 72

The Rule of 72 illustrates why you need more income every year that you're retired. Just divide the number 72 by the inflation rate to estimate how quickly the prices you're paying now will double. For example, if you need $50,000 to live on today and estimate a 3% average annual inflation rate going forward, in 24 years (72 divided by 3 = 24) your income need could double to $100,000 a year to maintain your current lifestyle.

One of the 10 things you should know is that once you stop working, you may need to either live on less income or generate additional income to offset the impact of inflation.

#6: TRANSITION YOUR GOALS

You can't control what the markets will do, or when they will do it. Asset classes and global markets are more correlated than ever before. And the timing of a market downturn, such as in the first few years of retirement, can have a dramatic impact on how long retirement assets may last. The retirement income phase differs from the accumulation phase of investing because, once retired, you no longer have the investment timeline to help you recover from the impact of a down market. Your goals should revolve around what it is you want your money to do for you in retirement. What is the purpose of it? To be comfortable and secure or to live in luxury?

Combine Growth Opportunity with Guarantees

Traditionally, as pre-retirees approached retirement they would transition assets from growth-seeking investments to more conservative fixed-income vehicles. This worked fine back when retirement was expected to last only five to ten years. However, given today's longer life spans, you can use your bonus lifetime to work for you in the markets; you just need to pair higher investment risks with sources of reliable income. Most retirees need growth to meet the challenges of a long life and the impact of long-term inflation, as well as sources of secure income to ensure that daily essential living expenses will always be met — regardless of market returns.

Sample Benefits Based on
Retirement Age

Starting Age	Monthl Benefit
62	$1,125
63	$1,200
64	$1,300
65	$1,400
66	$1,500
67	$1,620
68	$1,740
69	$1,860
70	$1,980

Continuing to work in order to delay drawing Social Security benefits also allows you more time to contribute to qualified retirement plans, potentially accruing higher gains than you might have otherwise.

Sequence of Returns

No matter how strong or how long a bull market runs, one fatal correction can have a resounding effect on retirement savings. For example, from the bull market starting in 1992 to the correction in 2002, more than 20% of retirees suffered enough market loss to put them in danger of outliving their assets.[19] Furthermore, 9% of pre-retirees who surveyed decided to retire later than originally planned due to the economic events associated with September 11, 2001.[20]

While you may devise a plan to retire at a certain age, you can't plan on how the market will be performing at that time. If your investments experience a decline when you're ready to begin taking income from them, it could dramatically affect how much income you can withdraw over the rest of your life.

One of the 10 things you should know is that today's retirement income plan generally features investments seeking more aggressive growth than in the past — investments that are paired with insurance components to provide more reliable sources of income.

#7: SOCIAL SECURITY BENEFITS

Perhaps the most impactful decision you can make regarding Social Security benefits is at what age to begin drawing them. You may be able to apply for Social Security benefits as early as age 62. However, doing so will permanently reduce the payout you are eligible to receive. If you wait until full retirement age, you'll be eligible for the maximum amount of payout available based on your lifelong earnings. Delaying benefits as long as you can will increase the amount you are eligible to receive, as illustrated in the accompanying table.

Spousal Benefits

Once you reach full retirement age, you may claim either your own benefit or a derivative (50%) of your spouse's benefit, whichever is higher. When it comes to Social Security benefits for spouses, the determining factors are the length of marriage, work history, and the age of both spouses. Each spouse needs 10 years of work history (40 credits) to qualify for individual benefits, which will be based on an average of the 35 years of highest earnings.

Are you eligible for benefits based on your former spouse's work history?[18]

Divorce Facts

For a divorced spouse to receive benefits based on the ex's work history, the couple must have been married for 10 years or longer and both must be age 62 or older. The death of a spouse increases the survivor's benefit.

If a former spouse is eligible for a benefit but has not yet applied for it, the ex may still apply for the spousal benefit as long as they have been divorced for at least two years. Widows and widowers are entitled to the higher earner's full retirement benefit and may begin receiving benefits at age 60.

Once a divorced spouse remarries, he or she is no longer eligible to receive a benefit based on the first spouse's work history, unless the subsequent marriage ends in death, divorce or annulment. A surviving spouse may claim a reduced benefit on one working record and then switch to the other.

A former spouse may claim the highest benefit based on the work history of any number of ex-spouses as long as each marriage lasted at least 10 years. The higher earner can increase the survivor's benefit by waiting to receive any benefits until age 70.

A qualified, divorced spouse may receive the same benefit as the current spouse. The current spousal benefit is not reduced as a result of this.

When applying for Social Security benefits, each spouse will automatically receive the highest amount for which they are eligible. For instance, a wife may qualify for a higher benefit based on her husband's work history over her own.

To receive benefits based on a spouse's work history:

- Both spouses must be at least age 62.
- They need to have been married for at least one year.
- The spouse with the stronger work history must apply for Social Security retirement benefits in order for the other spouse to collect (although he or she may then choose to delay collecting benefits until later in order to qualify for a higher benefit).

If the higher earning spouse begins drawing benefits after attaining full retirement age, the other spouse may receive a spousal benefit of up to

50% of the higher earner's benefit. If the higher earner starts drawing early, his benefit and the spousal benefit will be reduced accordingly.

At this point, no one can predict whether Social Security will be funded well enough to provide this level of benefits in the future. Even the Social Security Administration admits that by 2040, there won't be enough young people working to pay for all of the benefits owed to those who are retiring (only 74 cents for each dollar of scheduled benefits).[22]

Are you eligible for benefits based on your former spouse's work history?[21]

Widow(er) Facts
The death of a spouse increases the survivor's benefit.

Widows and widowers are entitled to the higher earner's full retirement benefit, and may begin receiving benefits at age 60.

A surviving spouse may claim a reduced benefit on one working record and then switch to the other.

The higher earner can increase the survivor's benefit by waiting to receive any benefits until age 70.

#8: TAXES IN RETIREMENT
The income tax cuts enacted in 2001 and 2003 are scheduled to end in 2012, with 33% and 35% tax rates increasing to 36% and 39.6%, respectively.

Furthermore, the present 15% long-term capital gains tax rate is scheduled to return to 20%, while dividends will return to ordinary income rates in 2013 with a top rate as high as 39.6%. On top of those increases, capital gains will be subject to an additional 3.8% Medicare tax imposed by the Health Care and Education Reconciliation Act of 2010 for single taxpayers with incomes over $200,000 ($250,000 for married taxpayers). All combined, the total capital gains tax rate is scheduled to be 23.8% starting on January 1, 2013.

Many investors sold off some of their highly appreciated investments in 2012 in order to harvest gains and take advantage of that year's lower tax rate. And many are now rebalancing their current asset allocation and repositioning their allocations for a specific goal, such as retirement income.

Social Security

Social Security benefits are income tax free for the majority of beneficiaries. However, a portion of your benefits may be taxed if your combined income falls within established thresholds. Combined income includes your adjusted gross income, nontaxable interest, and half of your Social Security benefits.

Based on Internal Revenue Service (IRS) rules, if you file an individual federal tax return and your combined income is:

- between $25,000 and $34,000, up to 50 % of your benefits may be taxable.
- more than $34,000, up to 85% of your benefits may be taxable.

If you file a joint return and you and your spouse have a combined income that is:

- between $32,000 and $44,000, up to 50% of your benefits may be taxable.
- more than $44,000, up to 85% of your benefits may be taxable.

If you are married and file a separate tax return, you will likely pay taxes on your benefits.

Annuities

Annuity income from a non-qualified contract is considered a combination of return of principal and earnings, and only the earnings are taxed as ordinary income. If the annuity is purchased with pre-tax dollars in a qualified contract, such as a 401(k) or traditional IRA, the entire payout is subject to income taxes since the contributions were never taxed.

You may wish to reconsider your current asset allocation and perhaps reposition the allocation for a specific goal, such as retirement income.

#9: DISTRIBUTION STRATEGIES

Saving for retirement may seem like an insurmountable challenge in and of itself. It's like standing at the foot of a tall mountain and beginning the slow, steady climb toward your retirement savings goal. However, once you reach the top of that mountain and are ready to retire, you face an even bigger task: figuring out how to take the sizeable nest egg you've accumulated and dole it out over what may be a very long retirement. If you're not careful, you could run short of money midway through your descent.

This is what a distribution income plan is all about: how to descend the mountain as steadily, carefully, and securely as possible. How long your retirement income will last is significantly impacted by whether you stay within your predetermined budget and not withdraw more income than planned for each year.

One of the common ways of automating your income distribution is called the "spend-down" strategy. With this strategy, you set up a systematic withdrawal plan (SWP) to pay you a certain percentage of your account balance at specific intervals. However, if your portfolio balance loses significant value or the percentage you withdraw each year is too high, you risk running out of money.

To develop an effective distribution strategy, the first step is to identify the retirement income sources you have available to help pay for your lifestyle in retirement. On one hand, you're likely have some reliable income sources such as Social Security benefits, a pension, an annuity or income from a job. You may also have retirement assets designated to fund your retirement, such as a 401(k) plan, IRA, savings, CDs, mutual funds, and brokerage accounts.

One strategy is to position your reliable income sources — the income you have contractual guarantees to receive in retirement — to pay for your basic needs, so you know they'll be covered. Next, use your other retirement assets to supplement any gap in the income you absolutely need, and then pay for the things you want to enhance your lifestyle.

One of the 10 things you should know is that there's a difference between retirement planning and retirement income planning. The former is designed specifically to grow assets, whereas the latter is designed to grow assets with a risk-managed approach and then distribute them in an organized, disciplined manner to ensure that your money lasts throughout retirement.

Have you answered these questions?
- What is your "personal rate of return" – the rate of return, based on the income you need, that you have to earn to avoid running short of money during retirement?
- When should you begin receiving Social Security benefits?
- Will your income and savings last throughout retirement?
- What impact will taxes and inflation have on your income needs?
- If you pass away, will your spouse have enough income?
- How will a down market impact your income plan?

#10: THE PARADIGM HAS SHIFTED TO INCOME PRODUCTS AND STRATEGIES

The three strong legs of the retirement stool are not the only things that have changed in the 21st century. The way we design a retirement income portfolio has changed as well, with a shift from an accumulation mindset to distribution mode.

The closer you get to retirement and once you are in retirement, it is prudent to start limiting your downside exposure in exchange for upside potential as you transition to the income distribution phase. Consider allocating your assets among different types of products.

Product allocation is basically the strategy of transferring some of the risk of assets to an entity (such as an insurance company) in exchange for limiting the upside potential. Product allocation ranges from conventional savings vehicles to annuitized payout instruments.

When determining the portions of your product allocation, the following considerations should be taken into account:
- Your tolerance for market risk
- Your age
- A ballpark estimate of your life expectancy, based on your health and family history
- Actuarial life expectancy rate based on the overall population
- The amount you expect to spend in retirement for basic needs and discretionary purchases
- Desired value of inheritance you wish to leave behind
- The risk and return characteristics of risky and risk-free assets

It is certainly worth considering strategies to place assets in insurance vehicles, such as annuities that are designed to convert a lump sum of cash (or a series of premium payments) into a guaranteed stream of lifetime income (guaranteed by the financial strength and claims-paying ability of the insurance company). This strategy essentially moves a variable income resource into the reliable income category.

Some of the more retirement income-oriented products you may wish to consider include a systematic withdrawal plan from growth investments, lifetime income annuities, life insurance and long-term care insurance, and variable annuities with a guaranteed income rider.

IRAs

This year, more people are able to make contributions to IRA plans. The income limit for eligible tax deductions for a traditional IRA has increased to $58,000 for single filers or head of household (up from $56,000) and to $92,000 for those married and filing jointly (up from $90,000). As for the Roth IRA, single filers with adjusted gross income up to $110,000 (up from $107,000 in 2011) and joint filers with income up to $173,000 (up from $169,000 in 2011) can make a full contribution. The maximum contribution to a traditional or Roth IRA remains $5,000 ($6,000 for age 50-plus).

If you waiver back and forth between the wisdom of saving via a tax-deductible traditional IRA or a tax-free distribution Roth, consider using them in concert with a tax-efficient IRA strategy. For example, contribute to a traditional IRA to defer more income when taxes are higher, and then convert the assets to a Roth when taxes are lower so you position them for tax-free distributions in retirement. You may repeat this process indefinitely. (This is not intended to provide tax, legal or accounting advice. Please see professionals in these areas to see how this strategy applies to your situation.)

Annuity

An annuity is a contract you purchase from an insurance company. For the premium you pay, you receive certain fixed and/or variable growth options that compound tax-deferred until withdrawn. When you're ready to receive income, an annuity offers a variety of guaranteed pay-out options through a process known as *annuitization.*

The array of annuity contracts available in the market today includes immediate, fixed, variable, and indexed annuities. The choices allow you to match very specific, individual needs with a suitable product. Within each contract, you have the flexibility to select from a range of payout terms, death benefits, and income riders. An annuity purchase can be strategically positioned within your overall portfolio for any number of personal objectives, such as inflation protection, income for your spouse should you die or an inheritance for your children. Coverage is available for two people within one contract, so you don't have to purchase a separate contract for your spouse. All guaranteed benefits are backed by the financial strength and claims-paying ability of the issuing insurance company.

Annuity with a guaranteed lifetime withdrawal benefit
Today's annuities offer a variety of income options to ensure that your initial purchase offers income that can last the rest of your life. A guaranteed lifetime withdrawal benefit (GLWB) is available through a rider you can purchase with an annuity that allows for minimum withdrawals without having to annuitize the contract.

Fixed indexed annuity
The fixed indexed annuity combines a guaranteed minimum interest rate plus the opportunity for greater earnings based upon the market index to which it is tied. The principal in the annuity is not exposed to market risk, however. At the end of each contract year, the insurance company measures the growth of the annuity's linked index (such as the S&P 500) over the previous 12 months, and then credits your contract value with that growth, up to a predetermined percentage or cap. This way you receive the guarantee of a conservative return along with the opportunity

241

for additional growth. All guarantees are backed by the financial strength and claims-paying ability of the issuing company.

Municipal Bonds

Tax-exempt municipal bonds are an excellent tax-advantaged investment, especially for those in high income-tax brackets. Interest earned on municipal bonds is exempt from federal income taxes and, in most states, from state and local taxes for residents of the issuing state. The main advantage of municipal bond investing is the after-tax yield compared to that of a taxable security. The yield advantage further improves with higher tax brackets and longer maturities.

Laddered Bonds

Laddering your bond portfolio is a way to stagger your assets for income or reinvestment at varying intervals. When you spread your investments across a range of short-term, medium-term, and long-term bonds, they will mature at different times, allowing ongoing access to funds. This also gives you the opportunity to reassess interest rates to determine if reinvestment is your best option for income at that given time.

Dividend-paying stocks

High dividend-paying stocks are particularly attractive be-cause they are more tax-efficient than bond interest. Dividends paid out by stocks are taxed at the lower long-term capital gains and qualified dividend income rate — currently 15% at the federal level. Bond interest, on the other hand, is taxed at your ordinary income tax rate — currently as high as 35%.

Life Insurance

Whole life insurance provides a component for accumulating assets within the contract, which is referred to as the cash value. The cash value of a whole life insurance policy can be considered a fixed-income asset. As such, a 2009 study demonstrated that an asset strategy comprised of both fixed income instruments and the cash value from a permanent life insurance policy yielded higher expected returns and with less incidence of risk than a portfolio with only traditional fixed income vehicles.[23] Additional advantages that the cash account of a whole life insurance policy can offer include tax-deferred accumulation over the long-term and the potential for dividends. These advantages are guaranteed by the financial strength and claims-paying ability of the issuing company.

A universal life insurance policy (flexible premium whole life) allows you to vary the amount and timing of when you pay premiums, and may also permit you to change the amount of the subsequent death benefit. A variable universal life policy includes an investment feature, which allows the death benefit and cash value of the policy to fluctuate based on the investment performance of a separate account fund that offers a variety of investment options.

Long-term care insurance
Long-term care insurance (LTCI) may offer flexibility and a viable choice for Baby Boomers still enjoying good health and relative wealth. LTCI is designed to help people pay for short- or long-term care and housing costs at an assisted living facility, nursing home or even in your own home — by far the preference of most seniors. The best time to buy a policy at lower rates is around age 55, but late is better than never because an LTCI policy can make the difference between institutional care and something far more comfortable, flexible, and personal.

Have you answered these questions?

- Which assets will you hold in tax-deferred accounts versus taxable accounts?
- From which accounts should income be withdrawn first?
- When will you start taking Social Security?

- Should you roll over a 401(k) to an IRA?
- Who should be your designated beneficiary (ies) for IRA or qualified plans?
- Would a Roth IRA conversion be appropriate?
- What tax decisions should you address when leaving an employer?

CONCLUSION

While the "Greatest Generation" experienced the burgeoning of government and corporate retirement income and health plans, Baby Boomers and future generations are seeing these safety nets being reduced or eliminated altogether. The Baby Boomer generation will continue to take on more responsibility for providing income for our own essential living expenses in retirement, like housing, food, and health care.

The market corrections of 2001 and 2008, followed by the lengthy economic downturn of recent years, have put many Americans' retirement security at risk. You might have had a plan, but the economy threw you a curve ball, so you need to rethink it. In fact, you may need to reposition your assets to accommodate a longer life with fewer assets than you previously thought. This is a good time to think about your true priorities and align your assets to support your personal goals (not just your financial aspirations).

Obviously, with the bulk of the responsibility for providing retirement income shifting to individuals and the asset strategy paradigm shifting to different types of products, there is a steep learning curve. The best advice is to work with advisors you trust to ensure that your financial plan has all of the checks and balances necessary to ensure that your retirement income will last as long as it's supposed to last.

1 Watson Wyatt Insider, "Pension Freezes Continue Among Fortune 1000 Companies in 2009," August 2009.
2 U.S. Chamber of Commerce, "Private Retirement Benefits in the 21st Century: A Path Forward," 2012
3 Life Expectancy for Social Security, http://www.socialsecurity.gov/history/lifeexpect.html; retrieved June 2012.
4 Annuity Mortality Tables, 2000.
5 Scientific American, "Why Women Live Longer," October 21, 2010.
6 Fidelity Investments, Retiree Health Care Costs Estimate, 2012.
7 Sun Life Financial Unretirement Survey; "Flying Blind: How Working Americans View Healthcare Costs in Retirement," pg. 3; May 24, 2011.
8 Bureau of Labor Statistics; Focus on Prices and Spending, February 2012, Volume 2, Number 15.
9 Fiserv Case-Shiller; Fiserv Case-Shiller Home Price Insights: For Many U.S. Markets, the Return to Peak Home Prices Will Be a Long, Slow Road," April 8, 2010. Standardandpoors.com; "2012 Home Prices Off to a Rocky Start According to the S&P/Case-Shiller Home Price Indices," March 27, 2012.
10 Urban Land Institute, "Housing in America: The Next Decade," 2010.
11 National Family Caregivers Association; 2010.
12 Genworth, 2011 Cost of Care Survey, 2011.
13 Senior Journal, "Thirteen Million Baby Boomers Care for Ailing Parents, 25% Live with Parents," October 2005.
14 American Association for Long-Term Care; The 2009 Sourcebook for Long-Term Care Insurance, July 2009.
15 Genworth Financial Cost of Care Survey, 2011; Seniorhomes.com, 2011.
16 FundQuest, "A Process-Centered Approach to Retirement Income," June 2010.
17 Mercer, "Guide to Social Security, 39th Edition"; January 2011
18 Mercer, "Guide to Social Security, 39th Edition"; January 2011.
19 Employee Benefit Research Institute, 2005 data.
20 LIMRA International, "Retirement Planning," 2003 data.
21 Mercer, "Guide to Social Security, 39th Edition"; January 2011.
22 Social Security Administration, 2012.
23 Ibbotson Associates, "Estimating Expected Return and Standard Deviation of New York Life Insurance Company General Account for Investors", 2009

Chapter XIV: The Social Security Decision

What, When, Who, How?

The biggest story in Social Security today concerns the large number of baby boomers set to retire over the next 20 years and the relatively smaller younger generations feeding Social Security payroll taxes into the system.

On average, today's seniors are living longer than any previous generation. While that's good news, it also presents several new challenges. A longer life increases the likelihood that you'll have increased medical and long-term care expenses throughout much of your retirement. This is particularly true if you've been active all of your life, as many of today's baby boomers have been.

Furthermore, the value of your nest egg could be more significantly impacted by cost of living increases over a longer term. Quite simply, you could outlive your savings. When you consider all of these factors, it is important to make informed decisions about when to begin receiving Social Security benefits within the context of your overall retirement income strategy.

Other sources of retirement income, such as pension plans, 401(k) plans, IRAs, annuities, and tax-exempt and taxable securities should be carefully evaluated in light of various factors. For example, generating a reliable fixed income versus variable, at-risk income. You may want to consider speaking with a financial advisor or insurance agent to help develop a retirement income strategy before you apply for Social Security benefits.

There are strategies you can employ to help reduce the risks of outliving your money. These strategies may be directly related to when you start taking Social Security benefits and how you should position assets for a surviving spouse.

WHAT'S THE STATUS OF SOCIAL SECURITY?

Social Security benefits are largely funded by today's workers via payroll taxes. In 2011, the Old-Age and Survivors Insurance and Disability Insurance Trust Funds collected $805.1 billion in revenues from the following sources:[1]

- 82.8% from payroll taxes and reimbursements from the General Fund of the Treasury
- 3.0% from income taxes on Social Security benefits
- 14.2% from interest earned on government bonds held by trust funds

The number of retired workers is projected to double in less than 30 years. Adding to the Social Security funding dilemma, people are also living longer and the national birth rate is low. As a result, the ratio of workers paying Social Security taxes to people collecting benefits is projected to fall from 2.9 to 1 in 2011 to 2.0 to 1 in 2034. The Trustees Report projects that there will be a shortfall in payroll taxes needed to fund benefits, yet the redemption of trust fund assets will be sufficient to allow for full payment of scheduled benefits until 2032. At that point, payroll taxes and other income will be sufficient to pay only 75 percent of program costs.[1]

WHEN SHOULD YOU DRAW BENEFITS?

As of 2013, full retirement age (referred to as FRA) is age 66 for any-one born in 1943 or earlier. If you were born between 1943 and 1962, full retirement age is 66 plus two-month increments de-pending on the month of your birthday. If you were born in 1962
or later, full retirement age is 67. You may begin taking benefits start-ing at age 62, but they will be permanently reduced.

In 2012, the maximum payout for any beneficiary was $2,513 per month.[2]

Covered workers need 40 credits to be eligible for their own benefit, which works out to about 10 years of work history. Your benefit is cal-culated based on your average earnings over the highest-earning 35 years.

Working up to full retirement age may increase your benefit while at the same time any contributions you continue to make to a 401(k) plan and/or investment portfolio will have more time to potentially accrue higher gains.

If you begin drawing benefits before full retirement age, they are re-duced as shown in the accompanying table.[3]

FULL RETIREMENT AND AGE 62 BENEFIT
BY YEAR OF BIRTH[3]

Year of Birth[1]	Full (normal) Retirement Age	Months between age 62 and full retirement age[2]	A $1000 retirement benefit would be reduced to	The retirement benefit is reduced by[4]	A $500 spouse's benefit would be reduced to	The spouse's benefit is reduced by[5]
1937 or earlier	65	36	$800	20.00%	$375	25.00%
1938	65 and 2 months	38	$791	20.83%	$370	25.83%
1939	65 and 4 months	40	$783	21.67%	$366	26.67%
1940	65 and 6 months	42	$775	22.50%	$362	27.50%
1941	65 and 8 months	44	$766	23.33%	$358	28.33%
1942	65 and 10 months	46	$758	24.17%	$354	29.17%
1943-1954	66	48	$750	25.00%	$350	30.00%
1955	66 and 2 months	50	$741	25.83%	$345	30.83%
1956	66 and 4 months	52	$733	26.67%	$341	31.67%
1957	66 and 6 months	54	$725	27.50%	$337	32.50%
1958	66 and 8 months	56	$716	28.33%	$333	33.33%
1959	66 and 10 months	58	$708	29.17%	$329	34.17%
1960 and later	67	60	$700	30.00%	$325	35.00%

[1.] If you were born on January 1st, you should refer to the previous year.

[2.] If you were born on the 1st of the month, SSA figures your benefit (and full retirement age) as if your birthday was in the previous month. If you were born on January 1st, SSA figures your benefit as if your birthday was in December of the previous year.

[3.] You must be at least 62 years old for the entire month to receive benefits.

[4.] Percentages are approximate due to rounding.

[5.] The maximum benefit for the spouse is 50 percent of the benefit the worker would receive at full retirement age. The percentage reduction for the spouse should be applied after the automatic 50 percent reduction. Percentages are approximate due to rounding.

WHO CAN DRAW BENEFITS?

No matter when you begin receiving Social Security benefits, your payout will receive an automatic annual cost of living adjustment when there is a comparative increase in the consumer price index.

250

Common sense may tell you that, among couples, the higher earner should claim benefits as early as possible and the lower earner should delay in order to receive a higher benefit. In reality, the exact opposite may be the better option because if the higher earner claims early and then dies first, he or she is likely to have shortchanged the lower earner's survivor benefit.

In this scenario, the higher earner should delay claiming benefits so the lower earner can claim the highest possible benefit for life — whether it's the lower earner's own benefit or a derivative of the higher-earner's highest available benefit. If the lower earner dies first, there is no lost benefit, as the higher earner simply keeps his or her own benefit.[4]

Spouse

Spousal or "derivative" Social Security benefits are determined by each of their work history and earnings, and the age at which they apply for and/or begin drawing benefits. (According to the Defense of Marriage Act, information presented applies to opposite sex spouses.)

When women take time away from the workforce to have children, raise children or even provide care for senior parents, years with part-time or zero earnings may factor into the 35 years and result in a much lower benefit than those who work full-time throughout their adult lives. This is why many women might qualify for a higher benefit based on their husband's work history.

The spousal- or derivative-benefit is 50 percent of the higher earner's accrued benefit at the time the spouse begins drawing payouts. Should the higher-earning spouse start taking benefits earlier than full retirement age, the spouse's derivative benefit will be less.[5]

In order for the lower-earning spouse to collect benefits based on the higher earner's history, the higher earner must apply for Social Security retirement benefits first. However, if the higher-earning spouse has reached full retirement age, he or she may apply for benefits and then file to suspend drawing benefits until later. This enables the higher-earner to accrue a higher benefit via more earnings contributions and Delayed Retirement Credits (DRC).[6]

Delayed Retirement Credits

If you do not feel the need to draw benefits at full retirement age and/or would like to continue working, you are eligible to earn Delayed Retirement Credits (DRC) on your future benefits for each full year that you do not start receiving benefits after you've reached full retirement age.

- Currently, the Delayed Retirement Credit is 8% per year.
- The credit stops once you reach age 70.
- A spouse may draw benefits while the higher earner accrues Delayed Benefit Credits.
- Derivative benefits for your spouse do not include any Delayed Retirement Credits

Spouse with Two Options (applicable to opposite sex spouse)

If you are married and have reached full retirement age, you have a couple of options. You may claim benefits either on your work history or your spouse's. You can also draw the spousal benefit and allow your own benefit to accrue Delayed Retirement Credits until you turn age 70. At that point, you can apply for your own work history benefit and switch over to yours (assuming it is higher than the derivative amount).[7]

Here is an example of how it works:
- Ed and Sarah both turn age 66 (full retirement age).
- Ed's monthly benefit is $1,400; Sarah's is $1,000.

- Ed files for benefits and Sarah begins drawing her spousal benefit (50% of Ed's = $700).
- Sarah continues working and earning toward her own benefits while also earning Delayed Retirement Credits.
- At age 70, Sarah applies for her own benefit based on her work history, which is now $1,370 a month.
- Her payout automatically switches to the higher benefit amount.

Restricted Benefit[8]

Once you reach full retirement age, you may apply for a restricted benefit based on your spouse's earnings as long as that earner is already receiving benefits. Even if you are the higher earner, you may instruct Social Security to restrict your benefit to your spouse's earnings, which means you will be entitled to up to 50 percent of the benefit your spouse is receiving. This strategy enables you to earn Delayed Retirement Credits up until age 70, at which time you can switch to your own benefit. This option is not available prior to full retirement age.

Divorced Spouse[9]

If a couple was married at least 10 years and then divorced, either one of the spouses may qualify for Social Security benefits at age 62 under the other's work history. Even if the higher-earning ex has not applied for benefits yet, the other may apply for the spousal benefit if they have been divorced for at least two years.

Once an ex-spouse remarries, he or she is no longer eligible to receive a benefit based on the first spouse's work history unless the current marriage ends in divorce, annulment or death. You are eligible for the highest derivative available from any number of ex-spouses as long as each marriage lasted at least 10 years and you are not currently married.

In 2010, the average annual Social Security income received by women 65 years and older was $11,794, compared to $15,231 for men.[10]

Widowed, Opposite Sex Spouse[11]

Among married couples, the age at which the higher-earning spouse applies for Social Security benefits is very important, since the surviving spouse is entitled to the higher of his or her own or the deceased spouse's benefit. The higher earner can increase the survivor's benefit by waiting to receive any benefits until age 70.

If the higher-earning spouse dies, the widow(er) is entitled to the higher earner's full retirement benefit and may begin receiving benefits starting at age 60 (or at any age if he or she has a child under age 16, or is disabled). Should the widow(er) remarry, the Social Security benefit for the widow(er) will terminate, but the benefit for the eligible child will not.

A surviving spouse may also claim a reduced benefit on the deceased's working record and then switch to his or her own later. The surviving spouse may wait until full retirement age to accrue a higher benefit, or even delay benefits until age 70 to accrue Delayed Retirement Credits based on his or her own work history. Once the survivor applies for his or her own benefit, the payout will automatically be at the highest amount.

Lower-wage earners receive a higher percentage benefit than higher-wage earners.[12]

How a Job Impacts Benefits[13]

Once you reach full retirement age, there is no longer an earnings limit, meaning you can earn any amount of income without it impacting your benefits.

However, if you begin drawing Social Security benefits before you reach full retirement age and your earnings exceed the eligible limit, your benefits will likely be taxed, yielding an even lower amount. You may earn up to $14,640 a year before your Social Security benefits will be reduced. Thereafter, $1 in benefits will be deducted for every $2 earned above $14,640.

In the year you reach full retirement age, you may earn up to $38,880 (in 2012) ending the month before your birthday before benefits are reduced. Thereafter, $1 for every $3 earned above $38,880 will be deducted from your benefits.

In both scenarios, however, your benefit will be increased at full retirement age to account for benefits withheld due to earlier earnings.

Where Do You Apply for Social Security Benefits?
Contact Social Security at (800) 772-1213 or TTY (800) 325-0778 about three months before the date you'd like your benefits to start. You may also visit your local Social Security office or apply online at: https://secure.ssa.gov/iCLM/rib.

HOW TO PREPARE FOR RETIREMENT BENEFITS
According to the 2011 Risk and Process of Retirement Survey by the Society of Actuaries, only 35% of Americans age 45 to 80 report they have a detailed retirement income plan designed to manage the risk of running short of money.[14] To help you prepare for a possible reduction in Social Security benefits and/or an overall shortfall in your retirement income, calculate the general amount of income you expect to need in retirement.

Add your monthly expenses and factor in a 3.23 percent long- term annual inflation rate (the average annual inflation rate from 1913 through 2012).[15] If the retirement age increases in the future, you may be able to continue working and delay your own retirement. However, if you need to retire before the full retirement age, you'll need to factor in the potential for reduced Social Security benefits during those years.

Check your level of estimated Social Security benefits accrued each year. This information is mailed to all eligible participants every year on their birthday. You can also check your Social Security Statement online at any time by setting up an account at: http://ssa.gov/mystatement.

Once you've identified your level of benefits, subtract this amount from the total income you've calculated that you need. The balance will give you an idea of the amount that may need to come from other sources.

(Please note, this is a general calculation and not intended to be the sole basis of any financial decisions.)

Other Income Sources
One way to supplement your Social Security benefits is to save and invest as much as you can now toward your retirement. Other ideas include maximizing your contributions to an employer plan, such as a 401(k) or 403(b), or contributing whatever you can to a Roth or traditional IRA. If you are not eligible for a tax deduction on IRA contributions due to your participation in an employer retirement plan, you may want to consider contributing to a Roth as well, so you can benefit from tax-free distributions in retirement.

2013 Contributions:[16]
- Participants in employer-sponsored retirement plans, such as 401(k)s, 4030s, 457s or Thrift Savings Plans may contribute up to $17,500 in 2013 ($23,000 for employees 50 or older)
- 2013 annual limit for all IRAs combined is $5,500 ($6,500 for age 50+)

Long-Term Care Insurance
Because Americans are living longer than ever before, the chances of needing long-term care are much higher, and this is an expense that

could be far greater than your Social Security benefits will cover. In fact, the median annual cost for care in an assisted living facility is $39,600 nationally.[17]

Medicare pays for acute care, but not long-term residency. Medicaid requires that you spend down your wealth before coverage kicks in. One of the ways that you can prepare for your future is to buy a long-term care insurance (LTCI) policy. Long-term care covers costs that Medicare and other health insurance policies don't cover, such as in-home care, assisted living, adult daycare, nursing home care, and hospice care.

Long-term care insurance can offer a more flexible and sensible choice for those who are still in good health. We recommend purchasing a long-term care policy before retirement as premiums get significantly more expensive with age. If you are in poor health or already receiving long-term care services, you may not qualify for long-term care insurance. The older you are, the higher your premiums will be. As a general rule, the best time to buy a policy at lower rates is around age 55.

Shopping Tips for Long-Term Care Insurance
When shopping for an LTCI policy, consider these tips:

- Buy from an issuing company with an "A" or better insurance rating. Ratings are determined by objective, third-party entities as an indicator of a company's overall performance and ability to meet its obligations to policyholders over a long period of time.
- Frequently, you can get a discount if both spouses buy policies at the same time.
- Policies typically cover a benefit period or lifetime dollar amount maximum, including two, three, four, and five years, and lifetime or unlimited coverage.

- In general, you may select a daily benefit amount (for example, $100/day). Most policies let you choose from $50/day to as much as $500/day.

- You may choose the type of coverage you prefer; for example, "comprehensive" (which includes payouts for in-home care) or "facility care only." Comprehensive gives you more flexibility, but at a higher premium.

- An important rider option to consider purchasing is Inflation Protection, which guarantees* that benefits will reflect the rising cost of care later in life.

Other options to consider include Guaranteed* Renewal, to ensure that you won't be turned down when you renew your policy, and a Non-Forfeiture benefit, guaranteeing you will still get paid a good portion of your benefit even if you terminate your policy or let it lapse unintentionally (not uncommon with seniors).

- Also, carefully consider the wait period that may come with your policy, which often ranges from one to 180 days. Choosing a longer waiting period may yield a less expensive premium, but during that length of time you will have to pay for long-term care on your own.

*Guarantees are backed by the financial strength and claims-paying ability of the issuing company, and may be subject to restrictions, limitations or early withdrawal fees. Annuities are not FDIC insured.

Life Insurance with LTC Payout Riders

Another alternative to the traditional LTCI policy is to purchase a universal life policy that offers a long-term care insurance rider and/or a return of premium rider for an additional fee. You generally purchase this type of policy with a one-time, lump sum payment, which will payout two or three times that amount in long-term care cost coverage.

Should you ever need to pay for long-term care, the policy will pay accelerated death benefits to help cover those costs. Furthermore, the "return of premium rider" allows you to access your initial purchase amount, should you ever need it. This would, however, reduce the death benefit. In contrast to a traditional long-term care insurance policy, a life policy also offers tax-free proceeds to beneficiaries upon your death.

Longevity Annuity
In early 2012, the Treasury Department proposed new rules to encourage plan sponsors of employer-based pension and 401(k) plans to enable retirees to use a portion of their 401(k) plan to purchase a Longevity Annuity. With this option, a portion of the balance would be reserved for conversion to annuity income starting later in life, around age 80 or 85. There may be no cash value on the death benefit during the deferral period; the rest of the account would be available for withdrawals for the first phase of retirement. This arrangement can assure that you have a second leg of income available should you run out midway through retirement.

Annuities with Long-Term Care Riders
There are also annuities available that offer long-term care benefit riders for contract owners who need additional care as they age, either at home or in a nursing facility. One example is a rider that increases the annuity payout for a specific period of time if the contract owner becomes unable to perform a certain number of basic activities of daily living set forth in the rider. This type of rider may have a waiting period and a physician's statement may be required in each of the years the contract owner exercises the rider. (Riders may be available at additional cost.)

Long-Term Care Annuity
There are also long-term care annuities you can purchase for a single premium that offer double (with inflation protection) or triple (no infla-

tion protection) the amount of long-term care coverage. Your premium will grow tax-deferred, and taxes are waived on distributions that are used to pay for long-term care. You may redeem the accumulated value at the end of the policy term or allow the policy to remain in force. When you pass away, your beneficiaries will inherit the greater of the accumulated annuity value if you have not made any withdrawals, or the single premium you paid initially minus the amount of any long-term care paid.[18]

Be aware that purchasing a long-term care annuity will tie up your premium for a specific period (up to 20 years), subject to penalty fees/surrender charges that may be longer and higher than annuity contracts with no long-term care rider, if you need to access cash.

They are also not known for generating significant credited interest. However, the underwriting is usually less stringent and does not require a physical. In addition, the annuity and the cost of your long-term care are fully funded, so you won't lose coverage if you forget to make a payment, which sometimes happens with long-term care insurance policies.

Obviously, it's important to build a savings/investment nest egg to help supplement Social Security benefits with your personal retirement income sources. However, given today's health and longevity among older Americans, it is equally important to create a long-term health care plan to help prepare for a more satisfactory quality of life in your senior years.

CONCLUSION

The simple fact is that Social Security may not always be straightforward. Just like every other facet of retirement planning, there are strategies you can employ to optimize the benefits you are eligible to receive, particularly among married couples.

Many people are hesitant to delay receiving benefits because they don't want to lose money they've contributed to the system for the last 35 years. While people who apply for Social Security benefits early may get more dollars if they die soon after, the opposite may also be true; they may receive less if they live significantly longer.

The monthly benefit paid out at age 62 is actuarially reduced to account for the eight more years that the recipient will be paid benefits as compared to someone who begins drawing payouts at age 70. Furthermore, the person who waits to claim benefits at age 70 will receive 76 percent more (real) dollars per month for the rest of his life than if he claimed benefits at age 62.

What's most important in making Social Security decisions for your situation is at what point you can no longer live comfortably without those benefits due to job loss, health care expenses or other issues.

The question isn't how to beat the system, but rather how to optimize the amount of income you receive for the length of time that you need it.

For this reason, it's important to consult with a financial professional experienced in Social Security distributions to review different payout scenarios to help determine the optimal time to file and when to begin drawing your benefits.

1 Social Security Administration; Fast Facts & Figures About Social Security, 2012; www.socialsecurity.gov/policy/docs/chartbooks/fast_facts/2012/fast_facts12.html#page35

2 Social Security Administration; Fast Facts & Figures About Social Security, 2012; www.socialsecurity.gov/policy/docs/chartbooks/fastjacts/20l2/fast_facts12.html#page 35

3 Social Security Administration, www.socialsecurity.gov/retire2/agereduction.htm, Retrieved January 8, 2013

4 Social Security Administration; Retirement Planner, October 18, 2012; www.ssa.gov/retire2/otherthings.htm

5 Social Security Administration; Retirement Planner, December 10, 2012; www.socialsecurity.gov/retire2/yourspouse.htm#aO=0

6 Social Security Administration; Retirement Planner, October 18, 2012; www.socialsecurity.gov/retire2/delayret.htm

7 Social Security Administration Publication No. 05-10035, July 2012.

8 Social Security Administration; Program Operations Manual System- GN00204.020 Scope of the Application; July 26, 2012; https:llsecure.ssa.govlpoms.nsf/lnx/0200204020

9 Social Security Administration; Retirement Planner, October 19, 2012; www.socialsecurity.govlretire2/yourdivspouse.htm

10 Social Security Administration, www.socialsecurity.govlpressoffice/factsheets/women.htm, retrieved June 28, 2012

11 Social Security Administration; Survivor's Planner, October 19, 2012; www.socialsecurity.govlsurvivorplan/onyourownS.htm#aO=1

12 Social Security Administration; Social Security is Important to Women; January 2012; www.socialsecuritY.9ov/Pressoffice/factsheets/women.htm

13 Social Security Administration; How work affects Social Security retirement payments; December 4, 2012; http:// ssa-custhel p.ssa .gov I appl answersl deta i II a_id/2361 - Ihow·work-affects-socia I·secu rity-retirement·payments

14 The Society of Actuaries, "The 2011 Risk and Process of Retirement Survey," 2012.

15 InflationData.com; Average Inflation Rates by Decade; November 5, 2012; http://inflationdata.comlInflationlInflation/DecadeInflation.asp

16 IRS; IRS Announces 2013 Pension Plan Limitations; IR·2012-77, Oct. 18, 2012; www.irs.gov/uac/2013·Pension-Plan-Limitations

17 Genworth Financial, Genworth 2012 Cost of Care Survey, 2012.

18 Bankrate.com. New: a hybrid annuity with LTC coverage. www.bankrate.com/finance/insurance/new·a-hybrid-annuity-with-Itccoverage-1.aspx Retrieved January 9, 2013.

Chapter XV: What You Should Know Before You Buy Gold

⤳

There are tax consequences to getting a gold purchase wrong, and there are other government issues to consider. The key discussion should be: What is a reportable vs. a non-reportable commodity purchase? Gold & Silver Bullion of any size is a REPORTABLE commodity. So, if you are fearful of the economy, or a possible future demise of the dollar, this money is "on the radar."

In 1933, the U.S. dollar was convertible to gold, rendering the government incapable of printing more money, as it is apt to do today. With fiscal discipline enforced by this convertibility, our faithful politicians (even back then) did the next best thing — they promptly confiscated American citizens' gold, via executive order 6102 (signed by Franklin Delano Roosevelt), while remunerating them for the then-fair market value of $20.67 an ounce. Upon the successful completion of its gold confiscation, the U.S. government adopted the Gold Reserve Act in January 1934, which revalued the nominal price of gold from $20.67 to $35.00 per troy ounce. What a risk-free, profitable trade for the Federal Reserve!

Let's say you have a shady seller who sells you a 32.15 ounce Johnson Gold Kilo Bar for $56,100 today and does NOT report it as required. Five years later, gold hits $5,000 an ounce. (Awesome for you!) BUT that dealer is gone. With more governmental enforcement, all buyers of gold will report (because they will face this same tax nightmare on their purchase if they don't) and they enter you into the system with a $160,750 sale. What's your capital gain?

Since you "worked" the system and stayed off the radar by getting a seller to not report; your basis is $0.00. Now when you sell, you are taxed on a $160,750 gain. This is NOT subject to debate; this is fact, and it is easily researched. You'll pay 20% (or, the then current capital gain tax rate). Buying reportable commodities sets you up for tax scrutiny (FYI, I am not suggesting you buy non-reportable metals to avoid taxes. You are subject to gains and losses, but, the record keeping is your responsibility.)

In addition, the government tracks reportable commodities and the last go-around proved that the seller (the American public) got a lousy deal. Does it make sense to buy gold coins? Please don't hesitate to contact me to help you understand your best options!

About the Author

John (Jay) E. Tyner Jr.

Jay Tyner is President and CEO of Semmax Financial Group, Inc., which is a full-service wealth management and retirement planning firm with offices located in Winston-Salem and Greensboro, North Carolina. With more than 23 years of experience in the financial industry, Jay founded Semmax in 2003 with a commitment to serving the complex financial needs of retirees and pre-retirees. Today, the company is comprised of three firms dedicated to addressing the unique and diversified financial needs of its clients, offering tailored, integrated solutions to help them achieve the financial growth necessary for a successful retirement.

Jay's dad, John Tyner Sr. — This photograph is from John Sr.'s tour of duty in the Korean War. He was a member of the 73rd Heavy Tank Battalion
U.S. Army.

Jay Tyner with sister,
U.S. Navy Reserve Lt.
Cmdr. Kimberlee Tyner,
at her recent
commissioning ceremony.

Jay Tyner with his sister, Kim.
Top photo: Jay, age 1
Bottom photo: Circa 1965, Age 3

Jay with his parents and sister, Kim, during a missionary trip
in Egypt, circa 1963.
Jay's parents, John Sr. and Gail, served 40 years as
missionaries in Africa and Europe.
Their travels included South America, Egypt, and Israel.

Jay's second passport, issued in 1969.

The Clark family with Gail Tyner, Jay, and sister, Kimberlee, in Athens, Greece, in 1964.
Jay was 25 months old.

The Tyners holding up the Leaning Tower of Pisa, 1972.

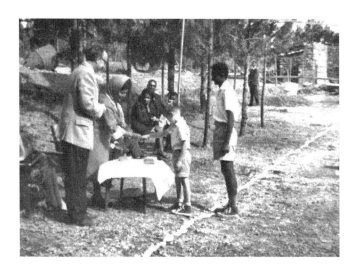

Jay receives an award for athletics at the British School he attended in Asmara, Eritrea, 1967.

Jay meets the Emperor Haile Selasie of Ethiopia, 1965.

Jay at Cambridge High School in East London, Republic of South Africa, 1978. (Back row, third from right)

2011 — Jay plays trumpet with the Triad Baptist Brass in Kernersville, NC. Jay is musically gifted and can play several instruments, including the trumpet, euphonium, and baritone.

Jay catches a 43-inch Northern Pike.
Lake of the Woods, Canada

Jay scuba dives with tiger sharks in the cool, 60°F water.
Off the coast of Chile, South America

Jay's Harley Sportster

Motorcycle Missions Fundraising Event at Triad Baptist

The Tyners enjoy camping all over the United States in their 2008 42' American Tradition.

Four-time Super Bowl winner Rocky Bleier lets Jay try on his Championship rings.

In 1983, while in college, Jay met the love of his life, Robin.
Jay and Robin married that same year, and they have cele-
brated more than 30 years happily married.

The Tyner family today

Jay & Robin's children (left to right):
Kristen, John III, and Candace

Easter at Jay's parent's in 2013

Candace, John, and Kristen

Jay & Robin with Jay's parents, John Sr. and Gail

Jay and Robin in 2012

Daughter Kristen's wedding (taken at Old Salem), married to Matt Landon on July 31, 2015

Jay and Robin Tyner are pleased to announce the wedding of Kristen Tyner to Matthew Landon held the evening of July 31st at Kernersville Moravian church with the reception at the Old Salem James A. Gray Auditorium. Kristen maintains her work as a cardiac ICU nurse while Matt continues his education in graduate school.

Married in August 2014, Candace and her husband, Drew, are adjusting nicely to married life. In the midst of life's business, they make every effort to spend time outdoors, as Candace loves to hike and take in the beauty of God's creation.

Jay and his team at Semmax Financial Group understand the uncertainty that surrounds retirement, especially in a daunting economic environment. Their mission is to coach retirees and pre-retirees through obstacles, to set and achieve financial goals, to provide tools, education, and guidance to get their clients through retirement and to strive to provide the highest standards of client service, results, and financial coaching through the ever-evolving financial landscape.

One of the services Jay offers to the North Carolina Triad community is free Financial Planning Seminars, where he explains the SIPS income strategy. With such serious topics to discuss and explain, it's nice to see Jay and wife, Robin, can also enjoy life and themselves!

Flat Jay

a.k.a John (Jay) E. Tyner Jr.

Appendix

THE DENVER POST

'Granny-to-jail' law

Repeal sought for measure limiting elderly's gift of assets

By Robert Pear
The New York Times

WASHINGTON — Clinton administration officials urged Congress yesterday to repeal a new law that makes it a federal crime to dispose of assets to qualify for Medicaid coverage of nursing home expenses.

They said that such abuses were not common.

Medicaid helps pay the bills for two-thirds of the 1.6 million people in nursing homes in the United States. Families can easily exhaust their assets on nursing home care because the costs average more than $100 a day.

Many elderly people give assets to their children. But the new law, added to a broader health insurance measure, makes that illegal if the purpose is to qualify for Medicaid. It is not entirely clear which transactions may result in criminal charges. Critics cite this ambiguity as a serious defect in the law.

Moreover, Bruce Vladeck, administrator of the Federal Health Care Financing Administration, which supervises Medicaid, said there was no evidence that large numbers of elderly people had given away assets to qualify for Medicaid.

Vladeck said Congress ought to repeal the criminal penalties, which took effect on Jan. 1. And he said that his agency would not press states to enforce the new restrictions on transfers of property by people seeking Medicaid.

The American Association of Retired Persons, the Alzheimer's Association, the National Senior Citizens Law Center, the American Bar Association and the bar associations of New York state and Ohio have all called for repeal of the law.

Patricia Nemore, a lawyer at the senior citizens law center, said: "The people likely to be jailed or fined are old, sick people needing nursing h me care. The typical nursing home resident is an 85-year-old widow."

Under the law, a person who "knowingly and willfully disposes of assets" in order to become eligible for Medicaid may be fined $10,000 and imprisoned for one year. In general, a person will not be subject to criminal penalties if he or she gives away assets more than three years before applying for Medicaid.

Some members of Congress say it is possible that some violators could be subject to much stiffer penalties, including a $25,000 fine and imprisonment for five years.

Rep. Steven LaTourette, R-Ohio, recently introduced a bill to repeal the provision, which he described as the "Granny goes to jail" law.

LaTourette, a former county prosecutor, said, "The new law has scared and confused senior citizens" and might discourage eligible people from applying for Medicaid. Moreover, he said, "Adult children who assist their parents could also be subject to criminal penalties."

The American Bar Association said that the language of the new law was "riddled

Key Medicaid Information for North Carolina for 2011

Last Updated: 4/1/2011 9:46:32 AM

Protections for the Community Spouse

Community Spouse Resource Allowance (CSRA):   Minimum: $21,912
Maximum: $109,560

Increased CSRA: Permitted in theory, but it is very rare.

Annuities: Actuarially sound annuities are permitted.

Monthly Maintenance Needs Allowance: Minimum: $1,821.25
Maximum: $2,739

Transfers

Average monthly cost of nursing home care according to state: $5,500

Income

Is the state an "income cap" state?   No

Estate Recovery

Has the state expanded the definition of "estate" beyond the probate estate?   No

Has the state included a hardship provision in its estate recovery plan?   Yes

Home Equity Limit

The state Medicaid program will not cover long-term care services for those with home equity above this limit, with certain exceptions. $506,000

An Explanation of the Legal Reserve System

The economic challenges that we face in today's world have become second only to the Great Depression. The recent collapses of banks and large corporations in our country have made people scramble for a place that has security. We are asked often, "Where can we place assets that provide safety and security in uncertain times?" One place that should be considered is life insurance companies that have a Legal Reserve classification.

The reserve liabilities are established as financial safeguards to ensure the company will have sufficient assets to pay its claims and other commitments when they fall due. These assets are kept intact for payment of living and death benefits to the insured. The reserve pool protects annuity investors as well as those who purchase other life insurance products or accident and health policies.

Every year all legal reserve life insurance companies submit annual statements to the insurance departments of each state in which they are licensed to do business. The format and contents of the forms used are prescribed by the State Insurance Commissioners, and they are a detailed report of an insurance company's financial status that is important in evaluating the company's solvency and compliance with the insurance laws. Every few years, depending on a company's home state law, all companies operating in more than one state undergo a detailed home office zone examination of its financial position. The audit is conducted by a team of State Insurance Department Examiners representing the various zones in which the company is licensed to do business. Companies licensed in only one state are subject only to an annual home office examination by that State Insurance Department.

A unique advantage of legal reserve life insurance is that if one company is purchased or merged into another, there is no change

287

whatsoever in the policy benefits or premiums. Legal reserve life insurance companies have established a public responsibility to respect both the letter and the spirit of laws and regulations so the interests of their policyholders are always protected.

If an insurance company's reserve levels fall short, and it goes into what is called receivership, the remaining insurance companies in the state legal reserve pool must assume the liabilities and obligations of the now-defunct insurer. The amount they are required to accept is based on the amount of insurance and annuities they have issued in that state. If one company has issued 10% of all insurance and annuities in that state, then they must accept 10% of any bankrupt insurer's obligations for the state.

Today, the life insurance industry provides more than a trillion dollars of death protection to American consumers. Through strict state insurance department regulations, the establishment of many state insurance guaranty associations and because of the insurance industry's history of financial stability and public responsibility to operate in a manner not detrimental to the welfare of the community your policy, principle and interest is guaranteed to be se-cure by industry safeguards. The Legal Reserve System was de-signed to insure a high level of safety for each of us. It was de-signed to insure that annuity and life companies have the cash when we need it.

SEMMAX FINANCIAL GROUP, INC.
RETIREMENT INCOME COACHING & 401(k) ROLLOVERS REDEFINED

Semmax Financial Group, Inc. is comprised of three firms committed to addressing the financial needs of today's seniors. Our offices are located in Greensboro and Winston-Salem, North Carolina. Over the past 20 years in financial services, our focus has narrowed to our current mission of coaching retirees and pre-retirees on how to protect, preserve, and effectively pass on their hard-earned assets.

We believe our clients should be able to live the remainder of their lives financially secure and at peace. That's why our Founder and President, Jay Tyner, RFC®, established the various companies that make up Semmax Financial Group, Inc. — to offer comprehensive financial solutions for valued clients.

Semmax, Inc. specializes in providing the most competitive insurance products and solutions available. From life and long-term care insurance to a host of annuity products from the top-rated carriers in the industry, Semmax, Inc. offers the insurance solutions you need.

Semmax Financial Advisors, Inc. is a Registered Investment Advisory firm — strictly regulated and audited by the Securities Division of the North Carolina Department of the Secretary of State — dedicated to managing our clients' stocks, bonds, mutual funds, REITs, ETFs, and any such equity that might be in our clients' portfolios.

Founded in 2004 as the third and final component of Semmax Financial Group, **Semmax Tax, Inc.**, a subsidiary of Triad Tax Advisory and Financial Services, Inc., offers full-service tax preparation for our clients.

All three companies and their associated specialists and staff coach you smoothly through your transition into a secure, tax-favored retirement. To schedule a time to discuss your financial future, contact us at info@semmax.com or call us at (336) 856-0080 today!

Corporate Office
1447 Trademart Blvd.
Winston Salem, NC 27127
PH: (336) 856-0080

www.semmax.com

Advisory services offered through Semmax Financial Advisors, Inc. a Registered Investment Advisory firm. Registration does not imply a certain level of skill or training. Insurance products and services offered through Semmax, Inc. Tax services offered through Semmax Tax, Inc. Futures offered through Semmax Futures Fund, LLC.

Acknowledgments

Thank you, Thank you, Thank you!

To The Lord Jesus Christ who saved me.

To my mother, Gail Tyner, who birthed me and gave 40 years to missionary work in Africa and Europe.

To my father, John Tyner Sr., who respects me and gave 40 years to missionary work in Africa and Europe.

To my wife, Robin Tyner, who loves and respects me more than anybody as she suffers from Lyme's Disease contracted over 14 years ago.

To my daughter Kristen, who's a great wife and nurse.

To my daughter Candace, who's a great wife and daughter

To my son, John Tyner III, who's going to be a great husband and make it big in New York, NY.

To my sister, Kimberlee Tyner, who is the best NAVY Nurse in the whole wide world.

To my closest friend & associate, Dr. Ron Smith, who for 20 years has worked on a "handshake."

To my Pastor, Dr. Rob Decker, who brings the most outstanding "messages" every Sunday.

To my now "estranged" friend Thomas J. McDermott who introduced me to the "business."

Endnote

Alpha Teach Yourself Estate Planning in 24 Hours
Keith R. Lyman, Alpha Books, 2002

Annuities and Insurance Values: Insurance Guaranty Fund Limits in the 50 States
Richard W. Duff, J.D., CLU 2000

Comeback America
Turning the Country Around and Restoring Fiscal Responsibility
David M. Walker, Random House Trade Paperback Edition, 2010

Elder Law in a Nutshell
Lawrence A. Frolik, Professor of Law University of Pittsburgh
Richard L. Kaplan, Peer and Sarah Pedersen Professor of Law University of Illinois, Thomson/West, 2006

Have You Been Talking to Financial Aliens?
Peter J. D'Arruda, Financial Safari Press, 2011

How to Turn Your Lunch Money Into $1 Million Plus Other Amazing Financial Strategies
Boardroom® Inc. 2004

Invasion of the Money Snatchers
A Practical Guide to Protecting Your $tuff from Creditors, Predators and a Government Gone Wild
Matt Zagula and Pam Smoljanovich, 2010

Let's Get Real About Money! Profit from the Habits of the Best Personal Finance Managers
Eric Tyson, Published by Pearson Education, Inc., 2008

The Medicaid Planning Handbook
Alexander A. Bove, Jr., Little, Brown and Company, 1996

Parlay Your IRA into a Family Fortune
Ed Slott, Viking, 2005

Tax-Free Retirement
Patrick Kelly, Strategic Financial Concepts, 2007

The 11 Be Attitudes of Prosperity
David B. White, JD, CPA, CLU, ChFC, Xulon Press, 2010

The Creature from Jekyll Island
A Second Look at the Federal Reserve
G. Edward Griffin American Media, 2003

The Wall Street Journal Guide to Planning Your Financial Future
Kenneth M. Morris and Virginia B. Morris
Lightbulb Press, Inc., 2002

The Wonder of America
Derric Johnson Honor Books, 1999

Whatever Happened to Penny Candy?
Richard J. Maybury, Bluestocking Press, 2000

Made in the USA
Columbia, SC
22 May 2019